A MADMAN'S MANIFESTO

AUGUST STRINDBERG

A MADMAN'S MANIFESTO

Le Plaidoyer d'un Fou

Translated by Anthony Swerling from the French in which
Le Plaidoyer d'un Fou was written

THE UNIVERSITY OF ALABAMA PRESS
University, Alabama

To Henry Bauer

Translated from *Le Plaidoyer d'un Fou,* published by
Editions Albert Langen (Paris, 1895) and by Mercure
de France (Paris, 1964). English translation copyright ©
1968 by Anthony Swerling. "Introduction" by B. G. Madsen
and Translator's Preface copyright
© 1971 by The University of Alabama Press.
ISBN 0-8173-8553-3
Library of Congress Catalog Card Number 77-158735
Manufactured in the United States of America

TABLE OF CONTENTS

INTRODUCTION TO THE TRANSLATION

August Strindberg's autobiographical novel *Le Plaidoyer d'un Fou* was written during the period from September 1887 through March 1888, which is to say during one of the most difficult periods in a generally tortured life. During the 1870's Strindberg had suffered many tribulations over the production and publication of his historical play *Master Olof,* but toward the end of the decade, in 1879, he made a great success in Sweden with his satirical novel *The Red Room.* Things seemed to be looking up for him both artistically and financially. In 1882, however, he offended the Swedish Establishment with a considerably sharper satirical work, *The New Kingdom,* which stirred up a storm of opposition against him in his native country. A still more serious personal crisis was precipitated in 1884, when he had to stand trial in Stockholm on charges of blasphemy arising out of some irreverent remarks about the sacrament of Confirmation appearing in one of the short stories in the first volume of *Married.* He was acquitted, to be sure, but the strain of the trial and a morbid fear of being imprisoned left him badly upset emotionally; the second volume of *Married,* published in 1885, is clearly the work of a gravely disturbed and unbalanced mind.

According to Strindberg's eldest daughter by his first marriage, Karin Smirnoff, his wife Siri von Essen was deeply offended by this second volume, with its savage attack on women, which marks the beginning of an implacable hostility between the spouses.[1] Especially noteworthy in this respect is the last story in the volume, "The Breadwinner," which is a graphic representation of Strindberg's marital situation as he himself saw it in 1885: it is the story of a distraught, hyper-nervous writer who works himself to death supporting his children and a lazy, cognac-swilling wife. In both its atmosphere and its one-sided portrayal of character the story is quite similar to *A Madman's Manifesto.*

By the middle 1880's, Strindberg's situation had indeed become rather desperate. His books were not selling at all well—some of his manuscripts were rejected outright by publishers—and he was in constant financial difficulty. It was during this period, discouraged by his slow progress in Sweden, that he toyed seriously with the idea of establishing himself in France and creating a name for himself as a French writer—hence the fact that *The Madman's Manifesto* was written in French rather than in Swedish. It was during this period also that he seems to have come to feel that "everyone" was against him, and quite frequently to take his frustration and hostility out on his wife: she had to agree with him in everything, apparently, for any disagreement at all could only mean that she was siding with his enemies! To all his

---

[1] Karin Smirnoff, *Strindbergs första hustru* (Stockholm, 1925), p. 213 ff.

other difficulties were added certain problems of a sexual nature. Specifically, Strindberg seems to have felt sexually inadequate and insecure in both his first and third marriages. This was undoubtedly one of his most nagging problems and probably a major cause of his celebrated misogyny: he compensated for his feelings of sexual inadequacy by decrying his female partners morally and intellectually. There is no reason to pass over this aspect of his first marriage in tactful silence, since Strindberg himself, in letters to Pehr Staaff,[2] was surprisingly outspoken about it. In two of these letters, which date from August 1887, he wrote at some length in the following vein:

... Who has destroyed my reputation, my honor in all respects? Siri, of course! I must hear incredible things! And I feel like going to court to clear myself thoroughly even of the accusation of not being a man. . . . Provoked in my very genital glands, I went to Geneva and brought a doctor with me to a brothel. Performed the feat of strength, not for the first time incidentally. . . . All this has been written in self-defense. Siri has created an opinion about my unmanliness and once [she even] humiliated me at a party—where, however, I took the liberty of replying that the screw is not necessarily too small because the nut is too large!

The antagonism between Strindberg and Siri von Essen seems to have reached its peak in that month of August 1887, and it was at about this time, apparently, that he conceived the idea of writing a novel about the marriage. In any case, he started work on this "self-defense," *Le Plaidoyer d'un Fou,* during the following month. In the novel, Strindberg's alter ego, the narrator "Axel," blames all his misery and suffering on his wife, the evil "Maria." "A crime has been perpetrated in the shadow or I am mad," the despairing Axel exclaims in his Introduction to the book. "The truth thus remains to be discovered." Since Axel's fear of going mad, like Strindberg's own, is very, very real, *to save himself* he must convince the reader that Maria is to blame for everything! Only by proving her guilty can he continue to regard himself as innocent (sane). Armed with the perspicacity and impeccable logic of a brilliant detective —so Axel is wont to conceive of himself—he proceeds to expose to public view all of Maria's many sins; ironically, in the process of doing so he succeeds mainly in proving that he is himself quite mad indeed.

It will not do, as some critics have done, to suppose that the novel *Le Plaidoyer d'un Fou* is a true-to-life account of actual events in Strindberg's first marriage, or to accept the one-sided portrayal of Maria as an authentic representation of the real Siri von Essen. Siri was *not* a Lesbian, an alcoholic, an unfaithful wife, a lazy, negligent mother, a poor housekeeper, and so on—not, at least, according to Karin Smirnoff's account of the marriage in her two books, *Strindbergs första*

---

[2] *August Strindbergs Brev,* VI (Stockholm, 1958), pp. 250–54.

hustru and *Så var det i verkligheten* (Stockholm, 1956). If it is argued that Karin Smirnoff is a biased observer moved by filial piety to come to her mother's defense against Strindberg's virulent charges, one can cite more neutral Strindberg scholars who have discussed the marriage: the Dane Harry Jacobsen, for example, likewise exonerates Siri von Essen from most of Strindberg's more serious charges.[3]

But if the Maria of the novel is indeed not a faithful portrait of Siri von Essen as she was in life, there can be little doubt that Maria is a reflection of the woman that a suspicious, unbalanced, and vindictive Strindberg had come to imagine Siri as being in the later stages of their protracted marital battle. In letters from Strindberg to Pehr Staaff[4] and Rudolf Wall[5] Siri is described in almost exactly the same terms as those used to describe Maria in the novel—as an unfaithful wife, Lesbian, etc. Thus, the portrait of Maria reflects Strindberg's hostile feelings toward Siri in 1887–1888, and most events treated in the novel have been post-rationalized to fit this jaundiced view. Sven Rinman[6] contends that there is less of this post-rationalization in the first part of the book than in the rest of it, and that for this reason the first part is more objective and less gloomy than the other three.[7] This is probably true, on the whole, but even so there are significant manifestations of post-rationalization in Part One. The following scene from the early phase of Axel's and Maria's relationship is a revealing example of this kind of technique:

What struck me, however, and in a manner prophetic for the future, was the exuberant gaiety the Baroness manifested on every occasion when an ambiguity escaped from the cousin's lips. Then a ferocious laugh, an expression of impudent voluptuousness lit up her features, testifying to a profound knowledge in her of the mysteries of debauchery. [I, 7]

In *A Madman's Manifesto,* then, Strindberg used a technique of distortion and exaggeration, just as he does so often in his dramas (especially in his late, "expressionistic" period). Another typical example of such distortion in the novel is this description of Maria's Danish friend, purportedly a Lesbian:

And one ought to have seen the object of that love! A redheaded type, male face, hooked, hanging nose, fat chin, yellow eyes, cheeks puffed out from an excess of drink, with a flat breast, crooked hands, the most detestable, the most execrable thing it is possible to imagine, a type with which a farm hand would not have contented himself. [IV, 3]

---

[3] *Strindberg og hans første hustru* (Copenhagen, 1946).
[4] August 1887, in *Brev,* VI.
[5] March 1888, in *Brev,* VII.
[6] *Svensk Litteraturtidskrift* (Lund, 1965), pp. 67–68.
[7] It is worth noting that in Part One we find the glowing, ecstatic praise of Maria's physical attractions [I, 24]—a hymn to female beauty that, in its unqualified enthusiasm, is rare in Strindberg's work.

The real-life model for this monster was Siri's Danish friend Marie David, who by accounts other than Strindberg's did not look at all that way. "The truth was," according to Harry Jacobsen, "that she had beautiful, golden hair, an attractive profile, a small well-shaped mouth, beautiful hands, was short, and had a delicate, fine complexion."[8] However, Strindberg detested Marie David and suspected her of all sorts of vices, and this hatred obviously colored his description of her in the novel.

How often Strindberg uses this technique deliberately as a stylistic device, and how often he is simply carried away by personal animosity, is hard to determine precisely; but that he often used it quite deliberately is indicated by a passage in a letter he wrote to Edvard Brandes on April 6, 1887. Brandes had sent him a copy of his play *Love*, and Strindberg was moved to comment in a forceful manner:

... thank you for the play. That's just it! You have been just—and have become flaccid! Justice seems to be only a mechanical concept which cannot be applied in life and on the stage. How would it have gone with *A Doll's House* if Helmer had received a little justice? How would it have gone with *Ghosts* if Mr. Alving had been permitted to live and tell the audience that his wife was lying about him? No, go ahead and accuse them; slander them; abuse them so that they don't have a clean spot—that's dramatic![9]

So Strindberg, the born dramatist, writes "dramatically" even when he is writing novels; justice is a "mechanical concept" and does not interest him. Indeed, in its one-sided portrayal of character (the wife cast in the role of villainess, the husband in that of martyr-to-the-marriage) and in its occasional violence *A Madman's Manifesto* is very similar to Strindberg's drama *The Father*, which he had completed just a few months before starting the novel. In December 1894, Strindberg wrote to his French translator, Georges Loiseau, about this play: "C'est écrit avec une hache au lieu d'une plume"[10]—a statement that applies equally well to *A Madman's Manifesto*, for both works are characterized by the same kind of monomaniacal power.

The two works are similar in another important respect, as well, for both *A Madman's Manifesto* and *The Father*, despite the rather gloomy nature of their subject matter, are notable for their grim Strindbergian humor. Indeed, passages of black comedy are not uncommon in Strindberg's works generally, even the most pessimistic of them (*The Dance of Death*, for example, and *A Dream Play* and *The Ghost Sonata*, among others). The reader of *A Madman's Manifesto* may well be thankful that Strindberg, though seemingly about to be overwhelmed by his monomania, had sufficient sanity and humor left in him to be capa-

---

[8] Jacobsen, *op. cit.*, p. 63.
[9] *Brev*, VI, p. 187.
[10] *Brev*, X, p. 323.

ble of writing such grotesquely funny pages as those on Maria's King Charles dog. His description of the "filthy beast's" funeral is especially hilarious.

The publishings and translatings of Strindberg's French manuscript *Le Plaidoyer d'un Fou* have run some checkered courses. The very first version of the novel to be published anywhere was an anonymous German translation, *Die Beichte eines Thoren,* which made its appearance in 1893. A pirated Swedish version, based on this translation, appeared in the magazine *Budkavlen* that same year. In 1894, the German translation was prosecuted in Prussia for obscenity, but Strindberg was acquitted. In 1895, *Le Plaidoyer d'un Fou,* corrected by Georges Loiseau, was published in Paris by Albert Langen. In 1910, a second German translation, that of Emil Schering, appeared in Munich, and in 1912, an English version by Ellie Schleussner, based on the Schering translation, was published in London. In 1914, John Landquist made the first of several translations of Strindberg's French into his native language; the second Swedish version, by Landquist and Erik Staaff, appeared in 1920, and the third, by Tage Aurell, was published in 1962. In 1964, Strindberg's French text of 1895 was reprinted in Paris by Mercure de France. An English version of the novel, prepared by Professor Evert Sprinchorn, was published in the United States in 1967 (Anchor Books, A492b) and in England in 1968 (Jonathan Cape). However, the Sprinchorn version of the work is based on the earlier English translation by Ellie Schleussner, which was based, in turn, on the 1910 German translation by Emil Schering. The first English translator to go directly to Strindberg's French text and to translate it in its entirety is Anthony Swerling, whose translation was first published at The Trinity Lane Press, Cambridge, in 1968, and is reprinted, with some minor typographical corrections, in the present volume.

A line-by-line comparison of Anthony Swerling's version and Strindberg's French text (Mercure de France, 1964) proves Swerling's translation to be a completely accurate and faithful rendering of Strindberg's original. Swerling has really succeeded in capturing and conveying to the English reader the peculiarly Strindbergian style and tone. A difference that one notices between the original and Swerling's translation is the use of certain verb tenses. Writing in French, Strindberg uses the present tense and the historical present very extensively. Swerling consistently renders most of these verbal forms by the English past tense. There can be no doubt that he does so quite deliberately—and I think properly—out of a feeling that for many of these descriptions the past tense is the more "natural" in English usage. A typical example, selected at random from among many, is the following paragraph, given first in the original French and then in Swerling's translation:

Aussitôt mandé le prêtre se présente. C'est un homme d'une trentaine d'années, type de valet de ferme endimanché. Avec ses cheveux rouges, ses yeux demi éteints, sa face parsemée de lentilles, il ne m'inspire pas de sympathie et je reste longtemps sans proférer une parole, ne sachant en vérité que confier à cet individu sans instruction, sans la sagesse de l'âge, sans connaissance aucune du coeur humain. Embarrassé comme un provincial devant un citadin, il se tient debout au milieu de la chambre jusqu' à ce que, d'un geste de la main, je l'invite à prendre une chaise. Alors seulement, il entreprend son interrogatoire. (Mercure de France, p. 109)

No sooner sent for, the priest appeared. He was a man of about thirty, a type of farm labourer in his Sunday best. With his red hair, his half-dimmed eyes, his face sprinkled with freckles, he did not inspire me with sympathy and I remained without uttering a word for a long time, not knowing indeed what to confide to this individual without education, without the wisdom of age, without any knowledge of the human heart. Embarrassed like a provincial before a citizen, he remained standing in the middle of the room until, with a gesture of the hand, I invited him to take a chair. Only then did he undertake his questioning. (*A Madman's Manifesto*, I, 7)

English and American readers have good reason to be grateful to Anthony Swerling for having gone back to Strindberg's original French text and rendering it so skillfully into English. *Le Plaidoyer d'un Fou* is a powerful novel about a tortured love/hate relationship. It is also interesting as a human document, one that sheds a good deal of light—more light, probably, than the author intended it to shed—on Strindberg's rather odd state of mind in the late 1880's.

University of California   BØRGE GEDSØ MADSEN
Berkeley, California

TRANSLATOR'S PREFACE

The specialist reader may cross upon several discrepancies in the *Manifesto* where fact is invested with fiction, for Strindberg's so-called autobiographies are in fact autobiographical novels in which the author has altered, added, or omitted to suit his creative bent. The few short translator's footnotes are intended to bear out fact rather than to shed light on fantasy.

Strindberg being prone to all the contingencies of subjectivity and afterthought in this alleged chronicle of documentary exactitude, the statements encased in the following pages should be approached as expressions of truth rather than as truth itself. Distortion, self-contradiction, and esthetic rearrangement are ingredients in the fluid and fluctuating state of mind of the protagonist, with his ambivalent attitude to detail. Further, the author's tempestuous imagination and his impatience as regards revision, coupled with the speed of his writing, left some minor obscurities of time and place in his text. Even so, transcription and typesetting might be as much to blame as any inconsistencies of recollection and reflection on Strindberg's part.

Although it is beyond the purview of this modest preface to supply a comprehensive listing of discrepancies, it will be readily noticed that at one place in Strindberg's French (and hence in our translation) the narrator's age in 1875 is given as 28, whereas Strindberg was born in 1849; that the reference (page 86) to the Ides of March as the thirteenth of the month departs from custom; and that, in consecutive sentences (page 155), the length of time during which the King Charles spaniel plagued the narrator diminishes from six years to three.

What Strindberg lacked in consistency he made up in genius.

University of Cambridge   ANTHONY SWERLING
April 25, 1971

A MADMAN'S MANIFESTO

INTRODUCTION

Seated at my table, pen in hand, I collapsed, overcome by an attack of fever. No serious illness having touched me for fifteen years, I was struck by such an untimely accident: not that I was afraid of dying, far from it, but having reached the end of a stormy career at thirty-eight, without having said my last word, without having accomplished all the vows of my youth, provided with plans for the future, this precipitate dénouement was not to my liking. Having lived the last four years with my children and my wife in almost voluntary exile, entrenched in a Bavarian hamlet, exhausted, recently summoned to court*, sequestrated, banished, held up to public obloquy—a single sentiment, that of revenge, obsessed me when I slumped onto my bed. A struggle began from then on within me, who was without strength to cry for help. Undermined by the fever which was beating me as one does with a feather bed, taking hold of my throat to strangle me, crushing my chest with its knee, scorching my ears to the point that my eyes seemed to be sticking out of their sockets, I remained alone then in my attic with Death which had no doubt slipped stealthily into my room and was charging at me.

But I didn't want to die. The combat became fierce as a result of the resistance I put up. My nerves were relaxing, the blood was streaming in my arteries. My brain was quivering like a polypus plunged in vinegar. Suddenly, persuaded that I was going to succumb during this dance of death, I let go and slipped backwards, abandoning myself to the terrible embraces of the monster.

Suddenly an indescribable calm took hold of my being, a voluptuous torpor coursed along my limbs, an ideal repose enveloped my soul together with my body, deprived of a salutary relaxation for toilsome years.

With what ardour did I hope that this was death! Little by little the will to live was vanishing within me. I ceased feeling, sensing, thinking. I was losing consciousness and only the welcome sentiment of nothingness filled the emptiness hollowed out by the disappearance of nameless pains, troublesome thoughts, and unadmitted trances.

When I awoke my wife appeared, sitting at my bedside, scrutinising my eyes with an alarmed look.

"What's happened to you then, poor friend?" she said to me.

"Nothing, I'm ill," I replied, "and it's good to be ill."

"What are you saying? . . . It's not serious? . . ."

"It's the end . . . at least I hope so."

"God forbid that you make us homeless," she exclaimed. "What would become of us in a foreign country without friends, without resources?"

---

* For blasphemy against religion relating to one of the stories in *Married*.

"I'm leaving you my life insurance," I hazarded by way of consolation. "It's little, assuredly, but it's still enough to return home with."

She had not thought of this insurance policy. In a slightly calmer manner, she continued:

"But, my poor friend, you cannot stay like this, I am going to call the doctor."

"No, I don't want to see the doctor."

"Because . . ."

"Because . . . I don't want to see him."

A whole procession of implied words passed in the looks we exchanged.

"I want to die," I concluded. "Life sickens me; the past appears like a tangled skein that I haven't the strength to unravel. May my eyes be filled with shadow and may the curtain be drawn."

She remained indifferent before my noble and courageous outpourings.

"Your old suspicions . . . still?" she said.

"Yes, still! Dispel the phantom! You alone have been able to chase it away until now."

She placed her soft hand on my brow with an habitual gesture and, simulating the little mother as before:

"Is it alright like that?" she said.

"It's alright like that, yes! . . ."

It was true, the simple contact of the light hand which had weighed so heavily on my destiny possessed the faculty to exorcise the black spirits, to repel the furtive worries.

Soon the fever took hold of me again, more intensely. My wife got up at once to prepare an elder infusion for me.

While I was alone I sat up to glance through the window which was opposite my bed. It was a large triptych-shaped bay, framed outside by bright green wild vine which disclosed a corner of the landscape: in the foreground, a quince tree swayed its beautiful vermilion fruit among the dark green leaves; further on, there appeared the apple trees planted amongst the lawns, the belfry of a chapel, a blue spot—Lake Constance—at the foot of the Tyrolean Alps. We were right in the heart of summer and all this formed a delightful tableau under the slanting rays of an afternoon sun.

From below rose the twittering of the starlings perched on the props in the vines, the cackling of the young poultry in the yard, the chirping of the crickets, the crystalline little bells of the cows, and, mixing in this gay concert of nature, the peals of laughter of my children, the voice of my wife giving orders, discussing the illness that was breaking me with the wife of the gardener.

Then I returned to the sweetness of living and the fear of

4

annihilation seized me. I didn't want to die, decidedly not. I had too many duties to fulfil, too many debts to settle. Overwhelmed with remorse, I felt a pressing need to confess my life, to implore the forgiveness of everyone for what I had done, to humiliate myself before someone.

I felt guilty, with a conscience racked by unknown crimes: I burned with a desire to unburden myself through a complete avowal of my imaginary guilt.

During this attack of weakness which came to me from an inborn timidity, my wife returned, carrying my infusion in a bowl and, alluding to the mania for thinking myself persecuted by which I was slightly attacked formerly, she sipped the beverage before offering it to me.

"You can drink it," she said smiling, "there's no poison in it."

I was ashamed. I didn't know how to reply; I emptied the bowl in one go to satisfy her.

The soporific elder tea, the smell of which recalled memories of my country where the mysterious shrub is the object of a popular cult, brought on a fit of sentimentality which gave way to an effusion of remorse.

"Listen to me carefully, darling, since I am soon going to die. I confess that I've always lived like a consummate egoist. I have broken your theatrical career in the interests of my literary renown . . . I want to admit everything now; forgive me . . ."

And as she was preparing to think up reasons to console me, I carried on, interrupting her:

"According to your wish we got married with the dowry system. Nevertheless, I have squandered your dowry to cover reckless guarantees: and what is tormenting me the most is that in case I die you will not be able to receive the rights of my published works. Bring a lawyer quickly so that I can leave you my wealth . . . Finally, promise me to return to your art afterwards which you abandoned for me."

She did not want to hear any of it, making a joke of the matter, advising me to rest a little, assuring me that everything would be arranged and that death, in any case, was not so close.

At the end of my strength, I took her hand. I invited her to sit down beside me, while I was going to doze off: and, begging her again to forgive me for all the wrong I had inflicted upon her, with her little hand pressed into mine, an exquisite torpor lowered my eyelids. Then I felt myself melting like ice under the rays of her large eyes which reflected an infinite tenderness. Her kiss was imprinted on my burning brow like a cold compress and I sank down into the depths of ineffable bliss.

When I awoke from this lethargy, it was broad daylight. The sun was warming the blind daubed with a Cockaigne landscape. I could tell from the morning sounds from below that it must have been about five o'clock. I had slept through the whole night without dreams and without waking up.

The infusion bowl was still on the night table and my wife's chair in the same place. Only I was wrapped in her fox fur-lined wrap, whose caressing and supple hairs tickled my chin.

It seemed to me that I hadn't slept for the last ten years, so much did my overworked head feel rested and fresh. My ideas, which formerly escaped in turmoil, were now rallying together, regular, ordered and vigorous troops, ready for resistance against those pangs of mobid remorse, the symptoms of a weakness of constitution in the degenerate.

And what haunted me immediately were the two black spots of my life uncovered yesterday, under pretext of a supreme confession, to my beloved wife—those two black spots which for so many years had ulcerated me, right up to my last moments.

And so, with no further delay, I wanted to examine in my brain the two avowals in question, accepted without discussion until now, seized as I was with a vague presentiment that everything, so presented, was perhaps not in strict fairness.

"Let's see a little," I said to myself, "in what I have sinned to consider myself from the outset as a cowardly egoist who might have sacrificed the artistic career of his wife to the profit of his ambitious ends. Let's see exactly what happened."

At the time of the publication of the banns, she already held only secondary rôles. Her situation as an actress was of the most modest, her second début having been pitiful, through lack of talent, aplomb, originality. She lacked all that was needed for the stage. The very eve of our wedding she had been given a further rôle; it was a chaperon of sorts in a play of sorts too. She only had two words to say.

However, how many tears, how much sorrow—to hear her—was this marriage to bring her which took away all the prestige of the actress, formerly so seductive as the Baroness divorced through pure love of art.

Certainly, some of the fault was mine, in this débâcle which was beginning to end later in a brusque refusal of re-engagement, after two years of tears shed over shorter and shorter rôles. I was reaching success as a novelist, incontestable success, at the very moment of the expiration of her engagement. I had formerly approached the theatre with unimportant playlets*. My first concern therefore was to compose a presentable play, I mean one of those machines which are suitable, specially prepared with a view to obtaining the desired re-engagement for the beloved. I began the task half-heartedly. For a long time I had been dreaming of opportune innovations in dramatic art. Still I wrote my drama*, momentarily sacrificing every kind of literary conviction. After that I had to impose my darling wife onto the recalcitrant public, throw her in its face with all the known artifices, forcibly introduce her into its favour. Nothing helped.

The play flopped. The actress failed before a parterre which reacted against a woman divorced, then remarried, and the director hurriedly rescinded a contract of no advantage to him.

"Is it my fault then?" I asked myself stretching out on my bed, very satisfied with myself after this first examination. Oh! how good it is to have a quiet conscience . . .

And I continued with a serene heart.

A sad, lugubrious year went by, spent in tears in spite of the joys that the birth of a hoped-for little daughter brought.

Suddenly theatre mania reappeared in my wife, more violent than ever. We ran from dramatic agency to dramatic agency, we forced the sealed doors of the directors, we advertised excessively, without any success, everywhere rebuffed, discouraged by everyone.

Disheartened by the failure of my drama, while making a fine position for myself in literature, I had sworn that I would never write a play to order again for an actor, deriving, moreover, no pleasure from it; and I limited myself to bearing my share of irremediable worries, little disposed to disorganise my household for the satisfaction of a passing fancy.

In the end, however, this exceeded my strength. I managed to get my wife engaged for a series of performances, profiting from my contact with the management of a Finnish theatre.

It was truly giving myself whips with which to scourge myself. A widower, a bachelor, head of a family and of a kitchen for a month, I had two parcels of bouquets and wreaths which were brought back to the conjugal domicile as a mediocre consolation.

But she appeared so happy, so young and so charming that I had to send off a request for a re-engagement.

Bear this in mind. I was going to abandon my country, my friends,

---

* *Hermione* (1869), *In Rome* (1870), *The Outlaw* (1871), INTER ALIA

* *The Secret of the Guild* (1880). Six performances.

my position, my publisher . . . why? for a woman's caprice . . . but it's like that. One loves or one doesn't.

Fortunately, that good man the manager couldn't fit an actress without a repertoire into his troupe.

Was it my fault, really? I rolled over in my bed with satisfaction at the thought. Ah! how good it is from time to time to look into things as the English do. It completely relieves the heart and there I was at once rejuvenated.

But let's see the outcome. The children arrived at short intervals: one, two, three. One sowed thick and fast.

And still, still the theatre mania manifested itself. One must really reach one's ends. Just then, a new theatre opened concurrently. What simpler indeed? Could I not offer it a play with a beautiful female rôle, a sensational play on the emancipation question since, in fact, this question was the order of the day!

No sooner said than done.—For, as I have already said: "One loves or one doesn't".

A drama appeared, beautiful female rôle, brilliant costumes by request of course, with cradle, moonlight, a bandit as foil, a subjugated husband, cowardly, in love with his wife (it was me); a pregnant woman on stage (that was something new), the interior of a monastery . . . and the rest, believe me.

Hence a colossal success for the actress, and for the author a fiasco, a black fiasco . . . Alas, yes.

She was saved. I was lost, sunk. And in spite of everything, in spite of the supper at a hundred francs a head offered to the director, in spite of a fine of fifty francs paid to the police for cheering at an undue hour of the night in front of the manager's door, we did not see any proposal of engagement forthcoming.

Still, I was not to blame for all that. But the martyr, the victim was me, however. Naturally I was a monster in the eyes of all the decent ladies, for I had sacrificed my wife's career. I have suffered remorse over it for years to the point that I cannot end my days in peace.

How often, moreover, has the bitter reproach been flung in my face in the middle of a drawing-room! And it's always I who am the guilty one . . . The thing happened quite differently, however . . . A career had been broken, that's true, I admit it . . . But whose and by whom?

A cruel suspicion arises and the irony evaporates when I think that I could have passed into posterity as responsible for that broken career, without an advocate to put matters right.

The wasting of the dowry remained.

I recall having been the subject of an article entitled: "A Dowry Squanderer". I also remember very clearly an occasion when it was said to my face that I was "kept" by my wife, when married. A pretty word which led me to slip six cartridges into the barrel of my revolver. Let us examine this then, since an examination is desirable; let us judge, since a judgement also has been found necessary.

My wife's dowry amounted to ten thousand francs represented by doubtful shares which were pledged in my name in a mortgage credit bank for a sum representing fifty per cent of their nominal value. The universal crash came. The titles remained almost valueless, which we already knew—since we had not sold at the opportune moment. So I was obliged to pay out the integral amount of my loan: that is fifty per cent. Later the banker holding the shares reimbursed my wife twenty-five per cent of her credit, forming her bank's active bankruptcy dividend. Here is a problem for the mathematicians: "How much, frankly, have I been able to squander?"

Nothing, in my humble opinion. Non-negotiable effects entitle their owner to their real value, whereas I, by providing them with my personal guarantee, had given them an effective enhanced value of twenty-five per cent.

Truly, then, I am innocent of this crime as well as of the other.

And the remorse, the despair, the suicide attempts so frequently projected. And the suspicions, the old distrust, the atrocious doubts incessantly reborn. Ah! I become furious when I think that I almost died like a wretch. Overwhelmed with worry, with work, I had never had the time to pay attention to the thousand rumours, the implications, the underhand jibes. And while, absorbed by my daily toil, I lived in ignorance, a legend was being sketched, was taking shape, perfidiously, based on the sayings of the jealous, on café chatter. And I, the good fool, believed everybody except myself. Ah . . .

Could it not really have been that I was never mad, never ill, never degenerate? Could it not have been that I was simply the dupe of an adored trickster whose little embroidery scissors cut the locks of Samson while he rested on the pillow with his brow weary from the task fulfilled and tired from the weight of the worries which came from her and her children? Trusting, suspecting nothing, he would have lost his honour in the arms of the charmer during his ten years' sleep, together with his virility, his will to live, his intelligence, his five senses, and still more, alas!

Could it not have been—oh! I am ashamed to imagine it—that a crime was secretly committed in those mists, in the midst of which I writhed like a phantom for years? A very small, unconscious crime, provoked by very vague desires for power, by a hidden tendency in the female to get the better of the male in the struggle between two called marriage.

Without any doubt I had been the dupe. Seduced by a married woman, forced to marry her to justify her pregnancy and thereby

9

save her dramatic career; married with the dowry system and with the stipulation that each would contribute half towards the necessities of the home, I was, after ten years, ruined, plundered, having after all carried alone the economic burden of our association.

Now that my wife is repudiating me as a good-for-nothing, incapable of contributing to the needs of the community, and depicting me as the waster of her imaginary fortune, she owes me forty thousand francs, her share according to our verbal contract made on the day of our nuptial benediction.

She is my debtor.

I got up, resolved to learn everything at last, I jumped from the bed like a paralytic who throws the crutches he thought he had in his dream far away, and hurriedly dressing, I went down to see my wife.

From the half-open door a ravishing tableau presented itself to my charmed eyes.

Lying on her unmade bed, with her pretty head buried in the white pillows, over the covers of which her wheat-blonde hair snaked; with her shoulders slipped out of the fine chemise, where her virginal breast appeared beneath the lace insertions; with her elegant and frail body rippling beneath the soft cover with its white and red stripes; with her foot uncovered, a minute and arched, perfect foot, whose rosy toes were enhanced by transparent, faultless nails; a truly accomplished work of art, moulded in human flesh in the manner of antique marble—so did my wife appear to me. Carefree and smiling, with an air of chaste motherhood, she watched her three podgy little ones climbing and diving between the spray-decked feather cushions, as in the middle of a newly-mown pile of flowers.

I was disarmed before this delightful spectacle and I thought deep down within me: "Let's watch out, the she-panther is playing with her cubs!"

I made an awkward entrance, as timid as a schoolboy's, subjugated before the majesty of the mother.

"Ah! already up, my little man," she said by way of greeting, with an expression of surprise, but less agreeable surprise than I would have thought. I sketched a muddled explanation, suffocated by the children who were toppling over my back while I was bending down to kiss their mother.

"What? she a criminal?" I asked myself as I went off, conquered by the arms of chaste beauty, by the frank smiles of that mouth which no lie had ever tarnished. No, a thousand times no! . . . I stole off, persuaded to the contrary.

Alas, the ferocious worries dogged me.

Why had my unexpected cure left her cold. Why had she not enquired after the progress of my fever? Why had she not asked for details of the night gone by? How could I explain her downcast face, that almost disagreeable expression at seeing me recovered and well? . . . And that mocking smile of superiority and condescension! . . . Had she conceived some hope of finding me dead one fine morning, to be rid of an idiot who was incessantly making her life insupportable? Did she hope to draw the few thousand francs of my life insurance which could then pave a new way for her towards some new goal? Ah! a thousand times no! . . .

And doubts still persisted within me, doubts about everything, about the virtue of the wife, the legitimacy of the children, doubts about the integrity of my mental faculties, doubts which still assail me without respite or mercy.

In any case it is time to finish; this flux of hollow ideas must be stopped. I must be certain or die. A crime has been perpetrated in the shadow or I am mad. The truth thus remains to be discovered.

To be a cuckolded husband! What would that matter to me, if I knew it? The important thing is that I might be the first to laugh at it. Is there a man in the world who could say with certainty that he is the favourite of a woman? . . . When I review the friends of my youth, today married, I cannot find a single one who is not slightly deceived! And they don't suspect anything, lucky men! One mustn't be touchy of course. To be two, to be alone, no matter! But not to know is to be ludicrous. And there's the principal point, one must know.

If a husband were to live for a hundred years he would never know anything of the true existence of his wife. He might know the world, the immense universe, but he will never have a straightforward idea of the woman whose life is rivetted to his own. That's why that poor M. Bovary is so beautifully placed in the memory of all happy husbands.

As for me, I want the truth. I want to know . . . To avenge myself? What madness! On whom? . . . On the favourites? But they have only used their male rights.—On my wife? I have already said, one mustn't be touchy. And do you think I'd touch a hair of the mother of my angels?

What I need is to know absolutely. And for that I am going to make a profound, discreet and scientific enquiry into my life. I will seek out everything at last, using all the resources of the new science of psychology, profiting from suggestion, thought-reading, mental torture, without discarding any such well-known old tricks as burglary, theft, seizure of mail, forgery and falsification of signatures. Is that monomania, the angry explosion of a maniac? It's not my business to judge.

Let the enlightened reader pronounce in the last resort, having read this bona fide book attentively. Perhaps he will discover in it some elements of the physiology of love, some indications of pathological psychology, with, moreover, a curious fragment of the philosophy of crime.

FIRST PART

(1)

It was the thirteenth of May 1875 in Stockholm.

I can still see myself at the Royal Library, which occupies an entire wing of the palace of the King, in the vast hall with its beech wainscoting brown with age like the meerschaum of a well-tanned pipe. The immense hall decorated with rococo beadings, garlands, chains and armorial bearings, surrounded by a gallery of Tuscan pillars to the height of the first floor, opened out, yawning like a chasm beneath my feet, the image of a gigantic brain, with the hundred thousand volumes which it held, where the ideas of vanished generations were ranged in cases.

The two principal quarters of the hall, fitted out all along the walls with shelves three metres high, were separated by a passage which cut the room down its entire length. The spring sun filtered its golden shafts through the twelve casements, lighting with a flash the Renaissance bindings in white and gold parchment, the black moroccos mounted in silver of the eighteenth century, the thick red-edged calf of the eighteenth century, the green leather which was modish under the Empire and the cheap cardboard covers of today. Here the theologians were neighbours of the apostles of magic, the philosophers of the naturalists, the poets made a good home with the historians. A bottomless geological deposit where, as in pudding-stone, the successive layers have agglomerated, marking the renewed stages of human stupidity or human genius.

I can still see myself. Mounted in the circular gallery, I was classifying a collection of old books, the recent donation of a collector, famous and prudent, for he had taken care to insure his immortality by signing on the verso of the bindings his ex-libris, where this device was displayed: "*Speravit infestis*".

Superstitious as an atheist, I couldn't help being impressed by this phrase, which had been reappearing before my eyes for a week, whenever I happened to open a volume. He kept up hope even in his reverses, that good man; and that was happiness for him . . . As for me, I had lost all hope. My tragedy in five acts and six tableaux, including five transformation scenes—I could not get staged. As for promotion to librarian, I had to bury seven supernumeraries, all in perfect health, four of whom had private incomes, in order to obtain a position. With a salary of twenty francs a month, a tragedy of five acts at the bottom of a drawer in an attic, one is, when past twenty-eight, only too inclined to indulge in the contemporary pessimism, in this renewal of scepticism, so comfortable for all the failures who find there a compensation for all the missed meals and

13

who replace an overcoat pawned before the end of winter by admirable, detached reasonings.

A member of an erudite, bohemian group, the residue of an older, artistic bohemian group, a collaborator in serious newspapers and solemn reviews which paid badly, a shareholder in a limited company formed to translate Edward Hartmann's *Philosophy of the Unconscious,* an adherent to a secret league of love free and paying, wrapped in the valueless title of secretary of the King, the author of two acts presented at the Theatre Royal, I managed with great difficulty to find the necessary income to sustain the course of this miserable existence. So much so that I had taken a detestation to life, without, however, having renounced living it—far from it—for I did my best to draw it out and to perpetuate my race and myself. One has to admit to oneself, however, that pessimism, taken literally by the crowd, and mistakenly confused with hypochondria, constitutes in itself a rather jolly and very consoling way of envisaging the world. Since Everything is only a relative Nothing, is it really worth making so much fuss about it; all the more since truth itself is only a second-hand truth? Has it not recently been discovered that the truth of the previous day is changed into stupidity the day after? Why then wear out one's strength and youth in discovering some new stupidities? The only verified point is that death remains for us. Let's live then!—For whom? For what? . . . Ah . . .

The restoration of all the old things, abolished at the end of the last century, having been accomplished with the coming of Bernadotte, a disillusioned Jacobin, to the throne, the generation of eighteen-sixty to which I belonged, had seen all its hopes crumble as the result of parliamentary reform, which came to light with such furore. The two chambers which had replaced the four estates were for the greater part composed of peasants and they had commuted the Diet into a municipal council where each one got used to dealing with his petty affairs by mutual agreement without ever caring for the vital questions and for progress. Politics then appeared to us as a compromise between communal or private interests, in such a way that the last traces of a belief in what was then called the Ideal, were decomposing in ferments of bitterness. Let us add to that the religious reaction which manifested itself the day after the death of Charles XV, at the coming to the throne of Queen Sophie of Nassau, and other motives will be found to justify the appearance of an enlightened pessimism, than those which resulted from individual causes . . .

The dust of the bestirred books was choking me and I opened a window onto the Lions' Court, in order to breathe a little fresh air and to have a corner of landscape under my eyes.

An embalmed breeze came to me loaded with the scent from the bestirred bunches of lilacs and from the gushing sap of the poplars.

The honeysuckle and the virginia creeper placed their carpeting greenery on the trellises; the acacias and the plane trees, which were not unaware of the dangerous caprices of the month of May, were late. It was spring all the same, although the carcasses of the bushes and the trees were still visible beneath the young frondage. And beyond the balustraded ramp, surmounted by Delft faïence vases, enhanced by the blue of Charles XII's insignia, the masts of the steamers anchored at the quay stood out, decked in honour of the feast of May. Further on, the bottle-green line of the cove between its two shores where the boles of the trees rose in tiers, with leaves on one side and needles on the other. All the ships anchored in the roads had displayed their national colours, more or less symbolising the diverse nationalities: England with the red of the bleeding beef; Spain yellow and red, striped like the blinds of its moorish balconies; the United States, a striped bed-tick; the joyous tricolour, a neighbour of the mournful flag of Germany, always in mourning with its ace of clubs near the flagstaff; Denmark's lady's chemisette, the disguised tricolour of Russia, all were there side by side, spread out under the navy-blue cover of a northern sky. And the hubbub of the carriages, of the whistles, of the bells and the cranes was added to this tableau, together with the odour of the oil of the engines, of the leather, of the salted herring, of the colonial produce, mixed with the perfume of the lilacs in the air which an easterly wind refreshed, rushing up from the sea where it had struck against the drift ice of the Baltic on its way.

I'd forgotten my books, turning my back on them, with my head out of the casement and I was bathing my five senses, when the mounting guard began to parade past to the March from *Faust*. Music, flags, blue sky, flowers, all inebriated me to the extent that I did not notice my office boy who was bringing up the mail. He touched my shoulder, handed me a letter and suddenly disappeared.

Hum! . . . Letter from a lady.

I hurriedly tore open the envelope, already scenting a stroke of luck . . . for here was one, for sure. Indeed:

"Be in front of 65 Regency Street at five sharp today. You'll see me there. Identification sign: a roll of music."

Having been mystified sometime previously by a little vixen who had led me by the nose, I did not appear difficult, having sworn to myself not to hold back another time. However, one thing shocked me, the imperative, decisive tone which came into conflict with the sentiment of my male dignity. How had this stranger got it into her head to capture me unawares like this? What the devil can those ladies be thinking with the unfavourable opinions they profess on our virtue? One does not ask permission, one intimates an order to one's conquest.

Unfortunately I was previously engaged to go on a picnic in the afternoon. In fine, I did not feel disposed to go and pay court to a woman in broad daylight in one of the central streets of the town. At two o'clock I went to the rendezvous fixed by my friends in the laboratory of one of our chemists.

They were already thronging in the anteroom, filled with doctors, aspiring philosophers or physicians, all eager to know the programme of the fête. I had been reflecting however. I apologised for not being able to join in the party. I was enjoined to give the reasons why I intended to be absent from the orgies of the evening. I brought out my letter which, held under the eyes of a zoologist, a recognised authority in the matter of love, only brought from him a shake of the head accompanied by an abrupt sentence:

"Nothing good! . . . That's for marriage, not for sale . . . Family, dear boy . . . Straight path . . . Do as you like! And you'd better go, you'll come and find us—later—in the Park, if you feel like it and the lady doesn't suit the horoscope."

So, at the appointed time, I was taking my stand on the pavement of the house indicated, waiting for the appearance of the beautiful stranger.

The roll of music was an invitation to marriage just like the advertisements on the fourth page of the newspapers and that caused me to hesitate while waiting, when I found myself in front of a lady.

My first impression—to which I gave enormous importance—was most imprecise. Her age, uncertain, floated between twenty-nine and forty-two; her dress was very adventurous. Artist or bluestocking? Family girl or free girl? Emancipated or cocotte? . . .

She presented herself as the fiancée of an old friend of mine, an opera singer, who wanted to place her under my protection, which I subsequently discovered was a lie.

She had a little bird-like quality, twittering without interruption. In half an hour I knew everything about her, what she felt, what she imagined, which was of mediocre interest to me; so that I asked her how I could be of use to her. On her reply:

"Me, serve as a chaperon to a girl?" I exclaimed. "But you don't know then that I'm the devil in person!"

"Ah! You think that, but I know you thoroughly," she retorted. "You're unhappy, that's all and you must be dragged from your black thoughts."

"Ah! You know me . . . Well, well . . . thoroughly? . . . Do you think so? In reality you only know the outdated opinion of me that your fiancé *could have* of my personality."

There was nothing to say, "my beautiful friend . . ." was in the know about everything, being able to read even from a distance into the heart of man. She was one of those viscous natures, avid to dominate minds by insinuating themselves into the secret folds of souls. She kept up an extraordinary correspondence, assassinating all the outstanding personalities with letters, distributing advice, lavishing admonitions on young men, fancying herself as conducting the destiny of man. Mad for power, directress of an enterprise for saving souls (highly recommended!), protectress of everyone, she had discovered a vocation to save me . . .

In short, an intriguante of the first water with little wit and a colossal feminine impudence.

I began by trying to put her off, joking about everything, about the world, about men, about God. She qualified my discourse as "dissolute".

"But you're not thinking, miss! Dissolute, my ideas? When on the contrary they're up to date! And yours, the residue of a past age, the commonplaces of my youth, the dregs of the dregs, appear new to you! Frankly, what you think you're serving up as early produce, is only preserves in badly-soldered tins. 'Take them away, for they smell.' You know the dictum."

Furious, taken aback, she left me without a good-bye. Since I had finished with her I hurried to rejoin my friends in the Park where we were to spend the night awake.

The following morning, slightly riled, I received a letter swollen with feminine fatuity, in which she overwhelmed me with reproaches and oozed commiseration, indulgence; she made vows in it for my spiritual health and her letter terminated with a new convocation to a rendezvous. We were to pay, she announced, a visit together to the old mother of her fiancé.

As a well-brought-up man, I resigned myself to undergo this second shower of words; and I donned a mask of absolute indifference as regards God, the world and the rest, to be let off more lightly.

O miracle! The damsel looked good with her fabric dress edged with fur and her Rembrandt hat, her moulded figure: full of the tender attentions of an elder sister, avoiding ticklish ground, she was charming, to the extent that, thanks to our mutual desire to please each other, our minds mingled in an amiable conversation which emanated sympathy.

The visit over, we made our way together under the stars, on that beautiful spring evening.

Caprice of the devil? . . . Either because I was seized with an imperious need for revenge or I was furious at having played a rôle of compère-confidant, I confided to her that I was almost engaged, which was merely a half-lie, since I was indeed courting at that time.

Thereupon, assuming the airs of a grandmama, she began to pity the girl, questioning me on her character, her looks, her status, her situation. I sketched a portrait susceptible of arousing her jealousy, which brought a slight relaxation in our warm conversation.—The interest I was granted decreased the more my guardian angel scented a rival for the saving of my soul. And so we separated, without having shaken off a coldness which had arisen without our knowing it. At the rendezvous next morning the conversation dealt exclusively with love and my fiancée.

After eight days of this intimacy, spent at the theatres and concerts, and on walks, she had reached her ends. Having entered my existence, her daily company now formed part of my routine, to the extent that it would have been impossible for me to renounce it. A conversation held with a woman by no means ordinary is an art. It is an almost sensual delight to caress souls, to embrace minds, to fondle mentally.

One fine morning she came up to me quite upset, with her memory filled with passages from a letter received the day before. Her fiancé was enraged with jealousy. She blamed herself for her imprudence; her fiancé had imposed upon her the strictest reserve towards me, my singer having had the instinct, the presentiment that things could turn out badly.

"I cannot understand anything about this frightful jealousy," she said with a heartbroken expression.

"It's because you understand nothing about love," I replied.

"About that love!"

"That love, miss, is the most elevated sentiment of ownership. Jealousy is only the fear of losing what one possesses."

"A property, ugh!"

"Common property, you see, since you possess each other."

But she did not want to understand love thus. Love for her was something disinterested, sublime, chaste, inexplicable.

She did not love, after all, her fiancé madly in love with her. Which I demonstrated to her.

She got angry and openly confessed to me that she had never loved him.

"And you will marry him just the same!"

"Of course, he would be a finished man but for that."

"Still the saving of souls then!"

She grew more irritated, claimed that she was not, never had been, his fiancée.

We had caught each other in the act of telling lies! What luck!

Nothing more remained for me than to open my heart to her by denying my engagement. We would be free afterwards to profit from our freedom.

Now, since it was no longer a question of jealousy on her part, the game was to resume—better than before. I addressed a written declaration to her. She sent it on in a sealed envelope to her lover who didn't delay in overwhelming me with insults by post.

18

I summoned the beauty to explain herself, to choose between the two of us.

She carefully avoided doing anything of the kind, preferring, and by far, to choose him, to choose me, and two, three, four others as well, to see us all at her knees, soliciting the great favour of adoring her.

She was only a coquette, a man-eater, a chaste polygamist.

I had become enamoured of her however, for lack of anything better, for I was sick of chance loves, and disgusted with my lonely attic.

Towards the end of her stay, I had invited her to pay me a visit at the library, with the intention of dazzling her, of appearing to her in a grandiose milieu, crushing for her little pretentious bird brain.

I dragged her from gallery to gallery, making a verbose display of my bibliographical knowledge. I forced her to admire the miniatures of the middle ages, the autographs of famous personages; I evoked the great historical memories, enclosed in manuscripts, incunabula, to the extent that she felt herself embarrassed by her inferiority towards me. In the end:

"But you're a wise man, sir," she exclaimed.

"But certainly, miss."

"My poor histrion! . . ." she let slip, thinking of my friend the actor, her fiancé.

Anyone else would have thought the actor ousted for ever . . .—Not at all.

Still by post, the histrion threatened me with his revolver; he incriminated me; it was I who had stolen from him his fiancée *whom he had entrusted to me.* I made him understand that nothing had been stolen from him, for the very simple reason that, not possessing anything, he couldn't keep anything in deposit. The correspondence ceased meanwhile and gave way to a menacing silence.

The day of the lady's departure approached. On the eve of the good-byes, I received from my beauty a triumphal letter in which she announced a stroke of luck to me. She had read my tragedy to people in high society, very much in favour with the administration of theatres. The play had so much impressed the said personages that they wanted to make the acquaintance of the author. Details would be given to me by word of mouth at the afternoon rendezvous.

At the appointed time, Miss X . . . took me for a walk among the counters of the shops for her final purchases, whilst conversing with me about the effects of my drama, and as I was enlightening her on the deep aversion I nourished for every kind of protector, she took extreme measures to convert me. And I, without stopping, blathered on :

"But it repels me, my dear child, to pull bell cords, to stay in front of strangers, to chatter about everything without tackling the important point, to arrive at strange houses like a kind of beggar, to solicit this or that . . ."

I was struggling as best I could, when she stopped in front of a young woman, well-dressed, even elegant, shapely and distinguished. She introduced me to the Baroness of Y . . . who threw some polite phrases to me, scarcely perceptible in the hubbub of the crowd on the pavement. I stammered a few disjointed words, uncomfortable at feeling myself led and trapped by an artful dodger. For it was a plot, for sure.

A minute and the Baroness was eclipsed, not without having repeated to me the invitation which had been handed on to me by Miss X . . .

What struck me in the appearance of the Baroness was her girlish air, her child face despite her apparent twenty-five years. She had a schoolgirl's head, a pretty face framed with saucy hair, blonde like ears of barley, princessly shoulders, a figure supple like a wythe, a way of inclining her forehead with frankness, deference and superiority. And to think that this virgin mother was safe and sound after the reading of my tragedy! Fortunately!—Married to a captain of the guards, mother of a little daughter of three, she had become infatuated with the theatre without the prospect of ever approaching it, in view of the elevated position held by her husband and father-in-law, recently promoted court chamberlain.

That's how things stood, when my May dream vanished. A steamer was carrying away my beauty into the vicinity of her histrion, who from then on would reassume his rights, amusing himself by going through the letters which I would address to his fiancée; a just revenge on similar curiosity exercised to the prejudice of his correspondence, read recently by us together.

On the gangway of the steamer, at the moment of the tender good-byes, my queen made me promise to go and pay a visit on the Baroness as soon as possible. It was the last word we exchanged.

The innocent reveries so different from the brutal debauchery of erudite bohemians had left a gap within me which had to be filled. The friendly intercourse with a woman considered an equal, that relationship between two individuals of different sex, had reawoken delicate tastes, long atrophied in the isolation into which I had plunged myself as a result of family dissension. The sense of the home abolished by the habit of café life had reappeared under the influence of my relations with that woman, very ordinary, but decent in the vulgar acceptance of the word. In short, I found myself one fine evening about six o'clock before the door of a house in North Avenue.

Fate! it was the old paternal dwelling where I had lived the hardest years of my youth, where I had experienced the internal troubles of puberty, of the first communion, seen my mother dead and replaced by a stepmother! Seized with a sudden uneasiness, I was tempted to turn tail, eager to flee through fear of seeing all the sadness of my adolescence reappear before my eyes. The courtyard opened, as before, with its enormous ash trees whose leafage I impatiently awaited every spring in front of the lugubrious house, leaning against a sand quarry, the inevitable collapse of which had determined the lowering of the rents.

Despite the depression which came to me from so many sinister memories, I recovered my courage; I entered, I went up, I rang. When the bell tinkled, I couldn't help thinking my father himself was going to open to me. A maid appeared and disappeared to announce me. An instant later the Baron was coming to meet me and was welcoming me with cordiality. He was a man of about thirty, corpulent, tall, with a noble carriage, with the manners of a perfect man of the world. His strong face, slightly swollen, was lit by two blue, infinitely sad eyes. The smile on his lips dissolved incessantly into an expression of strange bitterness, taken from deceptions, failed projects, disillusions.

The drawing-room—formerly our family dining-room—was furnished without a definite artistic taste. The Baron, who bore the name of a general famous in history, as is Turenne or Condé in this country, had assembled there a collection of family portraits, dating from the Thirty Years' War, heroes cuirassed in white and weighted with Louis XIV wigs, infiltrating amongst landscapes of the Dusseldorf school. Here and there old furniture, renovated and regilded, alternated with chairs and pouffes of recent date. From all the corners of the vast drawing-room a warm atmosphere of peace and home love emanated.

The Baroness made her entrance; charming, cordial too, simple and comely. There was, however, a certain stiffness in her, a trace of awkwardness in her bearing, which chilled me until I had discovered the reason for it. Voices, the bursts of which issued from a neighbouring room, told me of the presence of other people. I apologised for the disturbance I might have caused by calling at that time. Indeed, the relatives of the newly-weds had assembled there to play whist and I soon found myself in front of four members of the family; the chamberlain, a retired captain, the mother and the aunt of the Baroness. As soon as the old people were installed at their table of play, we youngsters made conversation. The Baron confessed his pronounced taste for painting. Having enjoyed a bursary offered to him by the late King Charles XV, he had studied awhile at Dusseldorf. It was a point of contact between us since I myself had been awarded a bursary, but in my capacity as dramatist, by the same king. And the conversation turned to painting, the theatre, the

21

personality of our protector. Our effusions grew gradually tepid, however, chilled by the reflections of the old people who joined from time to time in our talk, touching upon sensitive points or badly scarred wounds, to the extent that I felt troubled, out of place in this motley company.

I rose to take my leave. As they accompanied me to the threshold, the Baron and the Baroness seemed to lay down their masks, now that they were out of reach of the old people. They invited me to dine with them the following Saturday in a little group. And after a brief chat on the landing, we parted as declared friends.

2

When the Saturday came I set out at three o'clock for the house in North Avenue. Welcomed like an old, trusted friend, I was initiated without scruple into the intimacies of the home. The meal was seasoned with mutual confidences. The Baron, disgusted with his position, belonged to the group of malcontents of the new regime, a malcontent which had been born at the time of the coming to the throne of King Oscar. Jealous of the resounding popularity obtained by his late brother, the new prince had sought to relegate into the shadows all the projects with which his predecessor had toyed. In this way the friends of the old regime, with its frank gaiety, its spirit of tolerance, progressive aspirations, ranged themselves on one side and formed a reasoned opposition without mixing, however, in the petty struggles between electoral parties.

Our hearts drew closer as we reawakened our bygone memories. All my old petty bourgeois prejudices against the aristocracy which was beating a retreat since the parliamentary reform of 1865 were dissipated, giving way to a sympathetic pity for the downfallen grandeur. The Baroness, of Finnish origin, recently emigrated, could not take part in our first effusions. As soon as the dinner was over, she sat herself at the piano and sang ditties to us: then, the Baron and myself discovered in each other an unknown talent for the Wennerberg duets. And so the hours sped by, rapidly. Finally, we read a verse playlet, recently staged at the Theatre Royal and we cast the parts to each according to his capacity.

After those various distractions there was an inevitable pause for one is quickly exhausted when one makes sustained efforts to display one's merits and when one is set on conquering people. In the interval the old obsession took hold of me again. I fell silent.

"Whatever's the matter with you, sir?" the Baroness asked me.

"There are ghosts here," I said to explain my silence. "I lived in this apartment a century ago . . . alas, yes, a century for I am so old."

"And can't we chase away those ghosts?" she asked with a captivating air of motherly tenderness.

"No, my dear, for that," said the Baron, "is the privilege of a single person. She alone can dispel black thoughts. Come now, admit it—aren't you the fiancé of Miss X . . .?"

"Ah . . . No . . . You're mistaken, Baron . . . Love's labour lost . . ."

"Then she's engaged elsewhere?" asked the Baroness, examining me attentively.

"A good question!"

"Ah! That's a pity. She's a pearl, that girl. Anyway I'm certain that she's taken a fancy to you."

And I began forthwith to rail against that poor actor. From then on we all set on the luckless singer who intended to force a girl to love him in spite of herself and the Baroness ended up by assuring me that everything would be arranged as soon as she had finished a trip she had to make to Finland—a trip planned for the near future.

"That won't happen," she affirmed, angry at the idea of a forced marriage imposed upon a girl of the élite whose sentiments inclined in another direction.

At about seven I got up to take my leave. They pressed me so much to stay that I was tempted to believe that they were bored in that home which was three years old at the most and which heaven had blessed with a little angel. They were expecting a cousin of the Baroness in the evening and they wanted to arrange a meeting between us so as to know my opinion of the girl's personality.

During the conversation the maid handed a letter to the Baron. He tore it open, read it there and then and, murmuring incoherent words, handed it to his wife.

"I can't believe it," she exclaimed after reading it.

And to inform me as a friend, after a nod of the head which she made to her husband who agreed with her, the Baroness burst out:

"It's from my first cousin. Just imagine, my uncle and aunt won't let their daughter cross our threshold, with the excuse that it's causing gossip about my husband!"

"It's too much, isn't it?" added the Baron. "A child, nice, innocent, unhappy, who likes being with us, her allies, newly-weds . . . And that lends itself to gossip."

Perhaps a sceptical smile betrayed me. In any case the surge of the conversation slowed down, soon stopped, and was then replaced by embarrassment thinly disguised under an invitation to take a walk in the garden.

After supper, about ten, I left and once out of the door I began to reflect on all I had just seen and heard during that fateful day.

In spite of the apparent happiness of the couple, despite their public caresses, there must have been a black spot in the union. Sad airs, careworn looks, implications indicated hidden worry, and allowed me to imagine secrets I was afraid of discovering.

Why, I wondered, that isolation from the world, that relegation to the heights of a suburb? They both appeared shipwrecked by life, so much did they seem enchanted, delighted at having found a man, a newcomer, to whom they gave themselves from the start.

The Baroness especially intrigued me. In trying to evoke her image I was confused by a complexity of different characters I saw in her and which left me room for choice. Full of goodness, gracious, hard,

24

enthusiastic, expansive, reserved, cold, impulsive, she seemed to me to be sulking, brooding over dreams of ambition. Without being dull, without being witty, she imposed herself, however. Of a Byzantine slenderness which made her dress fall in the simple and grandiose folds of a St. Cecilia's, her body offered ravishing proportions to the eye: her limbs were of an exquisite beauty, and from time to time the pale and hardened features of her thin face were animated by shafts of overflowing gaiety. It seemed difficult to me to determine which of the two spouses had the upper hand in the home. He, the soldier accustomed to command but with a weakened constitution, seemed submissive more from inborn indolence than an absence of will. They certainly treated each other as friends but without those upsurges of first love and my appearance in their house had brought them the sweetness of rejuvenating themselves before a third party by the evocation of past memories. As far as one could see, they were living on left-overs and were bored together. As proof, the frequent invitations which were sent to me from the day after my first visit.

When the Baroness was on the eve of her departure for Finland, I called on her to say good-bye. It was a fine evening in June. I was entering the courtyard when I caught sight of her standing in a clump of birthwort, behind the garden enclosure and I was struck by the uncommon beauty of the sight. She was dressed all in white in a piqué frock with lace trimmings, the masterpiece of a Russian serf. Her necklace, her brooches and alabaster bracelets enveloped her in a glow which seemed to have come from a lamp through a fluor globe, and the green of the broad leaves, mingling with it, threw deathly hues in the brightness and shadows of this pallid face, where the black pupils of coal shone.

At that minute I was seized, troubled down to my marrow, as if before a vision. The sense of veneration which I bear in me emerged completely, with the desire for a cult. The gap left by dispelled religiosity was filled: the need to adore reappeared in a new form. God was relegated. Woman took his place, but woman, virgin and mother at once; for when I saw her little girl by her side I couldn't believe that that childbirth had been possible. The thought of the intimate relations between the two never reminded me of sensual behaviour, so much did their relationship seem not of the flesh. From that moment the woman presented herself to me as the incarnation of a Soul, pure, inaccessible, invested with that glorious body in which the Holy Scriptures enjoy dressing defunct souls. In fine, I adored her without wanting to. I adored her as she was; as mother and wife, just as she appeared to me; as wife of *that* husband, as mother of *that* child. Since, for the satisfaction of my need for adoration, the presence of the husband was a necessity. Without a husband, I told myself, she would be a widow and, if a widow, would I be certain of adoring her? Perhaps if she were mine, my wife . . ? No! Firstly I couldn't engender such a sacrilegious idea. And then when she'd wed me, she would cease to be the wife of *that* husband, the mother of *that* child, the mistress of *that* house. As she was and in no other way.

Whether it was because of the austerity of the memories attached to that former dwelling where she lived; whether it was because of my instincts of a man from the lower classes, the admirer of the superior, thoroughbred race—a sentiment which would be annihilated the day she would no longer be so highly placed—the fact still remains that the cult vowed by me to this woman resembled in every detail the religion from which I had just freed myself. I wanted to revere, sacrifice myself, suffer, without a hope of ever gaining anything other than the joy of reverence, of sacrifice and of suffering.

I appointed myself her guardian angel. I wanted to watch over her so that the force of my love might not succeed in carrying her away. I carefully avoided finding myself alone with her, so that confidences might not slip between us to the prejudice of her husband.

However, on that eve of her departure, when I perceived her in the shrubbery, she was alone. We exchanged some insignificant words. But, suddenly, my emotion was overriding and communicated itself. I saw, while I beheld her with inflamed looks, that a need to confide was being born in her. She spoke to me of the presentiment of the regrets she'd have · after her separation—however short—from her daughter and her husband. She begged me to devote my leisure to them, not to forget her herself while she was going to save my interests compromised with my young Finnish girl.

"You really love her from the bottom of your heart, don't you?" she said, wrapping me very slowly in her gaze.

"You're asking me?" I replied, but oppressed by the weight of that painful lie.

And I was persuaded from that moment that that spring love had only been a fancy, a whim, a pastime.

Through fear of tarnishing her with the contact of my so-called love, afraid lest I enclose her in spite of myself in the network of my sentiments, in order to safeguard her against myself, I brusquely stopped the course of this perilous conversation by asking news of the Baron. She grimaced, interpreting my rather curious solicitude absolutely in its true sense. Quite likely—I now suspect—she was amusing herself with my confusion before her crushing beauty. Perhaps too at that instant she felt the frightful enchantress's power she held over this Joseph, of glacial appearance, of obligatory chastity.

"You're bored with me," she resumed. "Come along, I'm going to call in reinforcements."

And in a clear voice she called her husband who had remained in his room on the first floor.

The casement opened and the Baron showed his friendly face, greeting us with a frank smile. He came down into the garden at once. Standing in his fine uniform of the Royal Guards he looked resplendent. His dark blue tunic was decorated with silver and yellow silk embroidery; his virile face, strongly developed, made a worthy pendant to the white vision, alabaster on white, which I admired at his side. They were truly a rare couple, the advantages of the one serving as foil to the advantages of the other. Indeed, to see them was a veritable enjoyment of art, a spectacle dazzling to behold.

After supper the Baron suggested that I accompany the Baroness the following evening on the steamship which was to carry her away. We would get off at the last station, the customs. The project, which I hurriedly accepted, seemed to delight the Baroness who was looking forward to the view of the Stockholm Archipelago from the top of the ship's deck on a beautiful summer's night . . .

. . . The following evening at ten o'clock all three of us were on the boat which had cast off from the quayside. The night was clear, the sky orange, the sea blue and calm. The wooded shores filed past, lit up by this half-day and half-night which allowed the mind of the onlooker to float between the two imprecise sensations of dawn or sunset.

After midnight there was a lowering of our ecstasy incessantly revived by new aspects from which memories surged up. We vigorously fought against the sleep which was overtaking us: our faces were pale in the daybreak and we were shaken with shivering in the morning breeze. A sudden sentimentality took hold of us. We declared eternal friendship to each other. It was destiny which had united us and already the fatal link which was to fetter us was appearing. In delicate health as a result of an intermittent fever, I looked poorly and I was treated like a sick child. The Baroness wrapped me in her plaid, she found me a place where I was to sit, she offered me a glass of her madeira and rebuked me with the fondness of a doting mother. I let her have her way. Lack of sleep was crushing me; my heart which I thought closed was opening up and, unaccustomed to this feminine tenderness of which no one has the secret like the mother-woman, I oozed respectful adoration and from my brain which the insomnia excited poetic reverie rambled on.

All the abortive dreams of that lost night were taking body, a dark, mystical, aerial body; all the expansion of a drowsed talent escaped in flimsy visions. I spoke uninterruptedly for hours, drawing my inspiration from two pairs of eyes which didn't leave me, never tiring. I felt my fragile body being consumed in the continual fire of the thought machine, and the sensation of my bodily existence was gradually evaporating.

Suddenly the sun rose and the islets swimming by the thousand in the sea bay lit up. The branches of the pines glowed with a copper tone which contrasted with the fine sulphur needles; the panes of the cabins on the shore flamed in the golden fires of the sun; smoke rose from the chimneys announcing the preparation of coffee; the fishermen set sail in order to leave to drag their nets among the waters of the gulf, and the seagulls screeched themselves hoarse, scenting the little herrings travelling under the dark green waves.

An absolute silence reigned on the boat. The travellers were sleeping on the deck and we alone had remained standing astern, eyed by the sleepy captain on his bridge, by the captain who was wondering what we could very well be saying to each other for such a long time.

It was three in the morning when the pilot boat brusquely appeared from behind a spit of land to part us.

The gulf was only separated from the open sea by a few islands, spread out, so that one could already feel the movements of the swelling tide and hear the roaring waves which pounced on the last steep reefs.

The time to say good-bye had come. They kissed, she and he, with heartbreaking emotion, she clutched my hand between her hands, passionately, with tear-filled eyes, entrusting me to the care of her husband and begging me to bring him some consolation during this fortnight of widowhood.

As for me, I bowed; I kissed her hand without thinking, either of the possible inconveniences, or that I would disclose to her, perhaps involuntarily, my most secret sentiments. The engine stopped, the boat slowed down and the pilot took his place between decks. Two steps to the rope ladder: I descended and found myself beside the Baron, in the pilot cutter.

The boat towered high above our heads. Leaning over the gunwale, the pretty head, with its child eyes filled with tears, greeted us with a smile on its lips, laden with regrets. The propeller started up, the monster advanced, dragging its Russian ensign over the sea, and we were rocking on the churned-up billows, waving our handkerchiefs soaked through with freshly dried-away tears. The thin face grew still smaller, the delicate features were effaced and only two large eyes followed us, which melted into two looks and then vanished. Already, with the passing of an instant, it was only a bluish veil in the air, floating above a Japanese hat, with a waving cambric handkerchief; then a white spot, a white dot, at last the monster, a shapeless hulk misted-up with filthy smoke . . .

The Baron and I went ashore at the pilots' and customs station, which formed a seaside spa for the summer. The village lay asleep; nobody on the landing-stage where we had stopped, to see in the distance the ship turning windward, seeking to veer to the right before disappearing behind the cape, the last rampart raised before the sea.

The moment the boat was eclipsed, the Baron hugged me, shaken with a fit of sobbing and we remained like this in each other's arms for some time without saying anything to each other.

Was it insomnia, the enervation of a sleepless night which was provoking these tears? Was it sinister presentiments, or quite simply regret? At this moment, I can't exactly say.

We went to the village, silent and mournful, in order to take a cup of coffee. But the restaurant wasn't yet open. We crossed the streets, whose little houses were shut up, their blinds drawn. When we arrived outside the hamlet, we reached a solitary place through which a channel ran. The water was limpid, which invited us to dab our eyes a little. I unbuckled my toilet case, brought out a clean handkerchief, a tooth brush, a bar of soap and a bottle of eau-de-Cologne. The Baron pulled a face as though he wanted to sneer at my refinement, which didn't prevent him from being grateful to me for procuring him the pleasure of making a toilet, however summary, by lending him what was necessary. While we were returning to the hamlet, I perceived an odour of burnt coal which filtered through the leafage of the alders planted on the shore. With a sign, I made him understand that there was the supreme good-bye, brought by the sea wind. But he didn't deign to seize the sense of my mimic.

Over coffee, the aspect of my friend appeared pitiful to me. His big head overwhelmed with sleep was drooping, his swollen features gave him an inconsolable expression. A certain embarrassment entered into our relationship, and he, in a sullen mood, kept an obstinate silence. At one moment he took my hand, apologising for his distraction, and the next moment he lapsed into an inappropriate reverie. I did my utmost to revive him, but we were off-key, no longer in touch. His face, still amiable and harmonious a moment ago, gradually assumed unexpected signs of vulgarity and coarseness. The reflections of grace, of living beauty from the adored woman were becoming effaced. The uncultured man was reappearing.

What he was thinking, I don't know. Did he see through me? To judge his interior state by the change in his behaviour, he must have been a prey to very divergent sensations; he was now shaking my hand, calling me his first, his only friend; now he was turning his back on me.

During this time I realised with horror that we were only living through Her and for Her alone. Since the sunset we had lost all individual colour.

Back in town I said good-bye to him. But he led me away in spite of myself, imploring me to accompany him to his house where I followed him.

Returning to the deserted apartment, it was as if we had penetrated into a mortuary chamber. We had a new fit of sobbing. Disconcerted, I didn't know how to extricate myself. I chose to laugh.

"Isn't it rather ridiculous—what do you think, Baron?—A captain of the Guards and a secretary of the King who are crying . . ."

"It does one good," he said to me.

Thereupon he called for his little daughter who was to resuscitate the bitter regret in us. It was nine o'clock in the morning. At the end of his strength, he invited me to have a little nap on the sofa, while he himself would go to his bedroom. Having put a cushion under my head and having covered me with his army coat, he wished me a good sleep, not without having thanked me again for not leaving him alone. In his brotherly affection, there were echoes of the tenderness of his wife; she filled his thought entirely. I fell into a heavy sleep, observing that at the moment when I was losing consciousness, he had stolen up on my improvised bed, in order to ask me once again if I was alright.

I woke up towards mid-day. He was already up. The solitude was making him afraid! He proposed that we go together and dine in the Park. Which we did. The day was spent in chatting about one thing and another, but particularly in talking about that being on the existence of whom our existences had been grafted.

3

For two consecutive days I kept aloof, seeking solitude in my Library whose basements, formerly rooms of the sculpture museum, offered a suitable refuge to my frame of mind. The vast room in the rococo style which overlooked the Lions' Court held the manuscripts. I tarried there for a long time, picking out at random what seemed to me old enough to distract my attention from recent events. But the more I pursued my reading, ·the more the present blended with the past, and the yellowed letters of Queen Christina whispered the avowals of the Baroness to my mind. In order to escape from the conversations of my friends, I avoided my usual restaurant. I didn't want at any cost to defile my tongue by confessing to heretics my new faith of which they must still have been ignorant. I was jealous of my person, uniquely vowed to Her henceforth. When I walked through the streets, I dreamt that I was preceded by choir children whose tinkling little bells informed the crowd of the approach of the Holy of Holies encased in the ciborium of my heart; I imagined myself wearing mourning along the pavements, mourning for a queen, and I was near to inviting everybody to bare their heads for the death of my stillborn love with no hope of ever being resuscitated.

On the third day I was dragged from my torpor by the rolling of the drums of the mounting guard and by the sudden sonorities of Chopin's Funeral March. I ran to the window. At the head of the procession I perceived the Baron who was commanding the guard. He greeted me, emphasising his nod with a roguish smile. It was he who had had the idea of getting his musicians to perform the Baroness's favourite piece: and those performers couldn't suspect that they were playing for the two of us in Her honour in front of this crowd even more unaware.

Half an hour later the Baron came and asked for me at the Library. I led him to the basement, through the dark corridors cluttered with cupboards, shelves, to the manuscript room. He appeared delighted and lost no time in communicating to me the contents of a letter from his wife. All was well and there was a small note for me which I devoured in all haste, dissimulating my emotion as best I could. In a cordial and frank tone, she thanked me for the care lavished on her "old man" and appeared flattered by the regret I had shown at her departure. She was for the present with my soul-saving angel to whom she had taken a warm liking. She did not stop praising her character and ended by inciting me to hope. That was all.

She loved me then, my soul-saving angel, a monster the memory of whom now sickened me, and I was going to be forced forthwith to play the man in love in spite of himself, condemned as I was to an abominable comedy, perhaps without end. For sure, one cannot toy with love with impunity. Ensnared, furious, I sought to undress in my thoughts the filthy beast, with her mongol eyes, grey face, red arms, who had forced me to love her. With diabolical satisfaction I evoked her seductive ways, her suspicious behaviour which had brought upon me ill-sounding questions from my friends: "What then is that tart," they had said to me, "which you take through the suburbs to the greenery?"

I recalled with malicious joy her tricks, her assiduity, her simperings to captivate me, her artifices, when she would take her watch out of her corsage in order that a fine bit of her underwear be uncovered. And that Sunday when we walked in the Park! We were going along the large avenues when she proposed to me that we go off into the undergrowth. My hair stood on end to hear such a suggestion, in view of the bad form of those woodland walks. But to my objections she had replied:

"Ah! A fig for convention!"

She wanted to pick anemones under the hazel trees. Abandoning the avenue, she ran off and vanished into the undergrowth. I followed her, rather embarrassed. She chose a well-sheltered corner under a buckthorn, sat down, spreading out her skirts and uncovering her feet, little, but deformed by chilblain bunions. A frightful time followed during which I was reminded of the old maids of Corinth who were enraged that the customary rape was being delayed. She looked at me, sillily and, upon my word, her virtue was only spared that day thanks to her extreme ugliness and the disgust I have for easy conquests.

All those details, repelled hitherto as odious, overwhelmed me at that moment when the prospect of seeing her fall into my arms again was opening up and I made vows for the happiness of the histrion in his amorous enterprises. However, I had to resign myself and don the mask again.

While I was reading his wife's note, the Baron had sat down in front of the vast table overloaded with books and manuscripts. He was playing with his captain's baton in carved ivory, with a distracted air as if he was aware of his inferiority in literary matters in the face of the civilian that I was. He withdrew before all the efforts I made to interest him in my scholarly work, declaring without conviction:

"Yes, that must be very interesting, indeed!"

As for me, humiliated before the insignia of his rank which were apparent in his neckpiece, his sash, his ceremonial dress, I sought to establish the balance by making a display of my knowledge without succeeding in anything else than to embarrass him.

Sword and pen! The falling noble, the rising commoner! Perhaps the wife unconsciously but clearsightedly foretold the future when she subsequently chose a father for her future children among the nobility of the intellect.

Despite all his attempts to treat me as an equal, the Baron felt an unavowed embarrassment in his relations with me. Sometimes he showed me due respect for my knowledge, a tacit avowal of his inferiority on this score: and when he sometimes also decided to tackle a question, a word from the Baroness sufficed to stop him in his ardour. In the eyes of his wife the inherited armorial bearings scarcely counted and the captain's parade uniform was to make way for the dust-sprinkled coat of the scholar. Had he not acknowledged it himself the day when he had donned the painter's blouse, classifying himself as the least of the pupils at the studio! Certainly, but there still remained a basis of refined education, an accustomance to the traditions, and the hatred born of the jealousy between students and officers had passed into his blood.

For the moment I was indispensable to him as the depositary of his sorrows and I received, for that very reason, an invitation to dine at home with him.

After the coffee he proposed that I write to the Baroness. He armed me with a pen and brought me paper. Although I was obliged to write, I racked my brain to find the requisite banalities to dissimulate what my heart was thinking.

The letter finished, I handed it open to the Baron, asking him to go through it.

"I never read other people's letters," he replied in a tone of mock haughtiness.

"And I," I replied, "I never write to other people's wives without the husband taking cognisance of the correspondence."

He glanced through the contents of the note and sealed it inside his own with an inexplicable smile.

I lost sight of him during the whole week. One fine evening I bumped into him at a crossroads. He appeared very glad to meet me, and we immediately looked for a café so that he could disclose his indispensable confidences to me.

He had been to spend a few days in the country with the famous cousin of his wife. Without ever having seen that seductive person, I at once discovered her personality in the reflections which the Baron had kept of her. He had left down there his mournfulness and his usual sadness. His face had taken on an air of joyous sensuality, like make-up. His vocabulary had become enriched with vulgar terms of doubtful taste and the intonations of his voice had become strikingly altered.

A weak mind, I said to myself, who is influenced by all impressions; a smooth tablet where the slightest woman's hand can, according to her fancy, inscribe either her follies or her shafts of embryonic genius. The Man in him had become a sort of operetta hero, who was witty, cracked jokes and larked about. In civils, moreover, he lost all his prestige, and when after supper, slightly tipsy, he proposed we see the whores, I found him repulsive. There was decidedly nothing to him but the bedecked clothing, the sash, the neckpiece and nothing else.

Having arrived at the culminating point of his drunkenness he got ready to tell me bedroom secrets, when I cut him short, stopping the performance, indignant although he assured me that his wife had left him every license to enjoy himself during his widowhood, which at first appeared to me very human and later corroborated the opinions I had on the cold nature of the Baroness. We separated early and I returned to my lodgings overwhelmed by the indiscreet revelations I had just heard.

So, that woman, in love with her husband, left him, after three years' union, bodily freedom without exacting the same rights for herself in return. It was strange, indeed, abnormal as love without jealousy, heads without tails. It was not possible! But something else. The Baroness had a chaste nature, he had confided to me. A new anomaly! She thus personified the virgin-mother whom I had divined in her. And wasn't chastity a quality, one of the attributes of the superior race: the purity of soul which had to ally itself to the correctness of behaviour in the upper classes? All that was found there, as I had imagined it during my youth, at the time when a young society girl inspired me only with veneration, without ever awakening my sensual instincts. A child's dreams, sweet ignorance of woman, a problem more complicated than a bachelor thinks!

At last the Baroness came back, radiant with health, rejuvenated by so many memories stirred by the contact with her childhood friends.

"Come on, here is the dove from the Ark who is bringing back a sprig of olive," she said to me, handing me a letter from my so-called intended.

I read the pretentious, colourless, heartlessly-styled chatter of a blue-stocking wanting to win her freedom through some marriage . . . or other.

After a reading begun with an apparent effusion, but without sincerity, I wanted to make a clean breast of the absurd story at once.

"Can you tell me for certain," I asked the Baroness, "if that person is engaged to that singer?"

"Yes and no."

"Is she engaged to him by a promise?"

"No!"

"Does she want the marriage to take place?"

"No!"

"Do her father and mother want it?"

"They detest your singer."

"Why then does she persist in wanting to give herself to that man?"

"Because . . . really, I don't know."

"Does she love me?"

"Perhaps."

"Then she is a husband-hunter. She has only one idea, to marry the last and highest bidder. That woman does not understand love."

"But you, sir, what do you understand then by love?"

"To tell the truth, a sentiment which predominates over all others, a natural force which nothing resists, something like the thunderblast, the rising tide, the waterfall, the storm . . ."

She looked me in the eyes, holding back within herself all the allegations prepared for the defence of her friend.

"And you love her with such violence?" she asked.

At that moment I was tempted to confess everything. But afterwards? . . . The link would be broken and the lie, my safeguard against that criminal love, had become indispensable to me.

To avoid a too categorical reply, I asked her not to speak to me any more of it. The beautiful beast would henceforth be dead for me and I would undertake the cruel duty of forgetting her. That was all.

The Baroness did her best to console me, without seeking to dissimulate from me that the singer was a dangerous rival, since he had the advantage of being close to the lady.

The Baron, tired of our chatter, interrupted the conversation, predicting that we would burn our fingers: "For," he said, "one ought never to interfere in the affairs of other people's hearts."

This was said in a tone of such brusqueness that flames of indignation were lit in the Baroness's cheeks and I was obliged to ward off an imminent tempest by changing the conversation.

4

The stone was rolling.

The lie, originally a fantasy, was taking on consistency; shame and fear were forcing me to dissimulate to the extent that this amorous adventure was becoming a poetic tale, which I was ending up by believing in myself. I was playing the rôle of a luckless lover in it which was not too difficult to sustain, in view of the situation, real in itself except in so far as the object of my sentiments was concerned. Now, I had gone so far that I was going to be caught in my own nets. One fine day as I was going back to my room I came across the letter of a Mr. X . . ., a registrar of the Customs administration, who was no other than the father of my "little horror". I returned his visit at once. He was a little old man, resembling his daughter atrociously, a caricature of a caricature. His first concern was to treat me absolutely like his future son-in-law. He questioned me on my family, my savings, my chances of promotion; in short, it was a veritable examination. The thing was threatening to take on a serious turn . . . What could I do? I belittled myself in his eyes as best I could, in order to deflect his paternal looks from me. The goal of his voyage to Stockholm appeared only too clear to me. One of two things: either he intended to get rid of the singer who displeased him, or the beauty had decided to honour me with her choice after having sent an expert to me with full powers for an estimate. I showed myself as disagreeable as could be, steering clear whenever possible, missing a dinner at the Baroness's, tiring out the luckless father-in-law by my incessant escapades, pretending absolute necessities of duty at the Library, hence—which I wanted—the departure of the furious registrar, before the time he'd fixed.

Did my actor guess to which rival he was indebted for his future conjugal misfortunes when he wed his madonna? No doubt he never learnt and proudly attributed to himself the honour of having ousted me.

This settled, an incident occurred which was not without consequences on our respective destinies. The Baroness suddenly left for the country, taking her little daughter with her. It was in the first days of August. For health reasons she had chosen Mariafred Spa for her stay, an isolated township, on one of the points of Lake Moelar, precisely where the young cousin was residing with her parents.

This precipitated departure, undertaken the day after her return from a long journey, seemed very strange to me; but as that was not my concern after all, I kept quiet. Three days went by and the Baron called for me. He was worried, nervous, bizarre. He announced the forthcoming return of the Baroness to me:

"Ah!" I said with more astonishment than I would have liked to disclose.

"Yes . . . she's agitated: the climate doesn't suit her. She has written me an incomprehensible letter which is tormenting me a lot. I have never understood, moreover, anything about her fantasies: she's haunted by senseless ideas. She'll even get it into her head that you're angry with her."

One can judge the face I must have pulled.

"Isn't it absurd, don't you think? In any case, I beseech you from the bottom of my heart, pretend you know nothing when she comes back, for she's ashamed of her instability. She is prodigiously proud, and if she ever suspected that you condemned her caprices she would do something silly."

"Well, things are taking a turn for the worse," I said to myself. And from that moment I thought of running away, not caring to be the hero of a novel of passion, whose dénouement would certainly not be long in coming.

I refused the first invitation I was given, on poorly-invented pretexts which were badly interpreted. The result was that the Baron demanded an interview in which he asked me for explanations of my unaffable conduct. I naturally did not know what to reply, and he took advantage of my embarrassment to extract a promise from me to accompany them on an excursion they were shortly to make out of town.

When I saw the Baroness again I found her looking unwell: her face was wilted, her eyes shining. I showed myself very withdrawn, speaking in a glacial tone, holding myself completely in reserve. After an outing in a steamer, we went to a well-known tavern, where the Baron had made a rendezvous with his uncle. The open-air supper was rather sad in front of this lugubrious stretch of the black lake, framed by black mountains, underneath the century-old lime trees with their blackened trunks.

The conversation, dry and dragging, dealt with futile matters and I thought I could perceive the echoes of an unsettled quarrel between the couple, a quarrel from whose imminent outburst I wanted above all to escape. Unfortunately the uncle and the nephew, having personal business to discuss, rose from the table. The mine was about to explode.

Now that we were alone, the Baroness leaned towards me and brusquely said:

"Do you know that Gustav appeared vexed, but really vexed, at my sudden return?"

"I didn't know at all."

"The fact is you also didn't know that he counted on his free Sundays to meet my hussy of a cousin."

"Please, Madame," I said interrupting the Baroness, "if you have any accusations to bring, let it be at least in the presence of the accused."

. . . What had I done, for God's sake! It was gross, that too-outright, intelligible reprimand, thrown in the face of the perfidious woman in favour of a member of my sex.

"Ah! That's too much, sir!" she exclaimed, alternatively red and pale with surprise.

"It's too much, dear Madam, indeed!"

All had been said between us. Forever!

As soon as her husband returned, she slipped up to him, grabbing his arm, as though she had wanted to implore help against an enemy. The Baron sensed something, although he understood nothing from this movement.

I left them at the landing-stage, alleging a visit to be made to a nearby villa. My return to town was made without my being able to explain how. My legs carried an inert body. The vital node was sliced. It was a corpse which went with me in its deathly convoy.

Alone! I was once more isolated, without friends, without family. And nothing to adore! God was not allowing himself to be recreated again by me. The statue of the Madonna was overturned: woman had been discovered behind the beautiful image, perfidious, unfaithful, claws outstretched! By inviting me to act as her confidant, she had taken the first step towards adultery, and the hatred of her sex had risen in me at that moment. She had outraged me as a man and male and I was siding with her husband against the feminine party. I did not flatter myself as being virtuous for all that. In the matter of love a man is never a thief, for he only takes what is given. Woman alone steals and sells herself and the only time she gives herself, really disinterestedly, is in adultery. The girl sells herself, the bride sells herself, the adulterous wife alone gives herself to her lover by stealing from her husband.

Moreover I had never desired her as a mistress; she had always inspired me with only feminine friendship. Protected from my eyes by her child, she was incessantly invested for me with the insignia of motherhood. And when she was beside her husband, I was not tempted to partake with her of pleasures, unclean in themselves, only ennobled by complete, exclusive possession.

Destroyed, crushed, I returned to my solitary room, more solitary, alas, than before, since I had broken with my erudite Bohemian friends, from the beginning of my relations with the Baroness.

5

Lodged under the roofs, I occupied a fairly vast room whose two garret windows opened onto the new port, the gulf and the rocky heights of the southern suburb. In the window-sills I had enjoyed doing a little gardening. Bengal roses, azaleas and geraniums always furnished me in turn with the flowers for the secret cult I had vowed to my Virgin with child. It had become a daily habit towards evening to lower my blind and, after having ranged my flower-pots in the form of an apse, to place beneath them the portrait of the Baroness lit by the lamp. She figured on this image as a young mother; her slightly severe features were of an exquisite purity under her pretty head crowned with its blonde hair; a light frock clothed her, rising to her chin, framing her face in a pleated frieze: on a table beside her, her little daughter all in white, eyeing anyone who gazed at her with the dolorous look of her profound eyes. How many letters addressed "To my friends" did I compose in front of that image—which left the following morning to the address of the Baron! It was at that time the only employment of my faculties as a writer. There, I had truly put the best of my soul. In order to direct the current of this artist manqué mind, I had enjoined the Baroness to seek an outlet for her poetic fantasies through literary form. I had brought her the masterpieces of all literatures, giving her into the bargain summaries, expositions, analyses, adding counsel, practical advice, the first indispensable notions of composition. She had shown mediocre interest in this, expressing from the outset doubts on her disposition for the art of writing. My only reply was to demonstrate to her that anyone who had received an education possessed the faculty of writing at least a letter, and that he thus contained within him a writer of more or less developed potential. All that served no purpose, theatre mania being too deeply innoculated in her tenacious brain. She affirmed that she had the art of speaking from birth; and because her situation did not allow her to embrace the footlights, which she did not want to let go, she had assumed attitudes of martyrdom to the detriment of her conjugal happiness. The husband was my accomplice in this charitable work which I had undertaken with the secret desire of preserving their home from a deplorable downfall. He had been very grateful to me but without daring to appear to be effectively interested in the matter. I pushed my idea further, despite the objections of the Baroness and in letter after letter I advised her to proceed to the excision of that interior abscess, to reveal herself through the novel, the drama or poetry.

"Give the substance of your life," I wrote to her, "if you have lived a life of moving peripeteia: take a handful of paper, your pen and above all be sincere, and you will become a writer," I pointed out to her, echoing Boerne's apostrophe.

"It is too painful to live a bitter existence over again," she had replied to me. "No, I want to find self-oblivion through Art, by cloaking myself in characters very different from my own."

I never asked myself what she might well have to forget; basically, I was ignorant of her past. Was she afraid of giving the word of her enigma, of delivering up the key of her character? By dramatic art did she mean a desire to hide herself behind masks, or did she want to amplify herself in rôles superior to her stature?

At a loss for arguments, I recommended that she begin as a translator; that would perfect her style and would furnish her with a means of introduction to publishers.

"Is one at least well paid as a translator?" she asked.

"Fairly well, but one must know one's job admirably," I replied.

"You think perhaps that I am a grasping woman," she rejoined, "but work which does not give tangible results does not attract me in the least."

She too was smitten with that mania of today's women to earn their bread themselves. The Baron had made a sceptical grimace, as if he had wanted to let it be understood that he would have preferred to see his home better kept rather than his wife occupied in bringing back a few pennies to the house, and that at the expense of a neglected domestic economy.

From that day, she had overwhelmed me with requests:

"Then find me a good book to translate and a publisher," she would say to me.

In order to extricate myself as best I could, I brought her two very short news items destined for a non-paying illustrated journal. A whole week went by, without the translation, a futile task which should have been polished off in two hours, being finished. The Baron, who sometimes dared to tease her, denounced her as a lazybones who liked to sleep in of a morning. And so he underwent one of those rebuffs which prove that one has just put one's finger on the wound. After that, I had stopped insisting, being scarcely inclined to act as the bone of contention between the two spouses.

Things stood thus when the rupture came between the two of us.

. . . At my table in my attic in front of the letters of the Baroness which I went through one after the other, my heart was wrung. She was, then, a soul in despair, an unused force, an unrecognised talent, just like me. Hence our sympathy. I suffered for her as through an organ adjoining my suffering, atrophied soul, incapable of feeling the cruel joy of pain by itself.

And what had she done, in short, to be exempted from my compassion? In a fit of jealousy she had complained to me of her conjugal disappointment. And I had snubbed her, browbeaten her, whereas I should have brought her back to reason, which appeared all the more feasible, since, according to the very words of her husband, she had left him every latitude in regard to the practice of his conjugal duties.

An immense pity overwhelmed me in favour of that woman who must have harboured dreadful secrets, anomalies in the development of her physical and psychic nature. I thought I would be committing a wrong if I let her founder. At the height of desolation, I decided to write to her to ask her forgiveness, to beg her to forget what had happened, explaining my deplorable impression as a misunderstanding. But the words did not come, my pen remained inert. I threw myself on my bed, crushed with fatigue.

When I woke up the following day, it was one of those sombre, tepid August mornings. At eight o'clock I went to the Library, dejected and disgruntled. As I had the key, I was enabled to spend three hours there alone before the regular opening. I wandered through the corridors between the double row of books, enveloped in that delicious solitude, for it was no longer isolation. An intimate rapprochement was established between the leading minds of all ages and my thought.

Taking out a volume here and there, I made prolonged efforts to fix my interest on some topic, in order to forget the painful impression that I had of the scene of the previous day. But I couldn't chase away the defiled image of the downfallen madonna from my brain. When I dragged my eyes away from the pages I perused, without recalling a single word of the text, I seemed to see her, appearing, as in an hallucination, going down the staircase which wound at the bottom of the low gallery, in the distance, in an infinite perspective. She descended, lifting the long folds of her blue dress, making a display of her tiny feet and elegant ankles, inviting me into treason with a sidelong look of her eyes, offering herself with that perfidious and so voluptuous smile that I had only discovered in her the day before. And the phantom evoked for me the Lust buried for three months, so much had her pure atmosphere rendered me chaste, proving that my ardent desires, as they say, were beginning to be individualised, to be concentrated around a single object. Ah! certainly, yes, I desired her. Suddenly, I imagined her naked, translating the supple line of her clothing that I knew by heart into white flesh. And my thoughts having discovered a goal, I went to seek an iconography of the museums of Italy, which contained a reproduction of all the famous sculptures. I wanted to try by scientific research to find the formula of that woman. I intended to recognise her species and the genus from which she came. There was room for choice.

Was she the Venus with firm breasts, with accentuated hips, normal woman who waits for her man, sure of the resounding triumph of beauty?—No ...

Juno? The fecund mother with her child, the child-bearing woman, spread on her childbed, making a display of the parts declared shameful of her magnificent body?—Neither . . .

Was she Minerva, the bluestocking, the old maid, who dissimulates her flat chest under a man's cuirass? In no way . . .

Diana then! The pale goddess, the Goddess of Night, afraid of the terrible brightness of day, cruel with her involuntary chastity, a result of a vicious constitution, too much of a boy, too little of a girl, modest of necessity, to the extent of harbouring resentment against Actaeon, who surprised her while bathing. Diana? Perhaps for the genus, but not for the species.

Let the future pronounce the supreme judgement! However, this frail body, those delicate limbs, that pretty face, that proud smile, that veiled neck, must have been burning with clandestine desires and exciting itself until it desired to see spurting blood. Oh! Diana! yes, that was it, that was really it!

I pursued my research; I went through all the collections of art published and stored in the rich treasure of the State; I wanted to rid the phantom of the chaste Goddess from my thought. I established comparisons, I verified my findings like a scholar, going from one end of the vast building to the other according to the references to such and such a work, so that the hour struck, dragging me from my fantasy. The arrival of my colleagues recalled me to my accustomed duties. .

(6)

In the evening I decided to go and see my friends at the Club. As soon as I entered the laboratory, I was greeted by an infernal burst of acclamations which restored my spirits a little. In the middle of the room a table was dressed as an altar, garnished with a skull placed in front of an enormous bottle of cyanide of potassium. A Bible defaced with stains of punch lay open beside the skull. Surgical bougies marked the leaves.

A row of punch glasses was displayed all around, filled from a retort: the friends were getting drunk. I was offered a matrass, of half-litre capacity, which I emptied in a single gulp and all the members, in unison, shouted the club motto: "Curse it", to which I replied by striking up the song of the "Ne'er do wells":

To booze
And to screw—
Is the only thing to do.

A general uproar, a monstrous shouting rose at this prelude and, amidst the acclamations, I began to deliver my well-known blasphemies. In sonorous lines, in anatomical terms, woman was glorified as the personification of the incapacity of men to enjoy themselves on their own.

I got drunk on coarse words, on the words of profanation I proffered against the Madonna, the morbid result of my unsatisfied desires. My hatred against the perfidious idol broke out so violently that I derived a bitter consolation from it. The convives, poor simpletons, who had never known love except in a brothel, were enchanted to hear the society women whom they couldn't approach being besmirched.

The drunkenness heightened. I was glad to hear male voices after months spent in sentimental purrings, in outpourings of false honesty, hypocritical innocence. It was as if I had dropped the mask, thrown off the veils with which Tartuffe covered his lubricity. In my thought I could see the Adored One delivering herself to all the fancies of conjugal love to dispel the boredom which came to her from her boring existence. It was to her, the Absent One, that I addressed my infamies, my insults, the spittings which I vomited in my vain rage, furious at not being able to possess her, since a force within me was stopping me on the brink of the crime.

The laboratory presented itself to my eyes, the vision of my over-excited senses, like the temple of an immense orgy with multiple sensations. The bottles shone on the shelves with all the shades of the rainbow; minium red, potassium chromate orange, sublimate sulphur yellow, verdigris green, sulphate blue. The air was saturated with tobacco smoke and the vapours of lemon-flavoured arrack punch, which awoke vague perceptions of the fortunate countries; the piano, expressly out of tune and attuned to an unknown tone, being mistreated, wailed Beethoven's march, to the extent that the rhythm was no longer recognisable; the pale faces of the drinkers oscillated in the blue mist which rose from the pipes. The gold sash of the lieutenant, the black beard of the doctor of philosophy, the smock of the doctor, the skull with its emptied orbits, the howlings, the hubbub, the abominable dissonances, the foul images which were evoked—all that grew muddled in my congested brain when, suddenly, out shot a single battle-cry, vociferated by the disunited voices:

"To the women, men!"

And for the departure the general chorus began the song:

> *To booze*
> *And to screw—*
> *Is the only thing to do.*

Overcoats and hats were donned. Then off we went.

Half an hour later the band burst in on the whores, and once the stout was ordered, the fire flaming noisily in the stove, my friends inaugurated the night of saturnalia with *tableaux vivants* . . .

When, in broad daylight, I awoke in my own bed, I felt marvellously self-possessed. Every trace of unhealthy sentimentality was dissipated and in the embraces of the night I had forgotten the cult of the Madonna. I then envisaged my imaginary love as a weakness of mind or of the flesh, which at that moment appeared one and the same thing to me.

After a cold bath and a restorative breakfast, I resumed my habitual functions, very satisfied to think that I had finished with all that. Slowly I accomplished my duty and the hours sped by.

It was half past midday when my office boy announced the Baron to me.

"Well then!" I said to myself, "and I who thought the incident closed!"

And I prepared myself to undergo some kind of scene.

The Baron, radiant, alert, shook my hand most cordially. He came to invite me to accompany him on a new steamer excursion to the spa of Soedertelje where the Society Theatre was to give an amateur performance.

I thanked him, alleging urgent business.

"My wife," he rejoined, "would be most obliged to you if you would come. Besides, Bébé will be in the party . . ."

Bébé was the famous cousin. He asked me with so much insistence, in such an irresistible, so touching way, softly casting his saddened looks on me, that I felt myself weakening. But instead of replying with a frank acceptance:

"Is the Baroness alright?" I asked.

"She was unwell yesterday, very poorly, but she's better this morning. Ah! Well, my dear chap," he added, "what went on then the other evening between you and her at Nacka? My wife claims that there was a misunderstanding in your conversation and that you grew angry without a reason."

"Upon my word," I replied uneasily, "I didn't understand anything about it. Perhaps I drank a little too much. I might well have made a blunder."

"Let bygones be bygones, alright?" he hurriedly replied, "and let's stay good friends as before. Women have strange susceptibilities at times, as you well know. Anyway, it's agreed, you'll say yes, won't you? So, at four o'clock this evening. We're counting on you."

I had said: "Yes!"

. . . Enigma without a key!

A misunderstanding? . . . She had been poorly nevertheless! Poorly with fear, with anger . . . with what?

The story was now acquiring a new interest through the appearance

45

on the scene of the little stranger and it was not without a beat of the heart that I embarked on the boat at four o'clock as arranged.

As soon as I met my friends, I was aware of the welcome of the Baroness who took a sisterly air with me.

"Really, you're not too angry with me for my hard words?" she said, turning towards me, "I get carried away so quickly . . ."

"Let's leave all that on one side," I replied, making a place for her at the back of the deck . . .

"Mr. Axel . . ., Miss Bébé!"

The Baron was introducing us. I had a young lady before me of about eighteen years, the blowsy type, as I had imagined her. Squat in stature, with vulgar features, she was simply dressed with a dash of affected elegance.

But the Baroness! Pale, with her cheeks sticking to her jaws and thinner than ever! The bracelets jingled around her wrists: her neck rose from her collar and her blue carotids could thus be seen snaking right up to her ears, even more prominent with her neglected coiffure. She was also badly dressed in a frock with gaudy, clashing colours. In a word she was ugly. She inspired me when I beheld her with profound pity and I cursed myself for my past conduct towards her. That woman, a coquette?—A martyr, yes! A saint overwhelmed beneath the weight of undeserved misfortunes!

The boat set off. The pure August evening on Lake Moelar inclined us to peaceful reveries.

By chance, involuntary or not, the cousin and the Baron had occupied two places side by side, but far enough away from us not to be heard. Leaning towards the girl, the Baron chattered, laughed, joked endlessly, with the rejuvenated, joyful look of a fiancé of the previous day.

From time to time he glanced roguishly at us and we exchanged a nod of the head and a smile.

"A lively one, the girl, isn't she, sir?" the Baroness said to me.

"She seems to be, indeed, Baroness," I replied without knowing exactly what expression to assume.

"She is wonderfully skilful at getting rid of my husband's wrinkles in his depressions. I haven't that gift myself," she added, addressing a smile of frank sympathy to the group.

And at that moment, undisclosed worries, tears withheld, a super-human resignation were portrayed on the lines of her face, and over her visage those imperceptible reflections of goodness, abnegation, self-oblivion, which are to be seen in pregnant women or young mothers, passed like clouds.

Ashamed of my unjust opinions, haunted by my remorse, nervous, I had difficulty in holding back the tears which filled my eyes and I sought to begin some sort of conversation .

"And you're not jealous?"

"Not in the slightest," she replied to me with a loyal air and without a shadow of wickedness. "It may appear strange to you, but yet that's how it is. I love my husband, a fine heart; I adore the little one, a sweet creature. And then all that is of an unparalleled innocence. Ah! Shame on jealousy which makes one ugly; then at my age one must really be careful."

Indeed, her ugliness was evident in a heartrending manner and under the influence of an unreflecting inspiration, I ordered her in a fatherly tone to put on her shawl, under the pretext of a draught which could chill her. I draped the hairy wool around her shoulders, framing her face to my liking, and so I brought out its dainty beauty.

How pretty she was when she thanked me with a smile! She seemed perfectly happy, as grateful as a child who begs caresses.

"My poor husband, I'm so delighted to see him a little gay. He's got such worries, alas . . . if you knew, dear sir."

"In the name of heaven, Baroness," I hazarded, "if I'm not indiscreet, tell me what is afflicting you, for, I can tell, there is a great worry in your existence. I can only offer good advice, but if I can be useful to you in the circumstances, use my friendship, I beg you."

Now these poor friends were harassed by worries. The spectre of ruination, a hideous spectre, was threatening them. The insufficient wage of the Baron was hitherto augmented by the Baroness's dowry. Quite recently they had realised that the dowry was, so to speak, imaginary, being represented by worthless titles. And he, on the point of handing in his resignation, was soliciting a post as a cashier in a bank.

"That is why," she ended, "I have spoken of utilising the talents I have: thus I will bring my share of the necessary revenue into the home. For the blame is mine. It's I who have put him in these straits, it's I who have broken his career . . ."

What could I say, what could I do in such a serious case, beyond my strength? I took it upon myself to embellish things and to lie to myself.

The whole story would work itself out; and, to reassure her, I drew her a tableau of a carefree future, full of smiling promises. I had recourse to economic statistics to demonstrate to her that better times were approaching, times when funds were likely to rise, for I invented enormous resources and I improvised as if by enchantment a reorganisation of the army accompanied by unexpected promotions.

That was pure poetry but, thanks to my fantasy, courage was returning to her, hope and even good humour.

At the landing, waiting for the theatre to open, we took a walk in the park in twos. I had not yet exchanged a word with the cousin.

The Baron, moreover, did not leave her. He carried her theatre wrap, devoured her with his looks, bathed her in a flux of words, warmed her with his breath, while she remained impassive, cold, her eyes without expression and her face hard. From time to time she appeared to let slip little words which excited the noisy laugh of the Baron, without a muscle of her face quivering. To judge by the salacious mimicry of her listener, she seemed always to be throwing asides, implications, even ambiguities. Finally, we were free to enter the hall and we went in to occupy our seats which were not reserved.

The curtain rose. It was a joy for the Baroness to see the boards again, to breathe the odours of distemper, canvas, rough wood, make-up and sweat.

They were performing *A Caprice*. A sudden uneasiness wrung me at the saddening memories of my existence as a failure for whom the stage was obstinately closed, a natural result also of my debauchery of the previous day. When the curtain fell, I left my seat and fled secretly to the Town Hall restaurant, where I brought myself round with a double absinthe which was prolonged until the closure of the spectacle.

My friends rejoined me for the supper arranged. They had the look of tired people and barely dissimulated their anger at my escape. The table was laid during a general silence. The conversation between the four of us had difficulty in getting going. The cousin remained silent, haughty, reserved.

Finally a discussion arose about the menu. After having asked me my opinion the Baroness chose hors d'oeuvres which the Baron cancelled in a brusque tone, a little too brusque for my tensed nerves. A prey to my gloomy thoughts, I pretended not to have heard and ordered "Hors d'oeuvres for two!" again for her and for me, since she had shown the desire to have some.

The Baron became livid with anger. There was a storm in the air, but not a word was spoken.

Whilst inwardly admiring my courage at having replied to an insolence with an outrage, which in a more civilised country would have rendered me liable to a serious request for an explanation, the Baroness, encouraged by my valiant defence of her rights, teased me to make me laugh. But it was in vain. All attempts at conversation were impossible: nothing could be found for us to say to each other and terrible glances were exchanged between the Baron and myself. In the end, my adversary began to whisper in the ear of my neighbour, who replied to him by nods of the head and monosyllables pronounced without a movement of the lips, while addressing disdainful looks at me.

This made my ears fairly burn and the lightning was about to

48

strike between us, when an unforeseen incident acted as a lightning-rod.

In a neighbouring room, a joyous company had installed itself. For the last half hour those people had been horribly banging away at the piano; that was not all, they struck up a filthy song, all doors open.

"Close the door," said the Baron to the waiter.

The door was barely closed when it was reopened and the singers continued their refrain, interspersed with provocative words.

The opportunity offered itself favourably to me to explode.

I got up from my seat; in two bounds I was at the door, which I brutally shut in the face of the howling band. Fire put to powder would have produced a similar effect to my resolute appearance before the enemies. A short struggle ensued, during which I held the handle of the door with a firm hand. But the door gave way, violently pulled, dragging me into the middle of the group of brawlers, who dashed at me, ready to come to grips. The same instant, I felt a hand placed on my shoulder and behind me I heard an indignant voice recalling to the laws of honour those gentlemen who were pouncing in number on a single adversary . . .

It was the Baroness, forgetful of conventions, of good manners, who, under the influence of the shock, was expressing warmer sentiments perhaps than she desired to show.

The scuffle was over. The Baroness beheld me with scrutinising looks.

"Ah! You're a valiant little man," she said to me. "I was very much afraid for you all the same."

The Baron asked for the bill and having called the landlord, he enjoined him to send for the mayor.

From then on, a perfect harmony reigned between us all. We vied in being the most indignant at the coarseness of the inhabitants of the place. All the silent rage of jealousy and wounded pride was transferred in concert onto those badly-brought-up rogues, and, around punch taken in one of our rooms, friendship flamed again to the point that one no longer thought at all of the mayor who didn't present himself.

The following morning we met at the café, sparkling with good humour, perfectly happy underneath it all to be rid of a disagreeable business whose consequences could not easily be measured in advance.

After breakfast we went for a walk on the embankment of the canal, still in twos, but at a respectable distance. Reaching a sluice where the canal took a definite curve, the Baron stopped and turning to his wife with a tender, almost loving smile:

"Maria, do you remember that place?" he asked.

"Yes, yes, I remember, my dear Gustav," she replied with an expression of passion and sadness.

And explaining this brief question to me:

"It was there that he made his declaration to me," she said. "One evening under this very birch, while a shooting star flashed luminously in the sky . . ."

"Three years ago," I said to complete the phrase. "And now, you are dwelling on your old memories. You're living in the past because the present has no longer anything to satisfy you."

"Enough, you're mistaken . . . I detest the past and I am grateful to my fine husband for having delivered me from a vain mother whose affectionate despotism almost ruined me. No, I adore my good Gustav and he has become a faithful friend to me . . ."

"As you like, Baroness, I am still of your opinion, to be agreeable to you."

The embarkation for the return to town was effectuated at the prescribed time and, after a trip on the blue lake with its thousands of green islets, we arrived at the quay where we separated.

I had promised myself to return to work, with serious intentions of extirpating from my heart this fleshly outgrowth which had donned the form of a woman, but I soon noticed that I had not counted on powers superior to myself. The day after our return, I received an invitation to dine at the Baroness's, whose wedding anniversary fell precisely on that day. I could no longer make excuses; despite the fear of seeing our friendship worn away, I accepted the invitation. One can judge my disappointment when, on entering, I found the house upside down for cleaning, the Baron in a sullen humour, and excuses from the Baroness for the lateness of the dinner. A walk in the little garden with the grumpy, famished Baron, incapable of disguising his impatience, exhausted my last resources of conversation, to the extent that all conversation was impossible after a half hour, when we decided to go up into the dining-room.

The table was laid, the hors d'oeuvres served, but the mistress of the house was not yet visible.

"How about us having a snack," the Baron said to me, "it would fill in the time?"

I did my best to ask him not to do anything of the kind, wishing to be careful of the susceptibilities of the Baroness. Nothing helped. Caught between two fires, I was obliged to obey him.

At last the Baroness entered: radiant, young, pretty, well-dressed, wearing a crêpe frock of transparent silk, of ripe wheat yellow and pansy violet, her favourite colours. Her dress, cut with perfect art, moulded her fine girlish figure, disclosed a glimpse of the roundness of her shoulders and sketched the delightfully modelled, curvacious line of her arms. I offered her my bouquet of roses with ardour and wishing her many happy happy returns of her wedding anniversary I eagerly put all the blame for our impolite impatience on the Baron.

She grimaced, noticing the disturbed cloth, and, in a tone more bitter than railing, she sent a rebuke to her husband who was not long in taking up this undeserved reprimand. I at once threw myself into the fray, evoking the memories of the previous day already stirred with the Baron.

"And let's see, how did you find my charming cousin?" asked the Baroness.

"Adorable!" I exclaimed.

"Isn't that child, dear friend, a veritable pearl?" the Baron exclaimed with a strong accent of paternal gravity, devoted sincerity, pity for that bedevilled wench, a martyr of imaginary tyrants.

But the Baroness was without mercy, despite the subterfuge employed by her husband who had purposefully used the word "child".

"Then look how that dear Bébé has changed the coiffure of my husband! . . ."

Indeed, the habitual parting of the Baron had disappeared from his hair. His hair was curled "à la cavalière", his moustaches turned up, to the point of disfiguring him. But, by a logical train of thought, I perceived, without letting on, that the Baroness had copied—she too—certain details of coiffure, of dress, and even ways from the enchantress of a cousin. One would have said the elective affinity of the chemists, fully functioning between two living beings.

However, the dinner dragged on heavily and clumsily, like a cart rolling on three wheels, the fourth having been detached but the thenceforward indispensable complement of our quartet which was beginning to disharmonise as a trio was awaited for coffee. At dessert, I raised a toast in honour of the couple, in conventional terms, without ardour, without piquancy, like flat champagne.

The couple kissed, exhilarated by the bygone memories, and when they counterfeited their gestures of affection, they became tender, loving, in the manner of the actor who ends up by becoming veritably sad while imitating the sincerity of true tears. Or was the fire lying beneath the cinder, ready to flame up again, revived on purpose by a skilful hand? Very hard to say exactly how things stood.

Having gone down into the little garden, we installed ourselves in a pavilion, whose casement opened onto the avenue. The conversation grew drowsy in the general torpor and the distracted Baron put himself on the lookout, watching through the window onto the street in case the cousin was coming. Suddenly, he darted out like an arrow, leaving us alone, apparently with the intention of going ahead to the awaited person.

Remaining alone with the Baroness, I felt troubled, not that I was timid, but she had a strange manner of devouring me with her eyes, of complimenting me on details of my dress. After a too-prolonged, almost embarrassing silence, she burst out laughing and pointing with her finger in the direction taken by the Baron:

"How he is in love, that dear Gustav!" she said.

"One would think so," I replied. "And you don't feel the fury of jealousy."

"Not in the least!" she affirmed. "Since I myself am in love with that pretty little kitten and how is your heart disposed to our charming cousin?"

"But perfectly well, Baroness. I'll be frank. Without wishing to offend you, your relative will never have the honour of my sympathy."

And that was true. From the first meeting, that young person of plebeian origin like me had taken a dislike to me. I was the importunate witness, or rather the dangerous rival, who was poaching on ground that she had reserved for herself to canvass an introduction into society. With her penetrating eye, a little pearl-grey eye, she had sized me up as a useless acquaintance, good for nothing; with her bourgeois instinct she had classed me amongst the fortune seekers. She was right up to a certain point since I had entered the house of the Baron with the avowed goal of finding patrons for my wretched tragedy, but the dramatic contacts of my friends were nil, invented at will by my Finnish damsel. There had never been question of my play, beyond the few vulgar compliments I was paid.

And so I was not long in noticing that the Baron, very mobile in his impressions, would change his attitude towards me in the cousin's presence, that he was beginning to regard me with the eyes of the cajoler.

There was not long to wait however; the two companions appeared at the railings, sprightly, laughing and chatting.

The little one was in a ribald mood, that evening. In a slightly coarse manner, swearing with a refined taste, she pronounced ambiguities of accomplished art with perfect innocence, seeming not to know the meaning of double-edged words. She smoked, drank, without, however, forgetting her position as a woman and a young one for a minute. She presented nothing virile, had no emancipated ways, no trace of prudery. In all, she was amusing and the hours flew softly by.

What struck me however, and in a manner prophetic for the future, was the exuberant gaiety the Baroness manifested on every occasion when an ambiguity escaped from the cousin's lips. Then a ferocious laugh, an expression of impudent voluptuousness lit up her features, testifying to a profound knowledge in her of the mysteries of debauchery.

While we were enjoying ourselves, the uncle of the Baron came to join us. A retired captain, long a widower, very gallant with the ladies, of comely manners, with a dash of risqué gallantry, a reminder of the old order, under the cover of his close kinship, he was the declared friend of those ladies, whose good graces he had known how to win.

He took the liberty of pawing them, of kissing their hands and tapping their cheeks. So that when he appeared the two ladies fell into his arms with little cries of joy.

"Ah! my little ones, be careful. Two at once . . . Eh! Eh! That's a lot for an old boy. Watch out, one gets burnt in the fire. Quickly, hands off or I'm no longer responsible for anything."

And the Baroness, handing him the cigarette which she held squeezed between her lips:

"Then a little fire, please, uncle!"

"Fire! Fire! But, alas, I can no longer give any, my child. It's five years since mine went out," he replied with a quizzical expression.

"Really?"

The Baroness gave him a friendly slap with her finger-tips. The old man took her arm, and, holding it between his hands massaged it up to the muscles of her shoulder.

"You're not so skinny as you look, my pretty one," he continued, feeling the soft flesh through the fabric.

The Baroness offered no resistance. She seemed to be enjoying the compliment. With her ferocious laugh of voluptuousness, she rolled up her sleeve, exhibiting an elegantly designed arm, of a charming contour and of milky whiteness.

But suddenly remembering my presence, she hurriedly pulled her sleeve down, yet not quickly enough for me not to notice a sparkle of the terrible flame which burned in her eyes, the expression of a woman possessed at the moment of amorous intoxication. At the same instant, by mistake, while lighting my cigarette, I dropped a flaming match between my waistcoat and my jacket. With a cry of distress, the Baroness rushed onto me and seeking to put out the burning with her fingers: "Fire! Fire!" she cried, very red.

Quite overwhelmed, I recoiled, pressing her two hands against my chest in order to put out the menacing fire: then, suddenly, ashamed, wrenching myself from her arms, I pretended to have been saved from a veritable danger, offering the Baroness, still under the sway of her excitation, my warm thanks.

We flirted continually until supper. The sun had set and the moon was rising behind the cupola of the Observatory, lighting up the apples of the orchard. Then we amused ourselves by guessing the names of the fruits hanging from the branches, half-hidden beneath the new green foliage, a reed green, in the electric brightness of the moon. The Calville, usually red, was only a yellow spot, the Astrakhan apple was verdigris green, the pippin a dark berry; the rest were in keeping. So it was with the flowers in the clumps. The dahlias offered nameless tints to the eye, the wallflowers shading of another planet; the tone of the China-asters appeared indefinable:

"Look, Baroness," I said in demonstration, "how everything is quite imaginary. There are no colours in isolation: everything is influenced by the nature of light. Everything is nothing but illusion!"

"Everything!" she repeated, stopping before me, looking me in the face with her eyes excessively magnified by the darkness.

"Everything, dear Madam!" I replied with a lie, bewildered before this real vision of flesh and bone which was frightening me at that instant by its extraordinary beauty.

Her blonde dishevelled hair rose like a radiant crown round her face illumined by the lunar rays: her figure, delightfully proportioned, rose tall and slender beneath the stripes of her dress whose colours had been modified, now black and white.

The stocks exhaled aphrodisiacal perfumes in the air, the crickets were calling in the grass moistened by the falling dew, a tepid wind was making the trees quiver, the twilight was enveloping us in its soft covering, everything invited love; honest cowardice alone held back the avowals on our lips.

Suddenly, an apple detached itself from a branch shaken by the wind. The Baroness bent down to pick it up and held it out to me with a significant gesture.

"Forbidden fruit," I murmured. "No, a thousand thanks, madam!"

And all at once, to amend the effect of that blunder which had escaped me in spite of myself, I hastened to improvise a satisfactory interpretation to my phrase, with an allusion to the miserliness of the landowner.

"What would the landowner say if he saw me?"

"That you're a knight without reproach . . . at least," she retorted, as if she had wanted to reproach me for my fear, while she slipped a sidelong glance towards the copse where the cousin and the Baron were taking shelter from indiscreet eyes.

Someone came to announce that supper was served. Rising from the table, the Baron proposed we all walk to accompany the "dear child" all the way home. At the door, the Baron offered his arm to the cousin and addressing himself to me:

"Give your arm to my wife, dear friend, and show yourself the perfect gentleman that you are," he added in a paternal tone.

I was anguished. As the evening was hot, she carried her mantle in her hand and from the contact of her arm, whose undulating contours made themselves felt through the silk, there emanated a magnetic current which awoke such an extraordinary sensibility within me, that I thought I could feel the spot where the sleeve of her chemisette came to an end at the height of my deltoid muscle. I could have retraced all the anatomy of that ravishing arm, so much was my over-excitation developed. Her biceps, the great elevator which plays the principal rôle in embraces, was pressing mine, flesh against flesh, with supple rhythms. While we were walking side by side, I could distinguish the roundness of her hip and of her thigh beneath the brushing of the skirts.

"You walk admirably with another, you must dance marvellously," she said to me to encourage me to break a too embarrassing silence.

And after some instants, during which she must have felt the quivering of my distended nerves:

"What! . . . You're trembling?" she asked with an air of mockery, in her superiority of a conscious woman.

"Yes, madame . . . I am cold."

"Oh! Dear child . . . you must put your overcoat on then."

And her voice became caressing, as if quilted.

I slipped on my overcoat—a veritable straightjacket—and thus found myself better safeguarded against that heat which transmitted itself from her body to my body. Soon the cadence of her small pattering feet, in step with mine, attuned our two nervous systems so perfectly that I had the sensation of walking on four feet, like a quadruped.

In the course of that fatal walk, a grafting was accomplished, of the kind that the gardeners call "ablactation" from the direct contact of two branches.

From that day I no longer possessed myself. The woman had inoculated her blood into my veins, our currents of nervous fluid had been placed in a state of tension, her female germs aspired to the motivating vigour which was to come to them from my male germs, her soul desired to be united to my intellect and my spirit desired to be spread at will in that subtle vase. Had all that really been done without our knowing it?

It was a grave question to resolve.

After I had climbed up to my room again, I wondered what remained to be done. Flee, forget, or seek to succeed in some distant land? And, at once, I sketched the plan of a journey to Paris, to the very centre of civilisation. Once there, I would bury myself in the libraries or I would lose myself in the museums. I would do my work there.

As soon as my project was decided, I sought the means to realise it. At the end of a month I was able to begin my farewell visits.

A most timely incident offered me naturally the difficult pretext to cover my flight. Miss Selma—that was the name of my Finnish girl, long since banished from my memory—was publishing the banns of her forthcoming marriage to my friend the singer. I thus found myself, I claimed, obliged to escape in order to forget and to seek some consolation faraway for the bruises of my poor heart. In short, this allegation was as good as another. However, I was forced to remain some weeks longer, for I had to give way to the repeated behests of my friends whom the habitual tempests of autumn frightened, when I informed them that I was resolved to embark on a steamer bound for Le Havre.

Finally there came the wedding of my sister, fixed for early October, so that my journey threatened to be eternally postponed.

During this lapse of time, frequent invitations were made to me. The cousin having returned to her parents, the three of us spent most of our evenings together, and the Baron, brought back by the occult will of his wife, began again to look upon me favourably. Finally, completely reassured by the expectation of my departure, he began to treat me amicably again.

One evening when we were in a little group at the home of the Baroness's mother, the former nonchalantly lying on the sofa with her head placed on her mother's knees, began to confess loudly the ardent penchant she felt for a then-famous actor. Was it to put me on the rack and be assured of the sensation that such an avowal would produce on me? I don't know. The fact remains that the old lady who was softly caressing her daughter's hair said to me:

"If you ever intend to write a novel, sir, I recommend this type of fiery woman to you. She is extraordinary. She must always have an inclination beyond her husband."

"It's true what mama is saying, you know," the Baroness added. "And for the moment, X . . . is my passion . . . Oh! he's an adorable man!"

"She's mad!" retorted the Baron smiling, with a more visible twitch than he would have liked to have shown.

A woman of fire! The word was engraved on my mind for, all joking apart, to be pronounced by that old woman who was the mother, it must have contained an element of truth.

However, my departure was near. The day before I assembled the Baron and the Baroness at a bachelor's supper in my attic. My little room was dressed up to disguise the poverty of the furniture and my simple retreat had the air of a consecrated temple. Against the wall, in between the two window recesses, one of which was occupied by my work table and my window-box, the other by my low library, I had placed my ramshackle wicker sofa, draped with a cover of imitation tiger skin, attached by invisible pins.

To the left, stood my large divan-bed, dressed in a gaudy tick coverlet, and on the wall above was displayed a map of the world, mottled with bright colours. To the right, my chest of drawers with its mirror, both in the Empire style, decorated with brass ornamentation: a cupboard topped by a plaster bust, a washbasin relegated for the occasion behind the curtains of the recess and the walls, with their adornment of framed drawings, offered an ever-varying spectacle to the eye, the ensemble of which gave the sensation of something archaic.

A porcelain chandelier with a floral design, hanging from the ceiling, discovered in a junk shop, recalled those seen in churches by its form. Its cracks were skilfully masked by means of a strand of artificial ivy that I had pilfered from my sister's some time previously. Beneath the three-armed chandelier stood the table. A basket of Bengal roses with abundant flowers, bright red among the dark foliage, on the very white spread tablecloth, struck a note of a flower fête, mingling with the drooping shoots of the ivy. Around the flower-laden rose-bush, red, green, opaline glasses were ranged, bought at random in a secondhand shop, at a low price, for they all had a flaw. So it was with the service, composed of plates, salt cellars, a porcelain sugar bowl from China or Japan, or Marienburg or else-where.

The menu of the supper only offered the guests a dozen cold plates, chosen rather with a view to decoration than from the point of view of consumption, since the main dish of the repast was oysters. I owed the small items indispensable to this extraordinary rejoicing under the roofs to the good offices of my landlady. In short, all that was rather pleasantly arranged, and the stage setting brought forth silent approbation from me: this mixture of sensations reminding me—in miniature—at the same time of the works of the poet, the research of the scholar, the tastes of the artist, gourmandise, the love of flowers which hid a trace of the love of woman in their shade. Were it not for the three places, one might have said that everything was prepared for an intimate feast for two, the prelude to a night of joy, when it was really only an expiatory Communion for me. For my room had not received a woman's visit since "the little horror" whose ankle boots had left their traces on the wood of the sofa. No feminine breast had been reflected since in that mirror on the chest of drawers. And now, a chaste woman, a mother, of good education, with delicate sentiments, was coming to purify this dwelling, a witness of so many troubles, miseries, pains. And, I thought poetically, it was a sacred repast as well, since, all in all, I was going to sacrifice my heart, my peace and perhaps my life in it, all that to safeguard the happiness of my friends.

All was ready, when I heard the noise of footsteps resounding on the landing of the fourth floor. I hastened to light the candles, to give a finishing touch to the basket, and, the instant afterwards, I could hear my guests panting in front of my door, exhausted after having climbed my four flights.

I opened. Dazzled by the burst of lights, the Baroness clapped her hands as before a successful opera décor.

"Bravo! You're a first-rate stage manager, my dear," she exclaimed.
"Yes, madame, I sometimes act and its to fill in time that . . ."
Having taken off her coat, having welcomed her, I invited her to
sit down on the sofa. But she couldn't stay in one place. With the
curiosity of a woman who had never visited a bachelor's room, led
to the nuptial chamber on leaving the paternal dwelling, she proceeded
to a veritable search of the house. For her début in my cell, she
handled my pen-holders, felt the blotting-paper, searched everywhere,
as if she were set on discovering some secret. She visited my library,
examining the backs of the books with a rapid look. Passing in front
of the mirror she stopped for a moment to arrange her coiffure and
to tuck a tip of lace into the cleavage of her corsage which disclosed
the hollow of her neck. After which, she reviewed the articles of
furniture one by one, sniffed the flowers, admiringly, with little playful
cries. Having accomplished this voyage round my room she asked
me, in a naïve tone, without a trace of premeditation, still looking for
an article of furniture which seemed to be lacking:
"But wherever do you sleep then?"
"On the sofa."
"Ah! How happy you must be to be a bachelor!"
And young girls' dreams were awoken in her mind.
"It's sometimes quite sad, yes," I replied to her.
"Sad to be one's master, to have one's own interior, to be free of
all control! Oh! I'm mad on freedom! This state of marriage is
infamous, isn't it, my love," she said addressing the Baron, who put
on a good face and replied:
"Yes, it's annoying!"
The table was served and the meal began.
With the first glass of wine gaiety overcame us. But suddenly
sadness took hold of us again, mingling with our pleasure when the
goal of this intimate reunion was remembered. And each of us in
turn evoked all our past happy recollections. We relived in thought
all the little adventures of our excursions, seeking in our memories
what we might well have said at such and such a moment. And our
eyes were lit, our hearts were kindled, our hands clutched together,
our glasses clinked together. The hours vanished and we silently
boded the minutes of the farewells to which every minute drew us
closer, with an increasing anxiety. Then, at a sign from his wife, the
Baron took a ring enriched with an opal stone from his pocket, which
he offered to me, raising the following toast:
"Here is, dear friend, a valueless souvenir which I beg you to
accept, however, with our gratitude, for the friendship which you
have been good enough to show us: may destiny fulfil all your desires,
such is my ardent wish, for I love you as a brother and esteem you

as a veritable man of honour! So, bon voyage, without an adieu and au revoir!"

As a man of honour! He had perhaps divined me! He had penetrated our consciences!—but no! far from it . . . for in chosen terms, by way of a commentary for his little speech, he let fly a volley of insults at poor Selma, "who had betrayed her oath, who had sold herself to a man who . . . anyway, to an individual, for whom she had no affection, a type who only owed his happiness to my excess of decency".

To my excess of decency! I was ashamed, but, carried away by the sincerity of that heart simple and prompt in judging, I passed myself off as most unhappy indeed, as inconsolable; and the lie flourished within me, decked out in all the trappings of reality.

Taken in by my skilful manoeuvres, misled by the coldness which I didn't renounce, the Baroness appeared to believe me and incited me to take heart with motherly tenderness.

"Eh! Let that girl go to the devil. There are others in the world and better than that faithless little person. Don't regret anything, my poor friend, she wasn't a good type, for she couldn't wait for you. Besides—I can really confess it to you now—what stories have been told me about her time and time again . . ."

And with a pleasure she had difficulty in disguising, she succeeded in disgusting me with the presumed idol.

"Just think! She wanted to treat herself to a lieutenant of the upper classes, and she declared her age minus more than a third . . . She was only a flirt, believe me."

At a movement of disapproval from the Baron, she realised her blunder and, clutching my hand, she beseeched me to forgive her with such profoundly tender looks that I felt myself racked to death.

The Baron, slightly tipsy, poured forth sentimental ramblings, cordial effusions, overwhelming me with his fraternal love, assailing me with interminable toasts which floated in ethereal spheres.

His swollen face shone, benevolent. He surveyed me with his caressing and melancholy eyes whose look dissipated all the doubts I could have had on the solidity of his affection. Indeed, he was a big, good-natured child, of irreproachable spiritual rectitude, to whom I swore to myself I would remain faithful at the risk of finishing myself off. We rose from table to be separated—for ever perhaps. The Baroness had a violent fit of sobbing and hid her face against her husband's chest.

"How mad I am," she exclaimed, "to be so attached to this little man to the point that his departure moves me so much!"

And, in a surge of love, pure and impure at once, disinterested and interested, passionate, with a tenderness that appeared angelic, she took me by the neck and kissed me beneath the gaze of her husband; then, blessing me with the sign of the cross, she bade me farewell.

My old maid who was waiting on the threshold of the door was dabbing her eyes and we all melted into tears. It was a solemn, unforgettable moment. The sacrifice was consummated.

I went to bed at about one in the morning without managing to fall asleep. The worry of missing the boat kept me awake. Exhausted by those farewell parties which had gone on for a week, nervous in the extreme as the result of my excessive drinking, my mind bewildered as a result of my idleness, frozen by all those commotions of the previous day, I writhed between my sheets until daybreak. Very conscious of the present weakness of my will, nourishing an absolute aversion to rolling in a carriage, the jogging of which is bad, so they say, for the spinal cord, I had chosen the sea route, and also a little in order to suppress all attempt at flight on my part. The boat was to leave at about six o'clock in the morning and the cab was coming to fetch me at five. I set off alone.

It was a windy, foggy and very cold October morning. The branches of the trees were covered in frost. Having arrived at North Bridge, I felt myself a prey to a vision. The Baron was walking in the same direction as my cab. It was really he, indeed, who, despite our agreement, was coming early to say a last farewell. Touched to the bottom of my heart by such an unexpected token of friendship, I felt unworthy of so much interest and filled with remorse for all the bad thoughts I had had about him. We arrived at the landing-stage. He climbed on board, visited my cabin, introduced himself to the captain and placed me particularly in his care. In short, he behaved as a veritable elder brother, as a devoted friend, and we kissed with great emotion.

"Take good care of yourself, old man . . ." he said to me, "you don't look all that well to me."

Indeed I felt rather uneasy. I held myself together, however, until the moment the boat cast off its moorings. Stricken with a sudden horror for this long journey without a reasonable goal, I felt myself seized with a mad rage, with a desire to throw myself into the water to swim back to the shore. But the strength was lacking for me to realise any desire whatever and I remained on the deck, irresolute, waving my handkerchief to answer my friend's greetings, which soon vanished behind the line of vessels anchored in the harbour.

The boat was a heavily-laden cargo steamer on which there was only a single cabin placed above the 'tween-decks. I arrived at my berth. I fell flat onto the mattress and huddled myself in the blankets with the fixed intention of sleeping through the first twenty-four hours, in order to cut off any hope of my escape. After half an hour in a complete daze, I woke up with a start, as if thunderstruck by an electric shock, the usual outcome of excesses of drink and of insomnia. All the sad reality came to light within me at that moment. I climbed back on the deck to take a walk. The shores filed past beneath my eyes, naked, brown, with leafless trees, fields of a yellowish grey and snow in the crevices of the rocks. The greyish water with sepia spots, the livid and sombre sky, the dirty deck, the impolite sailors—everything united to add to my discouragement. Furthermore an irresistible need to communicate my sentiments to someone, and not a passenger, not one! I climbed to the bridge in order to find the captain. He was a boor of the worst kind, absolutely inaccessible. I was imprisoned for ten days, alone, in the company of people without understanding, without heart. It was torture.

I began to walk on the deck again, up and down, as if that could accelerate our speed. My inflamed brain was functioning at a high pressure: ideas were being engendered by the thousand every minute: suppressed memories were rising up again, dashing together, pursuing each other and, amidst this jumble, a continual pain was assailing me, comparable with the paroxysm of toothache, which I couldn't place nor designate. The more the boat moved out to sea, the interior tension augmented. It was as if the umbilical cord which was linking me to the native land, to my mother country, to the family, to Her, was about to be severed. An abandoned being, floating on the swelling waves between the sky and the earth, I had the sensation that I was losing my footing and the solitude inspired me with a vague fear for everything and everybody. It was without any doubt a sign of inborn debility, since I recalled having cried hot tears when thinking of my mother, during a pleasure trip that I had undertaken when about twelve; and I was, however, of a physical constitution developed well before my age. To my mind this harked back to a premature confinement that my mother had had, or perhaps to unsuccessful attempts at abortion—a too-common accident in large families. The fact still remains that this defect had determined a pusillanimity in me which came to light whenever I happened to move about and, at this moment when I was dragging myself from my surroundings, I was overcome with a general panic before the future, the foreign country, the ship's crew. Impressionable as every abortive child whose exposed nerves await the still bleeding skin, shelled like a lobster at moulting time, who seeks a shelter underneath the stones and senses every degree of fall in the barometer, I roamed round the boat to discover a soul stronger than mine, the clutching of a robust hand, the warmth of a human body, the fortifying rays of a friendly eye. I wandered like a squirrel in its cage, on the foredeck between the capstan and the partition of my cabin and I pictured to myself the ten days of suffering which lay in store for me. I thought that it was no more than an hour that I had been aboard. An hour as long as a day of torment . . . And not a ray of hope of having done with this accursed journey! I tried to imbue myself with the necessary reason. I constantly reacted against it.

"What's forcing you to go away? Who then has the right to censure your actions if you decided to return? . . . No one! And yet . . . Shame, ridicule, the point of honour! No, no, all hope must be renounced! And besides the boat did not put in before the port of Le Havre. So forward and courage!" But courage is based on physical and psychical strength and both were lacking in me at that time. Pursued by my black ideas, I resolved to go for a walk astern since, moreover, I knew the front of the boat down to the slightest detail to the extent that the rails, the rigging, the cables displeased me like a finished book. As I was passing through the glass door I almost bumped against a person sheltering from the wind behind the cabin. It was an old lady dressed in black, with grey hair, with a careworn expression.

She was looking at me attentively, with a sympathetic eye. And so I advanced to speak to her. She replied to me in French and we became acquainted.

After an insignificant preamble, we made known to each other the purposes of our journeys. Her's was not a happy one. The widow of a timber merchant, she was returning from a visit to her relatives at Stockholm and was returning to her son, stricken with mental derangement, at Le Havre, where he was shut in an asylum. That woman's tale, so simple and so harrowing in its brevity, impressed me exceedingly, and I would not be astonished if that story, becoming impregnated in the cells of my already unhinged brain, was the point of departure for what subsequently happened.

Suddenly the lady stopped speaking to me and, beholding me with terror, in a compassionate tone:

"But you're ill, sir?" she exclaimed.

"Me, madame? . . ."

"Yes. You look ill. You should try to rest a little."

"To tell the truth, I didn't shut an eye last night and my nerves are affected. Sleep has left me for some time now and nothing has helped to bring the rest I need."

"Allow me then to try in my turn. Go at once and stretch out on your bed. I am going to make you take a drug which will make you sleep standing up."

She got up and pushing me with a gentle hand she obliged me to return to my berth. She disappeared for an instant and returned holding a phial in her hand which contained a sleeping-draught, a dose of which she administered to me in a spoon.

"And now I am sure that you're going to sleep."

After having received my thanks, she began to arrange my blankets.

How well she knew that task! And how that heat which little children seek at the breasts of their mothers emanated from her! The delicate touch of her hands calmed me and two minutes later a torpor was invading me. I imagined myself to have become a suckling again. I could see my mother once more busying herself with the little attentions for me around my bed; little by little the blurring features of my mamma merged into the exquisite lines of the face of the Baroness and the facial expression of the charitable lady who had left me at that instant and, under the protection of those visions of women, I felt myself fading like a colour, being snuffed like the glow of a candle. I was losing consciousness of my being.

When I awoke, I did not remember any dream, but a fixed idea as though suggested during the sleep, obsessed me: to see the Baroness or become mad.

Shaken by a long shudder, I jumped out of my berth, wet through with the salt air which was penetrating everywhere. Outside, the sky was a metallic grey-blue. On deck, the surging waves were washing the tackling, spraying the planks, sprinkling me in the face with the froth of their cream foam.

I consulted my watch and calculated the distance travelled during my hours of sleep. It seemed to me that we must roughly be crossing the Norrköping archipelago. All hope of return was thus taken from me. The landscape seemed completely unknown to me, from the islets dispersed in the bays to the rocky coasts and everything, the height of the cabins scattered beside the water, the cut of the sails of the fishing boats. And I felt the foretaste of homesickness before this strange nature. A silent rage was strangling me, the despair of being barrelled like a herring in this cargo boat, in spite of myself, by virtue of a case of force majeure, in the name of the imperious point of honour.

My fit of rage over, harassed, I was overwhelmed by prostration. Leaning against the rails, I let the waves whip my inflamed face while I avidly devoured the details of the coastline with my eyes, in order to discover a ray of hope there and, in my thoughts, I returned to my project of swimming ashore.

For a long time I contemplated the fleeting contours of the littoral. A calmness settled in my mind, flashes of peaceful joy illuminated my soul, and, without tangible reason, my congested brain no longer functioned with fury; visions of the lovely days of summer, memories of my first youth were resuscitated in it without anything being able to explain to me the motive of this caprice of my humour. The boat was going to round a promontory: the roofs of the red houses with their white cornices appeared above the fir trees, a flagstaff pierced through the patchworks of the little gardens, a bridge passed by, a chapel, a belfry, a cemetery . . . was it a dream? a hallucination? . . .

No, it was really the humble seaside resort, near to which, on an islet, I had passed the summers of my adolescence and, over there, was the very cottage where, last spring, I had lodged with Her and him for a night, in the evening after a day of boat-racing, of walking in the forest . . . It was really there, yes there, on that little mount, beneath the ash trees, on the balcony, that I had contemplated her pretty face all sunlit with the rays of her blonde hair, her little Japanese hat with its sky-blue veil, while with her hand gloved in kid skin she beckoned me from above that dinner was awaiting us . . . I could see her again even now, waving her scarf; I could hear her sonorous voice . . . and suddenly . . . how? . . . the boat slowed down, the engine stopped . . . a pilot boat came alongside us, rapidly . . . one, two, three! . . . a quick idea—only one—made me move as if under the sway of an electric force. With a tiger's leap, I climbed the ladder which led to the forecastle and planting myself resolutely in front of the captain of the steamer:

"Have me put ashore immediately," I said to him . . . "or else I'll go mad!"

He examined me with a keen eye, and without replying to me, amazed as if he had come face to face with an escaped lunatic, he hailed the mate to communicate this order to him without pondering his words:

"Have this gentleman taken down with his luggage. He is ill . . ."

Five minutes later I was sitting in the boat of the pilots who rowed hard and I touched land at once.

I possess a remarkable faculty. I can render myself blind and deaf at will. I had taken the road to the hotel without having seen or heard anything wounding for my pride, or an expression from the pilots telling that they were in the know about my secret, or a shocking word from the porters. At the hotel I installed myself in a room: I ordered an absinthe, lit a cigar and summoned myself to reflect.

Really, was I mad or not? Was the danger of such imminence that it had to occasion my immediate disembarkation?

In my present state, it was absolutely impossible to diagnose myself, seeing that the lunatic, according to the doctors, is unconscious of the aberration of his mind and that the coherence of his ideas is no proof against the anomaly of those very ideas. As an expert researcher, I examined analogous cases which had arisen in my past life. Once, at the time when I was still at the university, my nervous excitation, determined by troubling incidents, suicide of a friend, state of amorous delirium, anxiety for the future, had become so developed that I was taking umbrage at everything in broad daylight. I was afraid of remaining alone in my room, where I would appear to myself, which obliged my friends to look after me in turn during the night, the candles lit and the fire crackling in the stove.

Another time, in an outburst of contrition which followed calamities of every kind, I ran across fields, I wandered in the woods and finally, having climbed to the summit of a pine, I sat astride a branch and I made a speech to the fir trees which were spread beneath me to cover the murmur of their voices, picturing myself to be an orator coming to grips with the people. That happened quite close to here, on that very islet, where I had lived for so many summers and the headland of which rose over there in the distance. Recalling this incident with all its queer details, I was convinced that I was at least occasionally smitten with mental aberration.

What was to be done? Warn my friends in time before the rumour of my accident was spread through the town. But what shame and what dishonour to range oneself amongst the mentally under-aged! That I could never stand!

Lie then! Still take detours without succeeding in fooling anyone? That repelled me! Overwhelmed with scruples, buffetted between divers projects that I made to extricate myself from this maze without exit, I was seriously seized with the desire of escaping in order to hide myself from the fastidious inquisitions which were awaiting me, to discover for myself some shack in the forest in order to bury myself in it and perish there like a wild beast who senses the approach of death.

To this effect, I crept through the alley-ways; I climbed the soft slippery rocks with their covering of moss drenched by the autumn rains: I crossed a fallow field: I reached the enclosure where the cottage rose in which I had formerly slept. Its shutters were obstinately locked and the wild vine which carpeted it from ground to roof was now bare and disclosed the green trellis.

Finding again this place sacred to me, where the prelude to our liaison burgeoned, my love, shut away in the bottom of my heart as a result of other preoccupations, reappeared. Leaning against one of the supports of the balcony in fretwork wood, I cried, like an abandoned child.

I remembered having read in *The Thousand and One Nights* that young men could fall sick from the outcome of a thwarted love and that their cure depended only on the possession of the beloved. I also recalled those Swedish folk-songs in which the girls, despairing of ever being able to attain the object of their dreams, waste away before one's eyes, begging their mothers to prepare their deathbeds, and that old sceptic Heine who sang the tribe of the Asra who die when they love.

In fact my love was of a good quality since I had lapsed back into childhood, obsessed with a sole idea, with a unique image, with a predominant feeling which had rendered me feeble, unfit for anything except moaning.

To divert the course of my thoughts, I cast my looks onto the magnificent view which stretched at my feet. The thousands of islands, all bristling with fir trees intermingled with pines, swam in the immense gulf of the Baltic, decreasing by degrees, being transformed into islets, shelves, reefs, up to the limits of the Archipelago, where the green line of the sea stretched, where the waves broke against the escarped breakwater of the last outjutting rocks.

In the overcast sky, the floating clouds striped the surface of the waters with shadow in coloured strips, going from brown through the scale of bottle-greens, from Prussian blue to the snow white of the foam of the waves. Behind a fortress perched on an abrupt islet, a column of black smoke rose puffing in continual jets from an invisible chimney, then it would lie down beneath the wind, down to the living crest of the wave. Suddenly the cargo boat which I had just left showed its sombre carcass, wringing my heart, for it appeared to me as the witness of my dishonour. Then I took the bit between my teeth, like a maddened horse, and I fled towards the forest.

Under the ogival vaults of the fir trees where the breeze hymned through the spiked branches, distress anguished me increasingly. It was here that we would walk when the spring sun shone in the greenery, when the firs put forth their purple flowers which smelled of the perfume of strawberry, when the juniper cast its yellow dust to the wind, when the anemones pierced through the dead leaves beneath the hazel trees. It was here, on that brown moss, as soft as a woollen cover, that her small feet pattered as she sang her Finnish songs with a melodious voice. In a luminous flash of memory I found the two enormous pines again, intertwined as if in an embrace, and whose trunks rubbed together creaking under the thrust of the aereal wind. It was from there that she had left to make a detour and to go and pick a water-lily in the marsh. With the ardour of a veritable setter dog, I set out to seek the trace of that charming foot whose imprint, however light it was, couldn't escape me. I combed the terrain with neck bent, with nose to the ground, sniffing, examining, my vision strained, without picking up anything. The ground was trodden by the passage of animals and it would have been as easy to follow the track of the wood-nymph as to think of finding the place where the fine shoe of the Adored One had been placed. Nothing but cesspools, cow dung, flap mushrooms, fly agarics, puff balls rotting or rotten, petalless stems of flowers. I consoled myself for a moment, at the edge of the marsh, filled with blackish water, with the idea that this mud had enjoyed the honour of reflecting the most charming face in the world, and it was in vain that I sought to recognise the petals of the water-lilies among the dead leaves fallen from the surrounding birch trees. Then I turned back, plunging through the wood, the rustling of which deepened by a tone with the increasing girth of the trunks.

At the height of despair, under the acuity of pain, I howled while tears gushed beneath my eyelids. I trampled down the agarics and the mushrooms, like a rutting elk; I tore up the young junipers, I dashed myself against the trees. What did I want? Could I have said? An immoderate warmth was over-heating my blood; a limitless desire to see her again was taking hold of me. The one I loved too much to want to possess her had taken hold of my being. And now that all was ended, I wanted to die since I could no longer live without her.

But cunning as madmen are, I counted on dying in a happy fashion, by inducing pneumonia in myself or something similar and, bedridden for weeks, seeing her again, saying good-bye to her, kissing her hands.

Comforted by this clearly sketched plan, I made my way towards the cliff, which wasn't difficult for me, the roaring of the waves guiding me through the underwood.

The coast descended steeply, the water lay deep; all was for the best. I undressed, with an attentive care which did not reveal a sinister intention; I sheltered my clothes under an alder clump and hid my watch in the hollow of a rock. The wind blew sharply and in that month of October the water must have been at its minimum temperature above zero. After a run amongst the rocks, I flung myself head first, aiming at a cleft which was scooped between two enormous waves. I had the impression of having fallen into molten lava. I soon reappeared, bringing back strips of seaweed I had glimpsed at the bottom and whose vesicles were scratching my calves. Then I swam out to sea, offering my breast to the surging waves, greeted by the laughter of the sea-gulls and the cawing of the crows. At the end of my strength I swerved round and reached the cliff. The moment had come for the main operation. According to the warnings made to bathers, the essential danger consists in the prolonged stay out of water of naked man. Then I sat down on the rock most exposed to the wind, and letting the October gale lash my naked back, I felt my skin shrinking. My muscles contracted spontaneously, my thorax tightened as if the instinct of self-preservation wanted at all costs to protect the precious organs enclosed in its case. I was powerless to keep still. I grabbed an alder branch and passing the disordered movements of my muscular strength onto this tree which writhed beneath my spasms, I thus managed to hold myself in the same place. The glacial air burned my loins like a red iron. I hastened to put my clothes on again, convinced that I had done enough. Night however was approaching. When I returned into the wood it was dark there. Fear assailed me, and, knocking against the lower branches of the trunks, I was forced to grope my way back.

Suddenly, under the influence of my mad fears, the activity of my senses was sharpened to the extent that I could discern the species of the trees that surrounded me merely by the simple sound of the quivering of the branches. How low, that deep bass of the firs whose closely-set and solid needles formed gigantic Jews' harps: higher in tone were the long and mobile stems of the pines whose piping seemed the whistling of a thousand serpents; the dry clicking of the alder twigs evoked memories of childhood in me in which smarting torments and my first voluptuous experiences were mingled; the rustling of the dried leaves remaining on the oaks resounded like crumpled paper, and the whispering of the junipers almost imitated the voices of women speaking in each other's ears; the alders crackled in muffled tones when a branch split beneath the thrust of the wind. I could have distinguished a pine cone from a fir cone merely by the sound produced by the falling of the one or the other on the ground. I recognised the presence of a mushroom merely by the smell, and the nerves of my big toe seemed to discover what they were pressing, on touching on the ground, club moss or common fern.

I reached the enclosure of the cemetery, the stile of which I crossed, guided by my sensibility. For an instant I enjoyed the music of the weeping willows whose long whips lashed the crosses of the tombs which they sheltered. Finally, stiff with cold, quivering at every unexpected noise, I arrived at the village where the lights of the houses pointed out the way to the hotel to me.

Having gone to my room, I sent off a telegram to the Baron, informing him of the illness which had seized me and of my involuntary disembarkation. Then I made a complete confession of my cerebral state to him on some sheets of paper, mentioning the former attack and soliciting his discretion. In the first place, I indicated the engagement of my presumed intended, an engagement that I had learned of and which had withdrawn my hope forever, as the cause of my illness.

Exhausted, I got into bed, quite sure of having caught a serious fever this time. Then I rang for the maid and called for the doctor. As I was told that there wasn't one, I asked for the village priest to communicate my last wishes to him.

From that moment, I was prepared to die or to see madness break out.

No sooner sent for, the priest appeared. He was a man of about thirty, a type of farm labourer in his Sunday best. With his red hair, his half-dimmed eyes, his face sprinkled with freckles, he did not inspire me with sympathy and I remained without uttering a word for a long time, not knowing indeed what to confide to this individual without education, without the wisdom of age, without any knowledge of the human heart. Embarrassed like a provincial before a citizen, he remained standing in the middle of the room until, with a gesture of the hand, I invited him to take a chair. Only then did he undertake his questioning.

"You have sent for me, sir? You must have some worry?"

"Yes."

"There is no happiness but in Jesus . . ."

As I was aspiring to quite another happiness, I let him speak without protesting. He, evangelist preacher, discoursed alone, monotonous, like a weaver of words. The old phraseology of the catechism swayed me agreeably and the presence of a human being entering into moral correspondence with my soul, comforted me. The young priest, however, filled with sudden doubts on my sincerity, interrupted himself to ask me:

"Have you the true faith, sir?"

"No," I replied to him, "but keep on speaking, your words are doing me good . . ."

And he took up his task again. The continual noise of his voice, the radiance of his eyes, the heat emanating from his body had the effect of magnetic effluvia upon me. Half an hour afterwards I fell asleep.

On waking, the mesmerist had disappeared and the maid brought me an opiate found at the chemist's, with the strict instruction not to abuse it, because the phial contained a sufficient dose of poison to kill a man, she said to me, if taken in full. Remaining alone, I naturally swallowed the contents of the flask in a single gulp, and, resolved to die, I buried myself under the blankets, where sleep was not long in coming.

When I awoke in the morning I was not astonished to find my room lit by a brilliant sun: I had spent my night in very clearly drawn and coloured dreams. "I dream, thus I exist!" I said to myself: and I felt myself all over my body to discover the degree of my fever or the symptoms of pneumonia. But, despite my good intentions of seeing a fatal issue approach, I found myself in an approximately normal state. My head, although heavy, was functioning easily, less impetuous than before, and twelve hours' sleep had restored my vital strength, usually always lively, thanks to exercises of the body of every kind, practiced since my youth.

. . . A telegram was brought to me. My friends announced their arrival by the two o'clock boat!

Shame overcame me again. What was I going to do? and what face should I put on? . . . I reflected . . .

My reanimated virility was opposed to humiliating resolutions and, after a rapid meditation, I decided on the project of remaining in the hotel in order to recover and continue my journey by the next boat. So honour was saved, and the visit of my friends would only be another farewell—the last! However, when I returned in my thoughts to the incidents of the previous day, I hated myself. How could I, the strong mind, the sceptic, have let myself be drawn into those unlikely weaknesses! And, as for the assistance of that priest, how could such a folly be explained? Certainly, it was in his capacity as State employee that I had asked for him and he had only fulfilled the office of a hypnotiser with me. But, for the world, that would have the appearance of a conversion. Perhaps one would even believe in unavowable confessions concerning suspicious affairs, the last avowal of the rogue on his death-bed. What fine gossip for those villagers in direct communication with the town! What a treat for the caretakers!

A journey abroad, made without delay, was really the only means of breaking with this insupportable situation. While rehearsing my rôle as a castaway, I spent the morning walking beneath the verandah, observing the barometer, studying the timetables, in such a way that the hours sped by quickly: and the boat made its appearance at the mouth of the estuary, before I had made up my mind whether to go down to the landing-stage or remain in my room. As nothing was pressing me to make a show of myself in front of a forewarned crowd, I kept to my room. After a few minutes wait, I heard the voice of the Baroness who was asking the hotel proprietress about my health. I went out to meet her and she almost kissed me in front of the bystanders. With a heavy heart, she took pleasure in pitying me for that illness, a result of overwork, and strongly advised me to return to town and to postpone my journey until the spring.

She was at her best. In her fur wrap, she looked like a lama, so much did the long and supple furs hug her slim figure. The sea breeze had attracted the fine blood of her veins to her cheeks and, in her eyes enlarged by the emotion of seeing me again, an expression of infinite tenderness could be read. In vain did I defend myself against the apprehensions she had about my state of health, since I admitted to being quite restored; she found me looking ghastly, declared me unfit for any effort and treated me like a child. And that rôle of mamma suited her ravishingly . . . She had teasing intonations, addressed me with playful familiarity, wrapped me in her shawl: at table she put my napkin on, poured me out a drink, decided on all my movements. How she was a "mother" like this! Why didn't she devote herself to her child as she devoted herself to me? But I was only a disguised male, a seeking animal which the intractable autumn rut was harassing. Beneath this travesty of a sick child, I felt like the wolf lying in the bed of the grandmother whom he had devoured, while he was getting ready to have a bite at Little Red Riding Hood into the bargain.

I reddened before that naïve, loyal husband who was overwhelming me with attentions, sparing me painful explanations. Yet, all the same, all that wasn't my fault. My heart remained obstinately closed, and I received the thousand kindnesses of the Baroness with an almost wounding coldness.

At dessert, when the time for returning approached, the Baron proposed that I return with them. He offered me a room in his apartment, specially prepared for me. It must be said in my favour that I replied to him with a categorical "no", and suspecting the imminent danger, when one decides to play with fire like this, I informed them of my decision. I would remain a week here, and once restored I would return to occupy my old attic in town.

The reiterated protestations of my friends could not change any of the plan. A strange thing, as soon as I happened to leave my torpor, when I reassumed my virile will, the Baroness withdrew her friendship from me. The more undecided I was, the more I gave way to her caprices, the more she adored me, without ceasing to praise my wisdom, my kindness. She dominated me, bewildered me; the moment I put up a serious resistance to her, she would let go, testifying a repulsion towards me, almost rudeness.

While we were speaking of cohabilitation under the same roof, she drew a favourable picture of this arrangement, vaunting particularly the pleasure of seeing each other at any time and without previous invitation:

"But, madame," I replied, "what will the world think of this infiltration of a young man into a young home?"

"What does it matter to us what people say?"

"Well! and your mother, your aunt, etc. . . . . Besides, my manly pride is opposed to this sort of measure, suited to a minor at best."

"So much the worse for your manly pride! So you find it 'male' to let yourself perish without breathing a word?"

"But yes, Baroness, only men are worthy of showing themselves strong."

She flew into a rage, refusing to recognise, although it existed indeed, a difference between the sexes. Her feminine logic embroiled my ideas. I turned to the Baron who gave me, instead of a reply, a mocking smile in which could be read the small esteem he professed for the reason of women.

Finally, at about six, the boat lifted anchor, taking away my friends, and I returned alone to the hotel.

The evening showed promise of being magnificent. The sun was setting in an orange sky, the deep blue water was striped with white, a moon of copper rose on the horizon above the fir trees.

Leaning over a table in the dining-room, absorbed in my oscillating reflections, sad unto death, but sometimes gay, I didn't see the hotel proprietress approaching me.

"It was your sister, that young lady who has just left you, wasn't it, sir?"

"Not at all, madame!"

"Ah! . . . It's curious, however, how you resemble each other. One would have sworn you were brother and sister!"

I did not feel in a mood to prolong such a discussion. The conversation flagged, leaving only a ferment of ideas within me.

"Could it be," I said to myself, "that my constant preoccupation with the Baroness during these last days has left an imprint on my physiognomy?"

Was it indeed admissable that the expression of her face had become stereotyped onto mine, during this correspondence of soul pursued for six months? Had the instinctive desire to please each other at all costs produced an unconscious selection of the mannerisms, of the most seductive ways of looking, at the expense of the less favourable ones which had thus found themselves suppressed? It was quite possible, so much had the fusion of our two minds become effectuated, that we no longer possessed ourselves. Destiny or rather instinct was playing its wretched, unimpeachable rôle, and the stone was rolling, damaging everything, overturning everything in its passage, honour, reason, happiness, fidelity, wisdom and virtue.

. . . No, that candour of claiming to lodge an impetuous young man, at the age when the appetites are irresistibly rife, under her roof! Was she then a tart in disguise or had love obscured her reason? She, a tart? Ah! A thousand times no! I venerated her for her frank manners, her serenity, her motherly tenderness. That she was eccentric, unbalanced, she confessed herself when she spoke of her faults, but she, a rogue, no! Even in her little artifices to excite me, there was more of the mature woman who amuses herself by troubling someone timid than of the coquette who desires to awake carnal appetites.

Now it was going to be a question of chasing away the demons evoked again, and in order to continue to fool my friends I set about sketching a letter at my bureau, still dealing with the old theme of my luckless love. As supporting proof, I enclosed two poems in it, in the passionate genre, dedicated "To Her", poems with a double interpretation; the Baroness was free to take offence at them. Letters and verse remained unanswered, either because the means was hackneyed or the subject seemed uninteresting.

The days which followed, tranquil and calm, helped towards my recovery. The surrounding landscape had taken on the favourite colours of the adored one. That forest where I had spent hours of purgatory now smiled at me and, when I walked there in the morning, there did not remain the shadow of a painful memory in the folds of that ground on which I had struggled with all the demons enclosed in a human heart. Her presence and the certainty of seeing her again had restored life and reason to me at one and the same time.

Knowing from experience that a person who returns and is not awaited is never quite welcome, I presented myself at the domicile of the Baroness on my return, not without confusion, not without hesitation.

In the forecourt, the leafless trees, the absence of benches, the holes which the removal of the gates had left in the garden enclosure, the whirl of the detached leaves, the cellar holes stuffed with straw, all announced the arrival of winter. Penetrating into the drawing-room, I felt a heavy oppression in breathing the enclosed air, overheated by the porcelain stoves, which rose, tall and white, along the walls, like bedsheets falling from the ceiling. The inner windows were fitted, and their slits covered over with pasted paper: the cotton-wool spread between the window-panes, imitating snow, gave the aspect of a mortuary to this vast room which I tried to strip of its semi-lordly furnishing, in order to recall it with its former appearance of austere bourgeoisie: bare floors, rough wooden floor boards, with, around the black table of the dining-room, without a tablecloth, like a spider with its eight legs, the severe faces of my father and my step-mother.

The Baroness gave me a cordial welcome, certainly, but her saddened face revealed a worry. The father-in-law and the uncle were there: they were playing cards with the Baron in a neighbouring room. I went to greet the players and I found myself alone again with the Baroness in the drawing-room. She sat down underneath the lamp in an armchair and did crochet work. Taciturn, dull, not pretty, she left to me the care of holding the conversation, which, for lack of rejoinders, degenerated into a monologue. Huddled at the corner of the stove, I watched her leaning over her work without raising her head. Mysterious, introverted, she seemed sometimes unaware of my presence. I thought I had come at the wrong time, I thought that my return had perhaps produced the wrong impression that I had been afraid of producing. Suddenly I let my tired looks wander along the floor, and under the table cloth I glimpsed her leg, uncovered below the uplifted underskirts. The calf was delicate; a white stocking enclosed it: a garter embroidered in colours accentuated that charming muscle which turns our heads, allowing our fantasy to reconstruct the entire body from this single fact. The foot was arched with a vaulted instep, and was shod in a Cinderella shoe.

I thought this a mere chance then: I have since learned that a woman is perfectly aware that she is being looked at when she uncovers herself above her ankles. A little troubled by the fascinating vision, I veered the conversation round and, by a skilful manoeuvre, I came back to my imaginary love.

She drew herself up and, turning round, looked me in the face and said to me:

"Ah! You can boast of being faithful in your affections!"

My eyes wandered stubbornly underneath the tablecloth, there where the snowy white was shining beneath the cherry ribbon. However, I dragged them from their contemplation: I crossed them with the look of her pupils enlarged in the glow of the lamp and I replied to her in a firm tone, very resolute:

"Unfortunately, yes!"

The flicking of the cards and the exclamations of the players accompanied this brief confession.

A painful silence followed. She resumed her crochet and the underskirts, at a movement from the legs, fell back. The fascination was ending. There only remained an indifferent, ordinary, badly-dressed woman in front of me, and, after a quarter of an hour, I took my leave, pretending an indisposition.

Having returned home, I brought out my drama from the drawer, resolved to rewrite it, and to uproot that hopeless sentiment, by working frantically, for all that could only end in a crime which repelled me through disgust, through instinct, through cowardice, through education. And I prepared thenceforth to break off that more than dangerous liaison.

An unexpected chance came to my aid: two days later I was offered the cataloguing of a library at the home of a collector who resided out of town.

There I was then installed in a room of an old lordly manor of the seventeenth century, furnished with books from top to bottom. One could have made a patriotic journey there through all the epochs of history. The whole of Swedish literature was housed there, from the incunabula of the fifteenth century to the novelties of the present time. I plunged into it in order to encounter oblivion, and I was completely successful. At the end of the first week I had not noticed that I had missed my friends. On Saturday, the Baroness's "at home" day, a Royal Guards orderly brought me a formal invitation from the Baron preceded by friendly reproaches on my absence. I felt a bitter-sweet stupefaction at finding myself in a position to answer with a very amiable refusal, full of regrets that my time was no longer my own.

Another week having gone by, another orderly in full dress, who handed me a note, from the Baroness this time, couched in rather bitter terms, in which she begged me to come and see the Baron, bedridden following a cold: finally I was asked to be good enough to give news of myself. Impossible to get out of it. I went there at the appointed time.

The Baroness appeared poorly and the Baron, slightly sick, was bored in his bed, in the bedroom to which I was taken. The sight of that sanctuary, hitherto hidden from my eyes, revived my instinctive disgust for that matrimonial co-existence in a common room where the spouses exhibit themselves on those thousand occasions which demand solitude. The colossal bed where the Baron lay stretched betrayed all the turpitudes of secret life, and the pile of cushions, which rose up at the side of the patient, brazenly indicated the place of the wife. The dressing-table, the washstands, the towels, everything appeared defiled to me and I had to make myself blind to be able to hold back my nausea.

After a chat at the foot of the bed the Baroness invited me to take a glass of liqueur in the drawing-room, and since we were alone she overtook my thoughts as if she had guessed them. In chopped-up phrases she emptied the overflow of her heart.

"Isn't it sad?"

"What then?"

"Ah! You understand me well . . . That existence of a woman, without a goal, without a future, without an occupation! I will die of it!"

"And your child, Baroness, and her education, which will soon begin! And other children which may turn up . . ."

"I don't want to have any more children . . . Am I made to be a perpetual wet-nurse?"

"No, but a *mother* equal to her task, in the finest sense of the word."

"Mother or housekeeper! No thank you. They can be had. It's easier! And then, what do you want me to do? I have two maids who replace me marvellously. No: I want to live . . ."

"Become an actress?"

"Yes!"

"But your position is against it."

"I know it only too well, alas! And that's why I'm bored . . . why I'm becoming besotted . . . why I'm becoming nervy!"

"And literature! That's a trade less low than board-strutting."

"The art of speech is the elevated art par excellence for me. And so whatever happens, I shall never console myself for having missed my vocation. And why, Lord? . . . To find disillusion!"

The Baron called us back.

"What is she talking about?" he asked me.

"We are talking theatre," I replied.

"She's mad!"

"She's not as mad as one thinks," retorted the Baroness, leaving the room and slamming the door behind her.

"My dear chap," resumed the Baron in confidence, "she no longer sleeps at night."

"What does she do?"

"She plays the piano, she stretches out on the sofa or else she

75

chooses those hours to do the household accounts. Indeed, my young sage, tell me what must be done to put an end to those senseless ideas."

"Give her a child. What am I saying? A string of children!"

He grimaced. Then trying to put on a good face:

"Strictly forbidden by the doctor, because of the first confinement which went badly . . . and then . . . reasons of economy, dear fellow . . . You understand?"

I understood. I was careful not to insist on this too delicate subject, too young, moreover, to suspect that it is the sick women who order the doctors what the prescribe.

The Baroness reappeared, bringing back her little daughter whom she put to bed in a small iron bed near the Baron. The little one, who didn't want to sleep, began to cry. The mother, having made vain efforts to calm her, went to look for the birch.

I have never been able to see a child being beaten without losing my temper; I have even gone as far as to raise my hand against my father on such an occasion. I was carried away and, flying into a rage which I didn't dissimulate, I intervened.

"Pardon me," I said . . . "Do you think that a child complains without sufficient cause?"

"She is being naughty."

"The fact is she has reason to be. It may well be that she is feeling sleepy and that our presence or the glow of the lamp is annoying her."

Ashamed and perhaps conscious of her unbecoming pose as a shrew, she agreed with me. Upon which I retired.

That unexpected vision of the interior of that home cured me for some weeks of my love. I must admit that the scene of the birch added considerably to the odious impression that I carried away of that evening.

8

Autumn dragged on monotonously and Christmas approached. The arrival of a young couple (Finnish newly-weds of the Baroness's intimate circle) restored a little zest to our relations, whose charm was evaporating. I received numerous invitations thanks to the attentions of the Baroness, and I exhibited myself in evening dress at suppers, at dinners, even at a ball. During those incursions into a world whose distinction left much to be desired, I noticed that the Baroness, with boyish manners and under cover of an excessive frankness, herself paid court to young men, but always slipping a sly look at me, to make sure of the impression her conduct made on me. This brazen flirtation outraged me: I responded by keeping an offensive reserve, due as much to the sentiment of repulsion that bad form inspires in me, as to the pain that I felt on seeing the adored being degrade herself, cloak herself as a vulgar coquette.

She always appeared to be enjoying herself enormously and prolonged these reunions well into the night. My opinion was thus confirmed that she was a woman with unsatisfied desires who was bored in her home and that her artistic vocation was based only on the petty vanity of showing herself off and of enjoying life more. Smart, petulant, always in movement, she possessed the art of self-presentation and in the crowd of guests she was always the most surrounded, through the skill she showed in rallying people round her, rather than through her natural attractions. Her exuberant vitality, her nervous expansion obliged the most reluctant to listen to her, to notice her, and I observed that at the moments when her nerves abandoned her, when she went off into a shadowy corner, the fascination ceased. No one sought her any more then. In search of ambitious power, perhaps without a heart, she strove to be courted by young men, and neglected the society of the ladies. And so she had got it into her head to see me in love, dominated, sighing at her feet. One day, after an evening of triumph, she even took it upon herself, blinded with fatuity, to confide to a woman friend that I was madly in love with her.

As I was paying a visit to this friend some time later, I clumsily happened to say that I thought I would meet the Baroness by coming:

"Well, well," the mistress of the house said to tease me, "it wasn't me that you came to see. That's very kind of you."

"No, madame, indeed. To tell the truth, I have been asked to be here this afternoon."

"Then it's a rendezvous."

"If you like. You'll at least agree that I didn't fail to come."

And indeed it was she who had arranged the projected visit. I had obeyed her. She had simply compromised me to save herself.

I avenged myself for this adventure by spoiling a series of parties for her, where my absence no longer allowed her to enjoy my sufferings. Yet how I suffered! Roaming through the streets, under the windows of the houses where I knew she had been invited, I twisted the dagger in my wound, quivering with jealousy when I glimpsed her, bending on the arm of a waltzer, in her blue silk dress, with her blonde locks lifted by the wind of the dance, her ravishing figure spinning on the prettiest soles in the world.

9

We had rounded the cape of the new year. Spring was beginning to appear. We had spent the time in parties, in intimate gatherings, mortally sad, the three of us. There had been break-ups and makings-up, skirmishes and armistices, squabbles and effusions full of friendly cordiality. I went off and I returned.

The month of March was near, a redoubtable month in the countries of the north for rutting is terribly rife there and the destinies of lovers would then be accomplished of their own accord, freed of the formulated promises, crushing hearts, breaking all the bonds of honour, family and friendship.

The Baron, being on duty one day early in March, invited me to spend an evening with him at the barracks. I went at his invitation. In a son of commoners, an offspring of a petty bourgeois family, the insignia of the supreme power could only inspire respect. I traversed corridors at the side of my friend, saluted by officers at every step; I heard the rattling of the sabres, the "Who goes there?" of the sentinels, the rolling of the drums. We came to the orderly room. The warlike decorations which were displayed on the walls gave me secret emotions, the portraits of the great generals made me bow my head. The standards captured at Lutzen, at Leipzig, the flags of today, the bust of the present king, the helmets, the brilliant bucklers and the plans of battle—all that awoke in me plebeian uneasiness before the attributes of the reigning order.

And the captain seen thus in his imposing milieu, grew before my eyes, to the extent that I was close to him, ready to request his help in the event of an alert.

When the Baron went into his service room, his lieutenant came to pay his respects to him, standing, and I felt superior all the same to this hierarchy of lieutenants, the declared rivals of the men of letters for the ladies, the dreaded enemies of the sons of the people.

An orderly brought a bottle of punch and we lit cigars. The Baron showed me the golden book of the regiment to entertain me, a very artistic collection of sketches, water-colours, drawings, representing all the outstanding officers who had served in the royal guard for the last twenty years, the portraits of the very men whom the high school boys of my time envied and admired and whom they enjoyed imitating every day by playing at the "mounting of the guard". My instinct as a man of low extraction was delighted at contemplating all those privileged men whom we ridiculed and, counting on the assent of the democratised Baron, I allowed myself small sallies against those disarmed adversaries. But the line of demarcation of the democratic tendencies of the Baron was different from mine, and my sallies received a bad welcome. The *esprit de corps* prevailed;

and turning the leaves for me with a now readier hand, he stopped in front of a great composition representing the upheaval of 1868.

"Ah! Ah!" he said with a nasty laugh, "that's how we sabred the rabble!"

"You were there?"

"Was I there! I was on guard and charged with the defence of the tribune which stood opposite the monument attacked by the crowd. I got a stone on my helmet. I was dishing out the cartridges, when a dispatch rider from the King unfortunately came to forbid my volley fire, which made me stay a butt, like a sieve, for the stones of the populace. Ah! yes, I paid for loving the mob!"

And after a silence he continued, laughing, his eyes on mine.

"You remember that story well?"

"Perfectly, I recall it very well. I formed part of the students' procession."

What I kept quiet about was that I had, as a matter of fact, rallied to that mob which he wanted to shoot. I was furious that that tribune reserved for complimentary tickets had been erected, that the people had been excluded from a popular festival. I had then taken sides with the assailants, and I even retained the very distinct memory of the stones which I had thrown at the soldiers of the guard.

At that moment, when I was listening to him pronounce that word "rabble" in an aristocratic manner, I could understand the unconsidered fears which had seized me when I had penetrated into that fortress of the enemy; and the features of my friend which altered at my jokes only served to discourage me from continuing. The hatred of race, of caste, the traditions rose between us like an insurmountable wall, and when I watched him with his sabre between his knees, a sabre of honour decorated at the hilt with the crowned insignia of the donator, the King, I felt keenly all the artificiality of our friendship, the work of a woman, the only link between the two of us. His haughty accent, his physiognomy harmonising more and more with the milieu, were removing him from me, and I changed the conversation in order to draw us closer together. Apropos of boots, I questioned him about the Baroness and his daughter. Then his face lit up, became unwrinkled and his usual mien of a good boy reappeared. When I felt myself back on the territory of the past, I decided, beneath his benevolent look of an ogre fondling a dwarf, to pull three hairs from his giant's beard.

"Tell me, dear friend," I said to him, "cousin Matilda is expected for Easter, isn't she?"

"Certainly."

"Then, I'm going to start courting her," I hazarded.

He emptied his glass and, with his air of a good ogre, he said sneeringly:

"You can always try."

"What's that . . . always? Has she already perhaps some engagements?"

"No . . . not that I know of! . . . However . . . I think I know that . . . Anyway you can always try."

And in a tone of profound conviction:

"You'll get nothing for your pains, my lad."

There was something scornful in that advice given without caution. In reply to that kind of affront, an arrogant resolution was born in me, to brave that knight too bold in words, and to save myself from a criminal love by a happy combination, transferring it onto another object, which simultaneously offered a revenge for the Baroness, wounded in her legitimate feelings. The night had come. I got up to return to my dwelling. The captain accompanied me amongst the sentinels and we shook hands outside the gate of the castle which he pushed with a brusque blow, like a challenge.

Spring had come. The snow melted, the streets were rid of their pavements of ice. Already the hungry children were selling their bouquets of small liverworts on the streets. In the shop-fronts of the florists the azaleas, the rhododendrons and the early roses offered their coloured splendour to the eye; the oranges shone in the windows of the grocers; the lobsters, the radishes and the cauliflowers from Algeria appeared on the stalls of the greengrocer's. Under North Bridge, the sun lit the crests of the thin waves of the river with a strip of gold. On the quays, the steamboats donned their rigging, repainted in sea green and cinnabar scarlet. The men, numbed by the darkness, stretched out in the solar rays and the man-animal felt the goad of the rut pricking in him. Woe to the weak when selection is going to take place, when love is going to give free rein to the pent-up passions!

The pretty she-devil came. She stayed at the Baron's.

I made advances to her. As she seemed to be in the know, she was amused with me. We played a four-finger fantasia on the piano; she pressed her right breast against my left arm. The Baroness noticed this and she suffered because of it. The Baron was maddened with jealousy. He espied me with a wrathful eye. Now he grew angry because of his wife, now he took me to task because of the cousin. When he left his wife to whisper in a corner with the girl, I went and talked with his neglected wife. Then he lost his temper, asked us a clumsy question which broke off our conversation. I answered sneeringly; sometimes I didn't even listen to him . . .

There was an intimate supper that evening. The Baroness's mother was there. She took a liking to me and, circumspect as old women are, she smelled a rat.

On an impulse of motherly ardour, boding perils of which she was ignorant, she seized my hands and wrapped me in her gaze:

"Sir," she said to me, "I am sure that you are a man of honour. I do not know what is happening in this house. But, in any case, promise me to watch over my daughter, my only child: and if anything ever happens . . . something which ought not to happen, promise me to come and see me in order to tell me everything."

"I promise, madame," I said to her, kissing her hand in the Russian manner, for she had long been married to a Russian, dead for some years.

And I was to keep my promise!

(12)

We were dancing on the edge of a crater. The Baroness grew pale, thin, frighteningly ugly. The Baron was jealous, brutal, and uncouth towards me. If I went away, I was called back the following day, to be welcomed with open arms, everything to be explained as a misunderstanding, when, in fact, the day before, we had understood each other only too well.

What was happening in the house, the Lord only knows!

As that evening pretty Matilda had retired to her bedroom to try on an evening gown, the Baron had slipped off, leaving his wife alone with me. After half an hour's conversation, I asked where he might have gone.

"He serves Matilda as lady's-maid," the Baroness answered me.

I was emboldened. But at once she regretted what she had told me and she added:

"But that is of no importance between relatives. One shouldn't see anything wrong in it!"

Then changing her tone:

"Are you jealous?"

"And you, Baroness?"

"That will come to me perhaps."

"Would to God that that comes to you in time. That's the wish of a friend!"

The Baron returned and with him the girl in her light green evening dress, which disclosed the rise of the breasts at the cleavage of the bodice.

I pretended to be dazzled, lifting my two palms to my eyes and I exclaimed:

"Do you know that there is a danger in beholding you, miss!"

"Isn't she pretty?" asked the Baroness in a strange tone.

The Baron led Bébé out again and I remained alone with his wife once more.

"Why have you been so brusque with me for some time?" she said to me, her voice covered by tears, with the look of a beaten dog.

"Me? ... But I haven't noticed that ..."

"Yes: you have changed in your behaviour towards me; I would like to know why ... If I have failed in anything ..."

She brought her seat up to mine, contemplated me with shining eyes, trembled, and ... I got up.

"This absence of the Baron is extraordinary, don't you think? That confidence on his part is offensive."

"Which means?"

"That ... in short, that one doesn't leave one's wife like this

84

tête-à-tête with a young man, especially when one shuts oneself up with a girl in her room . . ."

"You are right, it's an insult to me . . . But your manners are . . ."

"Eh! What do manners matter? I detest that sort of thing. I despise you when you're not jealous of your dignity. What are the two of them doing in there?"

"He is seeing to Matilda's toilette!" she replied with an innocent expression and laughing up her sleeve. "What do you want me to do about it?"

"A man does not attend to the toilette of a woman without having amorous relations with her."

"She's his child, so he claims; she only sees a 'papa' in him."

"I would not allow my children to play papa and mamma and certainly not adults."

The Baroness rose to go and find her husband, who returned with her.

We spent the rest of the evening experimenting with mesmerism. I made passes over the forehead of the Baroness, who confessed to feeling calming effects on her nerves from it. Suddenly, at the moment she was about to fall into a cataleptic sleep, she shook herself, started up and looked at me with haggard eyes.

"Stop it! I don't want it," she exclaimed. "You're going to cast a spell on me."

"Then, it's up to you to try your mesmeric powers," I said to her.

She proceeded with manipulations on me identical to those which she had undergone.

While I was lowering my eyes, a prolonged silence reigned on the other side of the piano. I looked towards the feet and the lyre-shaped pedal of the instrument and . . . I thought I was dreaming. With a violent bound, I left my seat. At the same time, the Baron rose up behind the piano and invited me to take a glass of punch.

All four of us were going to clink our raised glasses, when the Baron said to his wife:

"Come on, drink to your reconciliation with Matilda!"

"To your health, little witch," the Baroness said smilingly.

And turning towards me:

"Imagine that we had quarrelled because of you!"

At first, I didn't know what to reply. Then:

"I will be obliged to you if you kindly explain yourself, Baroness," I said.

"Ah! Ah! No! No explanations," replied the chorus.

"It's a shame," I retorted, "for it seems to me that we have kept silent for too long, on the contrary."

The evening thus ended amidst general embarrassment and I returned home . . .

"Because of me!" I repeated to myself, searching my conscience.

What could that very well signify? Was it a naïve quip from that whimsical mind? Two women fallen out because of a man? They must be jealous of each other then over that man. Would the Baroness have been so mad as to betray herself in such a manner? Certainly not. Then? . . . There must have been other implications in it.

"What is happening in that house?" I thought, recalling the strange scene which had frightened me that evening without my being able to confess to having seen anything indecent, so much also did the adventure seem unlikely to me.

Those jealousies, without rhyme or reason, the fears of the old mother, the delirium of the Baroness excited by the spring air, all that was embroiled in my brain, was boiling in it, was fermenting, and, after a night of reflections, I came to the decision for a second time not to return to them in order to avoid imminent, irreparable disasters.

With this intention, I got up early to compose a sensible, sincere, deferential letter, couched in chosen terms which forewarned against an excessive abuse of friendship; explicit without giving any explanations, that letter asked for the absolution of my sins, accused me of having brought discord between relatives and the devil alone knows all that I scribbled down in it!

The result was that the Baroness came, as if by chance, to meet me, about midday, when I was leaving the Library. She stopped on North Bridge, held me back and led me aside into an alleyway on Charles XII Square. Almost in tears, she begged me to come back, not to ask any more explanations, to be simply theirs as before.

Ah! How charming she was that day! But I loved her too much to lose her.

"Leave me, do. You're going to cast a slur on your reputation," I repeated to her, examining the pedestrians whose looks embarrassed us. "Return home, at once, or I'll be the one to leave you."

She looked me straight in the eyes with such a pitiful expression that I was tempted to go down on my knees, to kiss her feet, to implore forgiveness.

But I turned my back on her and slipped off through a side passage.

After dinner, I climbed briskly up the stairs of my attic, my mind overjoyed at the duty accomplished, but with a torn heart. Oh! How she had a way of looking at a man, that woman!

A short siesta had restored my strength to me. I got up to look at the calendar hanging on the wall. It was the 13th March.

"Beware the Ides of March!"—Beware the 13th of March!"

Those famous words, quoted by Shakespeare in his *Julius Caesar*, were ringing in my ears when the maid entered and handed me a note from the Baron.

I would oblige him by coming to spend the evening with him, for the Baroness was poorly and Matilda was going out.

Not having the strength to resist, I went at his invitation.

The Baroness, more dead than alive, ushered me in, pressed my hands against her breast, thanking me with a warm effusion of words for not depriving them of the presence of a friend, of a brother, because of futilities, misunderstandings, nothings.

"She is becoming mad!" said the Baron mockingly, while he disentangled me from that embrace.

"Yes, I am mad, it's true, mad with joy at seeing our friend again who wanted to leave forever."

And there she was, crying!

"She has been so poorly lately!" said the Baron, embarrassed before this truly heartrending scene.

The poor woman seemed delirious. Her eyes shone with a sombre glow, filling her face: her cheeks were green. It was pitiful to see her. She had fits of coughing, a chesty cough, which shook all her fragile body.

The uncle and the father-in-law arrived unexpectedly and a large fire was lit in the stove, in front of which we prepared to "celebrate the dusk" without lighting the lamps.

She came to sit beside me while the three gentlemen started a controversy on politics.

In the shadow, I could see her eyes gleaming, I could sense the radiation of her body, by the heat that it probably gave off, after the fit of hysteria which she had just had.

Her dress brushed against my trouser, she leaned over my shoulder to be able to speak in my ear without being heard by the others, and in a murmur, she slipped this question to me without preamble:

"Do you believe in love?"

"No!"

And that "no" fell like a bludgeon stroke on her head, for I got up to change places.

"She is demented, a nymphomaniac," I said to myself, and seized with an apprehension lest she cause a scandal, I proposed to ask for some light.

During the supper, the uncle and the father-in-law expatiated wantonly on the qualities of cousin Matilda, her taste for the home, her dexterity in the graceful works of a lady. The Baron, having drunk several rounds of punch, launched forth in raptures, into furious eulogies, and with alcoholic tears in his eyes, he deplored the bad treatment that this little one was made to endure under the paternal roof. Which did not prevent him, at the height of his chagrin, from taking his watch out of his gusset and leaving us brusquely as if suddenly recalled to a duty:

"You will excuse me, gentlemen," he said to us, "but I have promised Bébé to go and fetch her in order to bring her back to the house. Don't trouble yourselves. I'll be back in under an hour."

The old Baron, his father, tried in vain to hold him back; the schemer got off with exclamations, claiming to be a slave to his word of honour. Upon which he escaped, expressly obliging me to await his return.

We remained at table for a further quarter of an hour. Then we moved into the drawing-room. The two old men, seized with a need for solitude, retired to the room of the uncle, who had been installed at his nephew's for some time.

I cursed destiny which had trapped me, in spite of so much trouble to avoid it, and I clothed my pounding heart in steel; as a cock bridles his comb I raised my head; I bristled my hair like a mastiff its fur, in order to ward off, by my approach, every attempt at lachrymose or amorous scenes.

With my back to the stove, I smoked a cigar, placid, cold, stiff, in the expectation of what was about to happen.

It was the Baroness who spoke to me first.

"Why do you hate me?"

"I do not hate you."

"Think a little of the way in which you welcomed me this morning."

"Let's leave that."

That extraordinary brutality in my replies, without reasonable motive, was a mistake. She guessed it and did not insist.

"You want to run away from me," she continued. "Now do you want to know what determined my brusque departure for Mariafred?"

A silence of two seconds and I replied:

"The same motive apparently as that which called me to Paris."

"Then . . . it's clear," she said.

"And what now!"

I was expecting a scene. She was there, tranquil, contemplating me with saddened looks. It was up to me to break this new silence, more dangerous than words.

"Now that you have dragged my secret out of me, a word. If you still want to see me sometimes in your home, very rarely," I said, "take care. My love is, you see, of such an elevated nature that I intend to live beside you, without asking anything other than to see you. If you forget your duties, if you betray what our hearts are hiding by an expression of your face, a gesture, I'll denounce you to your husband, and then come what may!"

Ecstatic, enthusiastic, she lifted her eyes towards heaven.

88

"I swear it to you! . . . How strong and good you are! . . . How I admire you! Oh! I'm ashamed! I would like to surpass you in loyalty, I would like . . . Do you want me to reveal everything to Gustav myself?"

"If you want to! . . . But then, we shall no longer see each other. Besides, that does not concern him. The sentiments which my heart feels are not criminal, and even if he were to know everything, is it in his power to stifle my feelings? No. If I decide to love a woman who pleases me, it's my business, until the day when my passions encroach on the territory of others. For the rest, do as you like. I am prepared, in any event.

"No, no; let him be ignorant of everything, and since he runs where it suits him . . ."

"Excuse me, I am not of that opinion and do not share your considerations on the similarity in this case. If he degrades himself, so much the worse for him. That is not a reason for . . . Ah! No! . . ."

The ecstasy had come to an end. We were coming back to earth.

"Ah! No!" I repeated . . . "Admit, at least, that that is fine, unheard of, almost original. We love each other, we disclose it to each other. And that's that."

"It's as beautiful as one reads in books," she exclaimed, clapping her hands like a child.

"Yes, but that is not usually found in serialised novels."

"And how good it is to remain honest!"

"That's the least onerous method of all!"

"And we shall still see each other, as before, without fear . . ."

"And without reproaches!"

"Then, no more misunderstandings! But at least it's certain that it isn't Matilda whom you . . ."

"Silence!"

The door opened. Oh! Height of banality! . . . The two old men appeared, returning from a secret place, holding a dimmed lantern in their hands. They crossed the drawing-room and returned into their room.

"Notice in passing," I said to her, "how life is blended of little miseries and beautiful moments. How reality differs from the poetic work. Would I dare, in a novel, in a play, to present such a natural scene without risking falling flat? Think then, a declaration without embraces, without going on one's knees, without big words, terminated in this appearance of two old men projecting the glow of their dimmed lanterns on the two lovers. And there, however, is the secret of the grandeur of Shakespeare, who shows Julius Caesar in a dressing-gown, in slippers, waking at night, frightened by childish dreams.

The little bell tinkled. It was the Baron with pretty Matilda. As he did not have a calm conscience, he overwhelmed us with kindnesses. And I, desirous of showing myself completely in my rôle, told him a bold lie:

"I've been quarrelling with the Baroness for the last hour," I said.

He examined us cunningly, and sniffing like a hunting dog, he went off, seeming to follow the false trail that I was indicating to him.

As for me, I retired.

What unparalleled candour to believe in chastity in love! That secret which we were guarding between us constituted a danger in itself! It was a child conceived in hiding: it took shape, after the union of our souls, it wanted to be born!

We longed more than ever to meet each other in order to compare our former feelings, to relive that year, spent in fooling each other. We invented ruses; I introduced her at my sister's, married to a high school teacher, who turned out to be slightly of her world, since he bore a name of the old nobility.

We made rendezvous with each other, innocent in the beginning, but the ardour grew increasingly and desires were awoken.

In the days which followed our declaration, she handed me a bundle of letters, written in part before the 13th March and partly after the avowal. Those letters, confidants of her sufferings and her love, I was never intended to possess!

(14)

Monday.

Dear Friend,

I am languishing for you today as everyday. Thank you for having allowed me to speak to you yesterday without your displaying that sarcastic expression, *de rigueur* with you. Why that air? If you could know how it angers me! When I turn to you, confidingly, at the moment when your friendship is more than ever necessary to me, you cover your face with a mask. Why? Must you then disguise yourself before me? In a letter, you have confessed of your own accord that it was only a mask. I hope so and I can see it, but that pains me however, for then the idea comes to me that I have committed yet another blunder . . . And I ask myself: "Whatever is he going to think of me?"

The fact is I am jealous of your friendship; the fact is that I am afraid of bringing your scorn upon me. But no, it isn't so, is it? You ought to be sincere and good towards me. You ought to forget that I'm a woman—don't I forget it myself too often! . . .

I was not angry with you yesterday for what you said to me, but it surprised and mortified me. Do you think I am capable of provoking the jealousy of my husband and of avenging myself in a dishonest way? Just imagine the risk to be run in order to reach such ends, seeking to bring him back to me by this means of jealousy! What would I have gained by it?—His resentment would have been turned against you and we would not have been able to see each other!—And what would become of me without your presence which is at present more dear than life to me?

I love you with all the tenderness of a sister, without the caprices of a coquette . . . It is true there were moments when I was longing, when it would have been pleasant for me to take your pretty little head between my hands, to look deep down into your sincere and wise eyes, and without any doubt, I would have gone as far as to imprint a kiss on that serene brow which I adore, but that kiss would have been the purest that you ever received.

This is due to my affectionate nature, and even if you were a woman, I would love you the same, provided that I could esteem a woman as I esteem you.

How happy I am at the opinion you have of Matilda! Must one be a woman to be able to enjoy that? What do you expect? Think of my position when they were all rallying beneath her banner! It's also my fault, what's happening. I authorised that inclination, seeing only a child's game in it from the beginning, and I left my husband free, sure of keeping his heart. The outcome served to prove the contrary to me . . .

92

He is in love with her and confessed it to me. The affair has passed the limit and I have laughed about it! . . . Imagine that after having seen you to the door he came back, clutched my hands, looked me in the eyes—a shudder seized me, for I have scarcely a quiet conscience—and with a pleading voice: "Maria . . . You won't be angry, will you? Allow me to go and join Matilda in her room this evening, I am too much in love with her!"—What can I do? Cry or laugh? And it's to me he comes to ask that, to me who am haunted by my remorse, to me who am reduced to loving you from afar, without hope of being able to ask you anything! What use are those stupid ideas of honour! Let him satisfy his carnal desire; you remain for me still, my dear love, and my feminine appetites are not so terrible as to make me forget my duties as wife and mother. But observe the contradiction, the duality of my feelings . . . I love you both, and I couldn't live without him, the brave, the loyal, friendly heart . . . nor without you now . . .

At last you have torn the veil which hid the secret of my heart. And you do not scorn me! Thank God! . . . You even love me. The word which you did not want to pronounce you have said. You love me!—And I am guilty, a rogue because I love you. May God forgive me! For I love him too, as well, and I will never be able to separate myself from him!

Oh! . . . How strange it is! . . . Beloved! Cherished! By him and by you! I feel so happy, so tranquil, that my love cannot be criminal! Otherwise I would feel remorse, or am I so hardened?

Ah! What shame! It was for me to be the first to make that confession! . . . Precisely at this instant Gustav is opening his arms to me . . . and I am going to kiss him. Am I sincere? Yes! Why didn't he protect me when there was still time?

All this is like a novel. How will it end? Will the heroine die? Will the hero marry another? Will they each go their separate ways? And will the dénouement have a morally satisfying ending? . . .

If I were beside you at this instant, I would kiss your brow with the devotion of the fanatic who kisses a crucifix and I would cast off from myself all the baseness and all the perversity that I find in me . . .

(15)

... Is it hypocrisy or am I fooling myself? Do these quasi-religious reveries beneath which the appetites are hiding come from concupiscence alone? No; not from that alone. The desire to perpetuate the existence received is more complicated and even with animals the psychic qualities are propagated by love. So it is both the body and soul which are in love, and the one is nothing without the other. If it is only bodily love, why prefer the frail, nervous and sickly adolescent that I am to the giant like him? If it is only love of the soul, why that covetousness of the kiss, why those adorations, of my little feet, of my beautiful hands, of my rosy, curved nails, of my high domed brow, of my abundant hair? Or could it be that the intoxications of her senses, excessively excited by the licenses of her husband, are procuring her those hallucinations? Or else does her instinct foresee that my juvenile ardour can provide her with more enjoyments than the inert mass of her husband? She is no longer jealous of the body of her husband, so she no longer loves him as a lover. She is jealous of all my person, so she loves me.

During a visit to my sister's, the Baroness fell a prey to a fit of hysteria. She fell onto a sofa and melted into tears. She was furious at the unworthy conduct of her husband, who was to spend his evening at a military ball with cousin Bébé. In an attack of delirium, she hugged me against her breast, kissed me on the brow, and I returned her kiss for kiss. She addressed me familiarly. The link held us and I desired her violently.

In the course of the evening I recited a piece of verse by Longfellow: *Excelsior*. Truly moved by that charming poetry, I felt her with my gaze and her face reflected all the nuances of my mimicry as with a hypnotised woman. She seemed a lunatic, a visionary.

After the supper, her lady's maid came to fetch her in a cab in order to accompany her to her home. I wanted to leave her in the street. She ordered me to get up into the carriage first, and told the maid to sit down beside the coachman, although I protested strongly. Alone in the carriage we kissed silently. I felt her delicate body contracting, quivering beneath my lips and, little by little, she abandoned herself to me. I still recoiled before the crime—why trouble the descendance of a family?—and I left her at her door, intact, ashamed, maddened with resentment perhaps.

Now all the doubts were dissipated. I could see it clearly. She had wanted to seduce me. It was she who had taken the first kiss, who had made the advances. But, from that minute, it was I who was going to play the rôle of the seducer, for I am not a Joseph, despite the rigid principles that I practice in the matter of honour!

(17)

We had arranged a rendezvous for the following day at the National Museum. I adored her, while she mounted the marble stairs underneath the gilded ceilings, when I could perceive her tiny feet pit-patting on the veined stucco squares, when I saw her approaching me, her princessly figure well fitted into a tailor-made top of black velvet, embroidered with trimmings in the style of the hussars. I approached in order to greet her, bending my knee in the manner of page boys. Her beauty exalted by my kisses appeared splendid to me. The skin of her cheeks was transparent, showing a glimpse of the flourishing blood of her veins beneath the epidermis: that almost spinster-like statue had become animated, warmed at the fire of life, beneath my caresses. Pygmalion had breathed on the marble and possessed a goddess.

We sat down in front of a Psyche, conquered at the time of the Thirty Years War. I kissed her cheeks, eyes, lips and it was with smiles, an intoxication of happiness, that she received my kisses. I played the rôle of the seducer-improvisor, employing all the sophistries of the orator, all the artifices of the poet:

"Desert," I said to her, "that house of adultery: run from that polluted room, break with that *ménage à trois,* or you will incur my scorn. (I didn't want to address her familiarly for it would be degrading her.) Return to your mother's, devote yourself to the sacred Art; in a year you will be able to make your début. Then you will be free and you will live your own life."

She poked the fire, she kissed me and I grew hot. I proffered an unbelievable quantity of words which culminated in a promise, that I wrenched from her, to confess everything to her husband, whatever the consequences we were to undergo.

"And if that turns out badly?" she objected.

"Then may everything be destroyed! But I couldn't love you without esteem for myself and you. Are you a coward then? Do you intend to obtain the recompense and withdraw yourself from the sacrifice? Have the sublimity of your beauty, risk the fatal leap, even if you perish. May all be lost except honour! Within a few days, if this is going to grow, I shall have seduced you, be sure of it, for my love is like a thunderbolt which will strike you, for I love you as the sun loves the dew . . . to drink it. So quickly to the scaffold! Give your head and keep your hands pure. Do not imagine that I will humiliate myself to share. Never! It's all or nothing!"

She made a show of resistance, in reality flinging a grain of powder right into the hearth. She complained of the wrongs of her husband, half-opening the doors of that bed-chamber, the very thought of which put me beside myself.

He, the idiot, poor like me, without a future, treated himself to the luxury of two mistresses, when I, the man of talent, the noble of the future, was moaning, was writhing beneath the blisters of my inflamed blood!

But suddenly she went off in the opposite direction, attempting to calm me, recalling to me our oaths exchanged to remain brother and sister.

"For others those dangerous games of brother and sister! Sillinesses of a little mother! Let's be man and woman, lover and mistress, that's the real thing! I adore you. I adore everything in you, the body and the mind, the blonde hair and the uprightness of soul, the smallest feet shod in suède, your frankness, your eyes lost in the shadow of a cab, your enchanting smile, your white stocking and your cherry garter . . ."

"Oh! . . ."

"Yes, charming princess, for I have seen all that. I want at present to bite you there at the hollow of the rising throat, in that loving dimple; and I promise you I'll stifle you beneath my kisses, strangle you between my arms, like a clasped necklace. Ah! I have the strength of a god when I breathe you! And you thought me a weakling perhaps! I was a hypochondriac, a hypocrite rather! Beware of the ailing lion! Do not approach his lair, he might caress you to death! Down with the infamous mask! I desire you and I want you, as at the first moment! A fairy-tale, a cock and bull story—the tale of Selma the Finn! . . . A lie, the friendship of our dear Baron . . . The bourgeois, the provincial, the outsider that I am? . . . He detests me as I execrate him myself, him, the noble!"

She did not seem to be moved by that avalanche of revelations which brought nothing new because we knew all that already without confessing it to each other.

And we separated with the firm resolve not to arrange any rendezvous before she had told her husband everything.

18

I spent my afternoon in anxiety, shut up at home, waiting for dispatches from the battle-field. To distract myself I emptied a sack full of papers and old books onto the floor and I stretched myself flat on the heap in order to rummage and classify. But my ideas could not fix themselves on this; I turned over, and on my back, with my hands supporting my neck, my eyes hypnotised by the candles which flamed in my old chandelier, I lost myself in reveries. I languished after her kisses and I drew up plans for the forthcoming seduction. Susceptible, bizarre, she must be adroitly tackled, left to come of her own accord, for if one tackled badly it would put a damper on the outcome.

I lit a cigar, imagining myself to be stretched out on a lawn, curious to contemplate my little room upside down. Everything in it like this presented itself in such a new way to me. The sofa, a witness of so many amorous victories, brought me back to my voluptuous suggestions, immediately paralysed by the fear lest everything collapse because of imbecilic considerations of honour.

Analysing the thought that put a bridle on my impetuosity, I discovered in it much cowardice, the dread of the outcome of the act, a little sympathy for a man who risked bringing up a strange child, a dash of repugnance for the unclean promiscuity, a trace of veritable esteem for the woman whom I didn't want to have vilified, some slight compassion for her daughter, a drop of mercy for the mother of the Adored One, in case a scandal should arise, and at the very bottom of my wretched heart a vague foreboding of the difficulties to come the day when I would wish to rid myself of a mistress so taken.

"No!" I said to myself. "It's all or nothing! Alone and for life!"

I was at that point of my musing, when I heard a discreet tapping at the door and I at once saw, framed in the doorway, a pretty head which enlivened my attic, and whose mischievous smille dragged me from my books and called me to the charming arms of the adored woman. After a hailstorm of kisses which fell resoundingly on her lips fresh with cold:

"Well then? . . . What has he decided?"

"Nothing! I have said nothing to him yet."

"Then you're lost. Leave me, poor woman!"

Holding her back, I took off her military dolman, the foretaste of the inevitable undressing. I took off her pearled hat and I led her to the sofa. Then she burst out:

"My courage failed me . . . I wanted to see you once more before the *débâcle,* for God knows if it will end in separation . . ."

I closed her mouth: and drawing up a pedestal table in front of her, I brought out a bottle of fine wine and two glasses from my cupboard. Beside them, I erected a basket of roses, two flaming candles, everything in the guise of an altar and for a footstool I gave her an old and voluminous edition of the poetry of Hans Sachs, priceless, whose leather binding, with gilded clasps, framed a portrait of Luther, an edition which I had borrowed from the royal collection.

I poured out some wine. I picked a rose which I planted among the blonde thicket of her hair. And after having moistened my lips in my glass raised to her health, to the delights of our love, slipping to my knees I adored her . . .

"How pretty you are! . . ."

It was the first time that she saw me as a veritable lover. She was overjoyed. She took my head and kissed me, passing her fingers through the long curls of my unruly hair.

Her beauty filled me with respect. She was like an imposing church image for me. And it was an enchantment for her to see me without the odious mask; it was an ecstasy before my outpourings and she loved me madly seeing me capable of a love warm, respectful and impetuous at the same time.

I kissed her feet until I dirtied my lips. I kissed her knees without touching the hem of her dress; I loved her as she was, fully dressed, chaste like an angel, as if she had come into the world fully clothed with wings above her tunic.

Suddenly tears came to my eyes without conscious reason.

"You're crying," she said to me, "what's the matter?"

"I can't tell you. I am too happy, that's all."

"Then, you can cry! . . . You, the man of bronze!"

"Alas! I know what tears are! . . ."

As a consummate woman, she thought she could penetrate the arcana of my secret pain! And she soon rose, affecting a curiosity for those papers spread on the ground; then, with a roguish expression :

"But you were spread out there, just as on the grass, when I entered. It's fun to go haymaking in the middle of winter, isn't it! "

And there she was, slumped on the pile of papers, with me beside her. Again a rain of kisses spattered down. The idol was bending, she was about to fall.

Little by little, I forced her down, imprisoning her beneath my lips so as not to leave her the time to free herself from the fascinating fire of my eyes or from the burning of my mouth. I hugged her and we stretched out—on the grass!—like lovers, and we possessed each other angelically, fully clothed, without the supreme coupling. We got up, relaxed, satisfied, without remorse, like unfallen angels. Ah! Inventive love! We thus sinned without sin. We surrendered without giving ourselves! Oh! The delicious charity of expert women!

99

Mercy for young pupils, which consists in giving with joy, not receiving! ...

Suddenly she took hold of herself, recalled to reality, and prepared to leave.

"Till tomorrow, then!"

"Till tomorrow!"

She has confessed everything to him. Now she declares herself guilty, for he has cried. He has cried with hot tears! Is he naïve, is he crafty? Both, no doubt! Love procures illusion, and the judgement which one bears on oneself is sometimes deceiving.

He is not angry with us, however, and is not opposed to the continuation of our intimate relationship, on the condition that we will be *chaste*!!

"He is nobler and more generous than we," she writes to me, "he still loves us both!"

What a weakling! He allows the presence beneath his roof of a man who has covered his wife with kisses and he judges us so sexless as to suppose that we are going to continue our relations as "brother and sister"!

It was an affront to my virility and I replied to it by a decisive, eternal farewell!

I remained in my room that morning, a prey to the pangs of the cruellest deception. I had bitten into the apple and it was wrenched from me. She, the superb one, had repented: she had remorse, she suffered from it; she overwhelmed me with reproaches, she, the seductress! A diabolical idea crossed my mind. Had she found me, by chance, too standoffish? Would she give up, distressed by my timidity? And, since she was unconcerned at the crime before which I recoiled, was her love, then, stronger than mine? Come back once again, beauty, and you'll see!

At ten in the morning, a note from the Baron summoned me to the Baroness who was, it appeared, gravely ill!

I replied that I wanted to be left in peace: "I have had enough," I said, "of being the troublemaker of your household; forget me as I am forgetting you".

A second missive about midday.

"Let us resume our former cordial relations. You still have my esteem, for, in spite of the error, I am intimately persuaded that you have behaved as a man of honour. We shall never say a word of what has happened. Return to my arms as a brother and let there be no more question of anything!"

The touching simplicity, the absolute confidence of that man moved me, and I forwarded him a letter full of scruples, with a request not to toy with love, to leave me my freedom.

At three o'clock in the afternoon, a final summons. The Baroness was agonising; the doctor had just left her; she was asking to see me. The Baron begged me to come and I went there. Poor me!

I entered. The apartment was stinking with the smell of chloroform. The Baron welcomed me with an accolade, weeping.

"What is the matter with her?" I asked him with the sangfroid of a doctor.

"I don't know. But she has seen death very near."

"And the doctor ... What has he said?"

"Nothing. He went off shaking his head and saying: "It is a case which is not within my competence."

"He has prescribed nothing?"

"Nothing!"

He led me into the dining-room, transformed into a sick room. There, on a chaise longue, I perceived her lying, stiff, destroyed, her hair untied, her eyes burning like coals. She held out her hand to me which her husband placed in mine. Then, he retired to the drawing-room, leaving us both. I remained, with an icy heart, not believing my eyes, circumspect before such an unaccustomed spectacle.

"Do you know that I almost died?" she said to me.

"Yes."

"And that does not make you suffer?"

"Yes."

"And you do not move, you haven't a look of compassion, not a cry of pain."

"Your husband is there!"

"Well then! Hasn't he brought us together himself! . . ."

"What illness are you suffering from, then, Baroness?"

"I am very ill. I must see a specialist in women's ailments."

"Ah!"

"It frightens me. It's so terrible! If you knew the horrible hours I have spent . . . Your hand on my brow . . . Ah! It's doing me good . . . Don't you want to smile at me now . . . Your smile gives life back to me! . . ."

"The Baron . . ."

"And you wanted to go off . . . leave me!"

"How can I be of service to you, Baroness?"

She melted into tears.

"You do not wish, however," I said to her briskly, "that I be your lover, in this place here, next door to your child and your husband!"

"Ah! You are a monster, heartless, a . . ."

"Farewell, madame!"

I went away. The Baron took me through the drawing-room, but not quick enough, however, for me not to catch sight of the end of a woman's skirt vanishing through the door of a room, and that glimpse of underskirt aroused in me the suspicion of a comedy.

The Baron closed the door behind me with a noise which resounded on the landings and which made me think of an expulsion.

There was no mistaking it, I had just attended a lacrimose comedy with a double dénouement. What was that mysterious malady? Hysteria? No. The German translation: "*Mutterwut*, the passion for motherhood!" Free translation: a violent desire to be pregnant, the rut of the female which has been diminished for years, disguised under modesty, but bursting forth, all the same, one day or another, through adultery.

A woman living in semi-celibacy, always guarding against fecundation, haunted by the fear of having children, incessantly unsatisfied by incomplete embraces, she was pushed towards the lover, led into the obligatory adultery by her unquenched appetites. And now, at the moment when the lover was going to belong to her, was conquered, he was escaping, leaving, in his turn, he too, the mistress unfulfilled!

Oh! miseries of marriage, pitiful love!

At the end of my analysis, I thus reached my conclusion: the frauds, the tricks of that union had driven them both towards the Other, that Other who promised them absolute Enjoyment. And her disappointment as a woman after my escapade had brought her back towards her husband who had returned all the more willingly to the practice of his duties because they seemed sweeter to fulfil, now that his wife was prepared by the Lover.

All was ended then, since they were reconciled.

Exit the Devil.

Curtain.

Well no, it wasn't.

She came to my room to lance me again and I withdrew a complete, brutal and frank confession from her.

During the first year of marriage she had understood nothing of the joys of love, of the intoxications of conjugal happiness. After her confinement, her husband had grown cold, and fearing a new pregnancy had had recourse to frauds.

"Then that man with the build of a giant has never made you happy?"

"Almost never . . . or sometimes . . . so rarely."

"And now? . . ."

She reddened.

"Now, the doctor has advised him to give himself completely."

She slumped onto the sofa, hiding her face with her hands.

Excited by the confession of those intimacies, I attacked her softly. She did not refuse herself, panting, palpitating, but at the psychological moment she was overcome by her remorse again and pushed me away.

Enigma without word, which was beginning to irritate me.

What did she want of me? Everything! But she was afraid of the real crime, of the illegitimate child!

I hugged her, kissing her enough to make her mad. She rose, still intact, but less disappointed, it seemed, than the last time.

And now, what was to be done?

Confess everything to the husband?—That had been done!

Give him details?—What was the use? . . . Since there were no details!

She continued to visit me.

And she always sat down on my sofa, pretending a sickly lassitude.

Then, ashamed at playing the timid one, mad at being humiliated, perhaps suspected of being impotent, I raped her, one day—if it was raping her!—and I rose up afterwards, superb, happy, swollen with pride, pleased with myself, as after a debt paid to a woman.

But she lifted herself up, with a pitiful, sheepish expression, moaning:

"Tell me, what has become of the proud Baroness now?"

And the fear of the outcome gripped her. Her saddened face betrayed a bitter disillusion, as always happens at the beginnings of chance love undertaken without the necessary calm.

"What! Was it only that? . . ."

She left, with slow steps; and, from the height of my window, I followed her, to the turning of the street, sighing too:

"What! It was only that?"

The son of the people had conquered the white skin, the commoner had acquired the love of a girl of breeding, the swineherd had mixed his blood with that of a princess. But at what a price! . . .

. . . A tempest was rising. The tittle-tattle was beginning to spread. The reputation of the Baroness was compromised.

Her mother prayed me to pay her a visit. I went.

"Is it true, sir," she said to me, "that you love my daughter?"

"It's the truth itself, madame."

"And you're not ashamed? . . ."

"It's an honour for me, madame."

"She has told me that she is in love with you."

"I know, madame. I pity you sincerely, I regret what might follow but what do you want to do about it? We love each other. It is no doubt deplorable, but neither of us is guilty. As soon as the danger appeared to us we warned the Baron. Wasn't that right and aren't we in order?"

"There is, indeed, nothing to be held against your conduct, but I must safeguard the honour of my daughter, of her child, of the family! You do not want our ruination, do you?

The poor old woman burst into sobs. She had staked her life on that single card, the elevation of her daughter to the nobility in order to raise the name of her family. It was pitiful and I succumbed before her pain.

"Command, madame," I said to her, "and I'll obey you."

"Flee far from here, go away, leave!"

"That's enough, madame, I promise you, but on one condition, however."

"Tell me, sir."

"It is that you ask Miss Matilda to return to her family."

"Then, it's an accusation?"

"Better still, a denunciation, for I think I know that the prolonged stay of that person at the Baron's does not add to the happiness of the home."

"Agreed, I accept. Ah! The wicked girl, I take it upon myself to tell her what I think of her. And you, you will leave tomorrow?"

"This very evening, madame."

It was then that the Baroness entered and, without warning, came to join in our conversation.

"You will remain, I want it!" she ordered me. "It's for Matilda to go away."

"Because? . . ." asked the mother in amazement.

"Because I have decided to divorce. Gustav treated me like a lost woman at Matilda's step-father's. I will prove to them that they are mistaken!"

Oh! The heartrending scene! What surgical operation is more painful than a rupture of the links between members of the same family! It is the childbirth of all the passions, of all the filth hidden at the very bottom of the soul.

The Baroness then took me aside and communicated to me the contents of a letter, written to Matilda by the Baron, in which he covered both of us with insults, in which he confessed to the girl his celestial love, in terms which showed that he had deceived us from the first moment . . .

. . . The stone now had the consistency of a rock. It was still rolling, crushing innocent and guilty.

23

It was a coming and going without hope of result.

New misfortunes arose. The bank did not give any dividend that year and ruination proclaimed itself. Penury was imminent and we profited from the incident in order to hatch a plan of divorce, based on the fact that the Baron could no longer support his family. So as to save appearances, the Baron enquired of his colonel if he could remain in the regiment in the event of his wife's entering the theatre. But the latter let it be understood that that was impossible. Which provided a good opportunity for railing against aristocratic prejudices. During this time the Baroness, who was having treatment for a uterine abscess, continued to live in the conjugal domicile, but carnally separated. Always suffering, agitated, dull, she rebelled against encouragement and I exhausted myself in injecting into her the overflow of my juvenile belief in better days. I painted the future of an artist for her, a free life in her own little room, like mine, where she would possess the liberty of her body and her thoughts. She listened to me, but without answering and it seemed to me that the flux of my words galvanised her like a magnetic current, but did not penetrate her intellect.

The plan of divorce was thus conceived. The legal arrangements terminated, she would retire to Copenhagen, where one of her uncles was living. There, the constatation of her pretended evasion from the conjugal domicile would be communicated to her through the intermediary of the Swedish consul, before whom she would express her intention of breaking her marriage. Then, free to decide on her future, she would return to Stockholm. The dowry would remain in the possession of her husband as well as the furniture, apart from some pieces of furniture that she reserved for herself, and the Baron would keep the child, until he decided to remarry, the Baroness retaining the right to see her child every day.

A serious incident was produced concerning the discussions under-taken on the financial question. With the intention of saving the débris from a squandered fortune, the father of the Baroness had, in dying, bequeathed his estate in the name of his daughter. By dint of intrigues the mother of the Baroness had secured the right to the estate by paying a percentage to her son-in-law. Now that the affair appeared trumped up by illegal procedures, the Baron insisted that the will take its full effect. The old mother-in-law, seeing herself reduced to living on a rather modest annuity, flew into a fury and, in a fit of rage, she denounced the amorous activities of her son-in-law to her brother, pretty Matilda's father. The storm broke out. The lieutenant-colonel threatened to have the Baron dismissed; a lawsuit was pending.

Then all the efforts of the Baroness were aimed at obtaining the safety of the father of her child. And to clear him of those accusations, the disagreeable rôle of scapegoat was foisted onto me.

In the end I was obliged to write a letter to the uncle, in which I took the blame for everyone and the responsibility for the disasters upon myself, swearing before God to the innocence of the Baron and the cousin, begging that outraged father for forgiveness for all the crimes which I alone had committed, I, the only repentant.

It was a fine and brave action; and the Baroness loved me after that as a woman can love a man who lays his honour, his self-esteem and his reputation beneath the bootees of the adored.

I was then, despite my intention of keeping myself clear of all those family goings-on which defiled me, condemned to odious proceedings.

The mother-in-law paid me visit upon visit, reminded me of my love for her daughter, incited me against the Baron—but in vain, since I no longer took orders except from the Baroness.—And besides I was on the side of the father. Since he had taken charge of the child, to him alone belonged the estate, imaginary or not . . .

Ah! that month of April! What a spring of love! A sick mistress, insupportable sessions in which two families washed their dirty linen which I had certainly not asked to see; tears, basenesses, a riot in which all the villainy hidden beneath the varnish of education was exhibited in the sun. That's what you get from sticking your nose into a wasps' nest! . . .

Love suffered by it, naturally. To meet a mistress always worn out with quarrels, her cheeks red from recent squabbling, with nothing but advocate's terms in her mouth, that's not a recognised aphrodisiac.

I gave her, and gave her again my consoling ideas, my hopes, sometimes spurious, since I was at the end of my nervous strength; and she received all that, sucked my brain, dried my heart. Conversely, she made me her rubbish-bin. She flung all her sweepings into it, all her worries, her setbacks, her problems.

Amidst that hell, I lived my life, I dragged my misery about, I sought to lead a painful existence. When she came to me, in the evening, she sulked at me if I got down to work, and then I had to waste two hours in kisses and in tears to convince her of my love.

Love for her was translated as a perpetual adoration, as a servile attention, as sacrifices offered.

An overwhelming responsibility weighed me down. I foresaw the moment when hardship, or the arrival of a child would throw a wife into my arms. She had only put aside three thousand francs for herself, for a single year, destined to pay for her preparatory studies for entering the theatre. And I feared for her stage career. Her diction was still terribly marked by a Finnish accent. There were unfortunate disproportions in her face for the stage. To take her out of herself I made her recite poetry. I appointed myself her teacher. But she was too taken up with her worries and the small amount of progress she realised she had made after the test plunged her into a complete affliction.

Oh! the lugubrious love! Her incessant fear of having children, joined to my inexperience of the mystery of frauds, combined to make a long suffering out of that love which should have been the source from which I could draw youth, the indispensable vigour for such depressing circumstances. The joy, scarcely born, vanished through a repercussion of her fear onto me, and we would separate dissatisfied, frustrated in our expectation of the supreme gaiety which we totally lacked. Poor mockery of love!

There were moments when I missed the whores, but my monogamous nature abhorred changes; our embraces, incomplete as they basically were, possibly procured for us even more serious psychic enjoyments, and those unquenchable desires were a guarantee of the longevity of our love.

24

1st May. All the necessary documents were signed. Her departure was fixed for the following day. She came to see me and, hanging round my neck:

"I am entirely yours now," she said to me, "take me!"

As we had never spoken of marriage, I did not exactly know what she meant by that. The position however appeared more correct to me now that she was going to leave her former domicile. And we remained seated, pensive and sad in my little room. All was allowed us now—the temptation was less. She accused me of coldness and I ostensibly proved the contrary to her. But then she complained of my sensuality. It was adoration, burnt incense, it was prayers that she needed.

A violent crisis declared itself and, in a new fit of hysteria, she claimed that I no longer loved her.—Already! . . .

An hour was spent in reticence, in adulations. Her reason returned to her, but she was completely restored only after having made me despair to tears. Then she resumed loving me. The more she saw me reduced, on my knees, small, weak, the more she adored me. She did not want to feel me virile and strong, and to attain her love I had to make myself wretched and unfortunate, in order that she might show herself superior to me, play little mother and console me.

We had supper in my lodgings; she spread the cloth and prepared the meal. When night came, I claimed my rights as a lover. The sofa was transformed into a bed and I undressed her.

It was the renewal of love, for it was a virgin, a girl who vibrated in my arms! How subtle and imperceptible are the brutalities with the beloved! The animal really has no part in this mixture of souls. Can one ever say where the one ends or the other begins?

Reassured about her health by a recent consultation, she gave herself entirely, she radiated with supreme happiness; she was blissful, grateful; her beauty shone and her eyes expressed beatitude. My poor attic became a temple, a splendid palace and I re-lit the broken chandelier, the work lamp, the candles in order to illumine the felicity, the Joy of Living, the only joy which makes this base life worth living.

For it is those intoxicating minutes of appeased love which follow us along the painful road; it is the memories of those brief joys, denigrated by the jealous alone, which make us live and survive ourselves. They are pure love! And:

"Do not say anything wrong about love!" I said to her. "Venerate nature in its functions; respect the god who obliges us to be happy, in spite of ourselves."

She said nothing, for she was happy. The madness was appeased:

111

her face relived and reddened beneath the surge of the blood injected by the palpitating heart during the vigorous embraces: the flames of the candles were mirrored in her pupils, moistened by the tears of voluptuousness, and the irisate colour of her veins was emphasised more brightly, as are the feathers of birds at the fine time of love. She had the aspect of a girl of sixteen, so delicate and pure were her lines; and the pretty head, buried in the pillow, all covered with her unruly hair, like sheaves of ripe wheat, gave me the sensation of a child's head. Her little body, more frail than skinny, was there, half veiled by the cambric chemise (a reminder of the chiton of the Greeks), gathered at her waist in countless pleats, hiding the thighs and disclosing the knees where so many beautiful muscles, tendons, ligaments met together, to the extent of recalling the bottom of a shell of mother-of-pearl by their entanglement of lines; and the lace trimming surmounted the breasts, like a trellis through which two twin goats stick their rosy snouts and the shoulders stood out like chiselled ivory handles to which palms are applied . . .

She posed as an idol and watched me adoring her, stretching out her arms, rubbing her eyes and sending me, furtively, half modest, half brazen glances.

How the adored woman was chaste in her nudity, yielding to the caresses of the lover! And, superior to woman in intelligence, man is only happy when he unites himself to the woman who equals him. My bygone loves, my couplings with girls of an inferior class, appeared crimes of bestiality to me, relapses, lowerings of the race. Are white skin, undeformed feet where the rosy nails are intact, regular like piano keys, hands without callouses a sign of degeneration? Compare with the wild beast, with its glossy fur, with its fine paws, which shows few muscles and many nerves! The beauty of woman is the ensemble of qualities worthy of being perpetuated, in unison with the man who is best able to appreciate those qualities. The husband had cast this woman aside and, from then on, she no longer belonged to him, having ceased to please him. Her beauty no longer existing for him, it was for me to evoke that flower visible only to the clearsighted Elected One!

What a satisfaction without scruples does one feel in possessing one's adored! She comes to you as after the accomplished duty; and to say that that is a crime! The suave crime, the sweet infraction, the divine wickedness!

Midnight was going to strike! At the neighbouring barracks the "Who goes there?" of the relieving guard was resounding. The mistress had to be conducted to her home again!

All along the long road, I hugged her with the fire of my inspirations, of my new hopes; I bewildered her with my projects grown in the heat of our embraces: she pressed herself against me, as if she wanted to draw strength from my contact and I restituted to her what I had received from her. And now that we had arrived in front of the high railings she noticed that she had forgotten the key. What bad luck! Mad to prove my courage to her, by penetrating into the lair of the bear, I shinned up the railings, and, crossing the yard in three bounds, I knocked at the door of the house, ready for a stormy meeting with the Baron. My timorous mind was exalted at the idea of a clash with my rival in front of the adored one and the chosen lover was converted into a hero! Fortunately, it was a servant who came down to open, and our respectful farewells were exchanged in a perfect tranquility, beneath the disdainful looks of the maid, who did not even return our good-evening.

25

She was now sure of my love and abused it!

She came to see me that day. She was forever praising her ex-husband. Overwhelmed with worry after the relegation of the cousin, he had given in to the behests of the Baroness and promised to safeguard her honour by accompanying her to the station where we would be present, he and I, at the departure, which would thus lose its character of a flight. Moreover, the Baron, who was no longer angry with me, had committed himself to receiving me that evening at his home and in order to reply to the rumours, he consented to show himself in public places in my company during the following days.

While appreciating the generosities of that big simpleton with a loyal heart, I was revolted for his own sake:

"How could one inflict such an opprobrium upon him! Ah! It can never be," I said to the Baroness.

"Remember that the honour of my child is at stake," she replied to me.

"But, darling, his honour is also something!"

Pooh, she didn't care for the honour of others! I was decidedly a queer chap.

"But it's too much! You underestimate me, you'll end up by degrading us all! It's all absurd! It's disgusting!" I exclaimed.

And she wept! But the tears made her irresistible to me, so that after an hour spent in sobs, in incriminating me, I promised her all she wanted. And I railed against the despot, I cursed those crystal drops which increased tenfold, as they fell, the might of two fascinating pupils!

Certainly, alas, she was stronger than both of us. She was leading us by the nose into ignominy! What did she want with that reconciliation? Was she afraid of a war to the death breaking out between the Baron and myself and terrible revelations ensuing?

. . . To what torture had she vowed me by compelling me to see that devastated household again? She had no pity for the pangs of others, the cruel egoist! And to think that she made me swear to deny the whole story of the illicit liaison between the Baron and the cousin, so that one might affirm the non-existence of their blame! I went to that supreme encounter, with a sad heart, with shaking legs. The little garden opened with its cherry trees in flower, its narcissi in bloom. The shrubbery grew green where her fairylike apparition had seduced me; the raked black flower beds were displayed between the lawns like shrouds, and I called forth the abandoned child, walking there alone, beside a carefree servant, occupied in her

114

handiwork: and the daughter would grow, would awaken, until the day she would learn that her mother had left her!

I went up the stairs of that house hounded by fate, perched on the edge of the sand quarry where my memories of youth were resuscitated. Friendship, kinship, love, all was compromised, and adultery, despite our care to regularise it, had put its smear on the threshold of that home.

Whose was the fault for all that?

The Baroness came and opened the door to me and stole a kiss in the doorway, before going into the drawing-room. At that instant, for a second, for two seconds, I hated her and pushed her away with indignation, for this reminded me of the dirty tricks of servants at back doors and sickened my heart! Behind the doors! Dirty beast of a woman, without pride, without dignity.

She acted as if I was afraid of entering the drawing-room, she insisted with a loud voice that I go forward at the very moment when I was embarrassed by that humiliating situation, when I was planning to retrace my steps. A flash from her eyes broke my resolution: paralysed by the firmness of her attitude, I gave in.

In the drawing-room everything pointed to the dissolution of the home. Linen was scattered on the furniture, dresses, underskirts, clothing. On the piano, there, I noticed the chemisettes with cleavages I knew so well. On the bureau rose a whole pile of women's knickers and stockings, once my dream, now my disgust. She came and went, arranging, folding, counting, without modesty, without shame.

"Was it I who had corrupted her in so short a time?" I said to myself, contemplating that exhibition of a decent woman's under-clothing.

She examined some garments and put on one side what could still go to the mending. She took a pair of knickers whose tapes were ripped off and laid them aside. All that with perfect calm.

It seemed I was attending a capital execution and I underwent its atrocious sensations while she listened with half an ear to my insignificant chatter which dealt with futilities. I waited for the Baron who had shut himself in the dining-room to write.

The door opened at last and I started, for my emotion changed on seeing the child enter, who came to ask the reason for all this bustle.

She came to me, followed by the King Charles of her mother, holding out her forehead as usual. I reddened, I grew angry and in a broken voice, turning to the Baroness:

"You could have at least spared me this torture!"

But she didn't understand me.

"Mamma is going on a journey, my pretty one, but she will soon return and bring you back beautiful toys: you'll see!"

The King Charles came and begged a caress from me, he too!

And shortly afterwards the Baron appeared.

He came forward, broken, humped, greeted me amicably, shook my hand, unable to speak; I kept a respectful silence before his irreparable grief, and he retired.

Dusk fell. The maid lit the lamps, without greeting me. Supper was announced. I wanted to leave. But the Baron joined his prayers to those of the Baroness and in so sincerely touching a manner that I accepted to stay.

We sat down at table then, all three as before. It was a solemn, unforgettable moment. We spoke a little of everything. And the question was asked: "Whose was the fault?" while our eyes moistened.—Nobody's, destiny's, that of a series of small incidents, of divers motives; and we clutched hands, clinked glasses, declared ourselves friends, just as before. The Baroness alone kept her humour. She organised the arrangements for the next day, the rendezvous at the station, the walks in town, and we conceded everything she wanted.

At last I got up. The Baron accompanied us to the drawing-room and there, placing the hand of the Baroness in mine, he said to me, in a choking voice:

"Be her friend. My rôle is finished. Keep her, protect her against mundane malevolence. Cultivate her talent, you who are better gifted than I, a poor soldier, and may God be a help to you on your way!"

Then he retired, leaving us alone together and the door closed on him again.

Was he sincere at that moment? I believed it and I would still like to believe it today. A sensitive heart if ever there was one, he was fond of us and no doubt he did not wish to see the mother of his child in the hands of an enemy.

It is possible that later, under pernicious influences, he boasted of having tricked us. It would be, in any case, out of keeping with his character at that time and we know that after the adventure there is no-one who admits having been the dupe.

26

Six o'clock in the evening. I did sentry-go in the large hall of the central station. The train for Copenhagen was to leave at a quarter past six and I could not see the Baron or the Baroness coming.

I was like a spectator at the last act of a terrible drama. I was waiting for its dénouement with a ferocious joy. A further quarter of an hour and peace would settle on us again. My nerves, unhinged by all the successive crises, aspired to calm and that night was going to restore to me all the nervous fluid that I had dispensed, or wasted for the benefit of a woman-mistress.

At last, there she was. She came in a cab drawn by a mare which the coachman drove at full speed.

Always negligent and always late.

She dashed to meet me, flinging herself about like a madwoman.

"The traitor, he didn't keep his word! He is not coming!" she exclaimed noisily enough to attract the attention of the passers-by who became agitated.

It was deplorable; but basically I respected the man and, seized with a rage for contradiction:

"He's done right, by gad," I said. "He has reason on his side!"

"Quickly, go and get a ticket for Copenhagen or I'm staying," she answered me.

"Ah! No! . . . Let's see . . . If I accompany you, I might as well abduct you. All Stockholm will know tomorrow."

"I don't care . . . Hurry up!"

"No, I don't want to."

At that moment I was truly sorry for her and the situation was unbearable. A quarrel, a quarrel between lovers was inevitable.

She sensed it and took my hands, troubled me with her looks and the ice melted. The sorceress had floored me, she had suspended my will, I was wavering! . . .

"Then just for Catherinholm."

"If you like."

Meanwhile she was having the luggage registered.

All was lost, even honour, and I still had the prospect of a night of torture.

The train pulled out. We were alone in our first-class compartment. The absence of the Baron weighed on us. It was an unforeseen and ill-omened danger. A terrifying silence reigned in the carriage and we each waited for the other to break it. She was the first to decide:

"Axel, you no longer love me."

"Upon my word, perhaps," I said to her, dazed by the turmoil supported for a month.

117

"And I who have sacrificed everything to you."

"Sacrificed everything? . . . to your love, not to me! Besides, have I not sacrificed my life to you! You are only furious with Gustav, and you want to vent your anger on my head . . . Be reasonable, at least!"

She cried, cried! What a honeymoon! My nerves hardened, I donned my coat of mail. I made myself insensitive, impenetratable, hard.

"Be careful with your feelings! From today onwards you must use reason! Cry, cry, until you dry up the fount of your tears! And pull yourself together! You are only a simpleton and I have adored you like a queen, like a sovereign, and I have obeyed you because I thought myself the weaker one! Alas! Never cause me to scorn you! Never put the blame for what happened on me alone! Yesterday evening, I admired the great intelligence of Gustav. He understood that the great events of life have never a single motive as cause. Whose is the fault? Yours, mine, his, hers, imminent ruination, your passion for the theatre, your uterine ulcer, the inheritance of your grandfather, thrice divorced, the hatred of your mother for childbirth, which has given you an undecided nature, the idleness of your husband whose profession left him too much leisure, my instincts of a man born of the lower classes, the chance configuration of a Finnish girl, who pushed me towards you, an infinity of secret causes of which we have only discovered but little. Do not degrade yourself in front of the populace who will judge you tomorrow on a word. Do not be one of those simple minds who think they have solved such a complicated question by not attaching importance either to the adulteress or to the seducer! . . . And, moreover, have I seduced you? Be sincere towards yourself, towards me, while we are alone together, without witnesses."

But she did not want to be sincere.

She couldn't.

For it is not in the nature of a woman. She felt an accomplice, she was harassed by remorse. She had only one thought: to free her conscience by putting the whole responsibility for the debt contracted upon myself.

I let her be, enveloping myself in an exasperating silence. The night fell: I lowered the window and posted myself at the door watching the file past of the black firs behind which rose the pale disc of the moon. Then, it was a lake ringed with birch trees, a stream bordered with alders; corn fields, meadows, and still more firs for a long while. A mad desire seized me to fling myself through the door, to leave that gaol where an enemy held me, where I was garotted by a sorceress. But worry for her future haunted me like a nightmare, and I recognised that I was responsible for the existence of that woman who was a stranger to me, for the existence of her future children, for the upkeep of her mother, of her aunt, for all her race, in short, into the infinity of the centuries.

So I would set about making her succeed in the theatre; I would suffer from all her sufferings, from her deceptions, from her reverses, so that one day she might throw me on the scrap heap like a squeezed-out lemon, me, my whole life, my brain, my spinal cord and my blood, all that to pay me back for the love that I gave her, which she received and which in her thoughts she believed she was offering to me as a sacrifice. Amorous hallucination! Genetic hypnotism!

Until ten o'clock she sulked at me without relenting. A further hour and the moment for farewells would have come!

But she asked my forgiveness and placed her two feet on the cushion of my seat, pretending a sudden lassitude. Before her languishing looks, in the face of her tears, despite her spider-like logic, I had kept my composure, my virile strength. Everything was going to collapse. I had noticed her adorable bootees and a glimpse of her stocking.

On your knees, Samson! Place your head of hair on her knees, press your cheeks against her hips, implore her forgiveness for the hard words—which she did not understand—with which you have flagellated her, renounce your reason, abjure your faith, love her! Slave that you are! Coward, you are yielding for a glimpsed stocking, you who claim to have faculties for toppling the world! And she, she only loves you thus vilified; she buys you for a minute of spasms, with which she supplies you for a mere song, for she can lose nothing in emptying you of an ounce of the best of your blood!

The engine whistled, it was the station of the farewells. She kissed me like a little mamma, she made the sign of the cross on my forehead—although she is a Protestant—commended me to God, begged me to take care of myself and not to worry myself.

And the train thrust into the night choking me with its bituminous smoke.

I breathed—at last!—the fresh air of the evening and I enjoyed freedom. Alas! only for an instant. I was scarcely in the village inn when I broke down, crushed by regret. I loved her, yes I loved her, I loved her, just as she revealed herself at the moment of the farewells, for that moment awoke in me the sweet memories of the first days of our liaison, when she was the pleasurable, cherishing mother-woman, when she cajoled me and petted me like a little child!

And yet I loved her, I desired her, I wanted her as an ardent woman, ardently.

Was this an anomaly of instinct? Was I then the product of a caprice of nature? Were my feelings those of a pervert since I

119

enjoyed this possession of my mother? Was it the unconscious incest of the heart? . . .

. . . I asked for writing materials and I wrote her a letter in which I prayed the Lord for her prosperity.

Her last embrace had brought me back to God and under the impression of her last kiss whose savour I kept on my moustache, I disavowed the new faith which presaged the progress of humanity.

The first stage of the decadence of a man was accomplished: the others were going to follow consecutively as far as brutishness, as far as the confines of lunacy.

SECOND PART

1

The day after our departure, the whole capital was informed of the abduction of Baroness X by a librarian of the Royal Library.

That had been foreseen; that, however, was to be feared! And I who had wanted to save her reputation! But all had been forgotten in a fit of weakness!

She had ruined everything; it was for me to bear the consequences of this and now grapple with the outcome, disastrous for her theatrical career, all the more disastrous as she could only claim her début on a single stage, and loose morals did not constitute a recommendation to obtain an engagement at the Theatre Royal.

From the morning after my return, in order to prove my alibi, I went, under some futile pretext or other, to present my respects to my librarian-in-chief, kept at home through an indisposition of no gravity. Then I ran through the main streets and began my duties at the usual time. In the evening I went to the journalists' club where I spread the news of the Baroness's divorce for artistic reasons alone, proclaiming the incident without importance and confirming the excellent understanding between the couple, separated only through the fault of social prejudices.

If I had known what wrong I was doing myself when I spread those rumours in favour of the innocence of the Baroness . . . But no, I would still have done the same.

The newspapers fought for the scoop of this society gossip, but the public did not want to believe in that irresistible love of Art, which is not very frequent, especially with actresses. Women, particularly, were distrustful, and the abandoned child always remained the black spot.

In the meantime a letter reached me from Copenhagen. It was only a long cry of distress! Gnawed by remorse, by regret for her forsaken child, she ordered me to come and join her immediately, for her relatives were torturing her. They had, in concert, she thought, with the Baron, diverted the document indispensable for the accomplishment of her separation.

I sharply refused to leave, and, furious, I wrote in turn some indignant lines to the Baron. He answered me in a haughty tone, which brought a definitive rupture between us.

A telegram, two telegrams, and calm returned again. The document in question was found and the proceedings followed their course.

I spent my evenings in drawing up a detailed plan of conduct for her, to take her mind off her worries, advising her to work, to study her art, to follow the movements in the theatre and, to provide her with a supplementary occupation, I suggested that she write articles on what she had noticed, articles which I took it upon myself to have inserted in one of our principal newspapers.

No reply. I had every reason to believe that my precious advice had been badly received by that independent mind.

A week went by, a week of uneasiness, of worries, of work. One fine morning, I was surprised in bed by a letter postmarked Copenhagen.

She was calm, in a gay mood; she couldn't refrain from a certain pride in the quarrel fought out between the Baron and myself (as she received both letters, she could judge). She found smartness in the jousting and she admired my courage. "Pity," she said to conclude, "that two lads of that mettle cannot stay good friends!"—then she told me of the distractions she had had. She enjoyed herself, mixed in the circles of minor artists, which hardly pleased me. She spent an evening in an establishment of pleasure in company with young men who paid court to her, and she had already made the conquest of a young musician who had broken with his family in order to devote himself to his artistic tastes, "curious analogy with her own destiny!" Furthermore, a detailed biography of the interesting martyr and a plea for me not to become jealous about it!

"What did that mean!" I asked myself, disgruntled by the tone, both warm and mocking, of her letter, which appeared to me as composed between two pleasures.

Could it be that cold and voluptuous madonna was one of those born tarts . . . a coquette, a cocotte!

I at once administered a solid reprimand to her, in which her portrait was strongly etched. I called her a Madame Bovary, I begged her to wake up from the perilous slumber which she was sleeping at the edge of a precipice.

In reply, by way of a supreme confidence, she sent me the letters that she had received from her young enthusiast. Ah! Those letters of love! One could see in them the same antiquated use of the word "friendship", and the inexplicable sympathy of souls and all the repertory of the hackneyed terms which we had both employed: brother and sister, little mamma, comrades and the rest, warm blankets under which lovers creep in order to end up by playing the beast with two backs.

What could I think? Was she a lunatic? Was she an unconscious rogue, who had retained nothing of those severe lessons received during those two frightful months, in which the hearts of three men had burned for her. And I who had been found good as a scapegoat, as a dummy, as a man of straw, I was breaking my life to pave her the way which would lead her to the disorderly life that actresses led.

What a new suffering! To see what I formerly adored dragged in the mud!

Then an unspeakable pity seized me, and foreseeing the destiny which awaited that perverse woman, I swore to myself that I would establish her, uphold her and preserve her from a fatal downfall as long as I had strength left.

Jealous! Ugly word of a woman, invented to hoodwink a man fooled or about to be. One abuses one's husband, and at the first gesture which manifests his discontent, one throws this word in his face: "Jealous!" A jealous man, a duped man! And to think there are women who take their jealous husbands for impotent ones, so that they close their eyes and find themselves really impotent against accusations of this kind.

A fortnight afterwards, she came back. Pretty, fresh, sprightly, having only joyful memories to relate since she had enjoyed herself! There were however some loud colours in bad taste in her new dress. She so simple, so fine, so distinguished formerly, she was wearing gaudy colours!

The meeting was colder than one would have thought. And after a painful silence, the explosion came at last.

Strengthened by the admiration of her new friend, she behaved proudly, teased me, railed at me. Spreading her magnificent dress over my ramshackle sofa, she reverted to her old ways, and the hatred melted in the warmth of the embrace. Not enough, however, not to leave a residue of anger between us which burst out with gross imputations. Enervated by my immoderate petulance which was out of keeping with her lax nature, she began to weep.

"How can you think," she exclaimed, "that I was playing with that young man? I promise you never to write to him, although that will be held against me as an impoliteness!"

An impoliteness? There was one of her big words! A man was paying court to her, in other words, was making advances to her and she accepted, for fear of committing an "impoliteness! . . ." Scoundrel!

Unfortunately for me she had bought herself some tiny shoes and I was at her feet! Curse it! She was wearing black stockings, her calf had rounded out and her knee protruded white from amongst the shrouds! Those black legs, swirling in the cloud of the petticoats, were legs of a she-devil . . . Tired by her eternal fears of a child, I lied. After painstaking research at the Library, I had discovered some means of cheating nature. And I advised her of preventive measures and I alleged an organic disability which made me if not infertile, at least harmless. I ended up by believing all this myself; she left me the field free then, even though I was to undergo the fatal consequences.

She had installed herself with her mother and aunt, on the second floor in one of the most frequented streets of the town. As she incessantly threatened to go and see me at my place, I was admitted into the house. And there was nothing recreative in being supervised by those two old ladies whom I sensed behind the door as long as I was present . . .

Now, one was beginning to notice, on both sides, what one had lost. She, who was a Baroness, a wife, a mistress in her home, she had lowered herself to the status of a child, watched over by her mother, imprisoned in a room, living on the pension of the invalids. And every day, her mother reminded her that she had brought her up to an honourable position, and the daughter remembered the happy hours when her husband came to deliver her from that maternal prison. And bitter disputes resulted from it, and the tears and the hard words which fell back on me every evening when I paid her a visit . . . prisoners' visit beneath the eye of a guard-witness.

When we tired of those painful tête-à-têtes, we risked some rendezvous in a public garden; it was going from bad to worse, for we were exposed there to the disdainful looks of the crowd. And the spring sun which lit our misery became odious to us. We missed the darkness, we longed for winter to devour our shame, and only summer was near, which was bringing back the long nights without twilight!

Everybody forsook us little by little. Intimidated by the gossip, my sister herself took umbrage. At the last supper she offered us in a little group, the former Baroness, to dissimulate her weakness, began to drink, got drunk, raised a toast, smoked, and eventually attracted the aversion of the married women and the scorn of the men.

"She's a whore, that woman!" said a family man to my brother-in-law, who hurriedly repeated this remark to me.

Finally one Sunday evening we were invited to my sister's. We went there at the appointed time. Imagine our surprise, when the maid informed us that the master and the mistress were not at home, having accepted an invitation elsewhere. It was the height of humiliation. We spent our evening shut in my room, crying with rage and despair, planning to commit suicide. I lowered the blinds to shield us against the brightness of the day and we waited for the night and the darkness to return but the sun set late, and at about eight o'clock hunger overtook us. I had no money. Nor had she, and nothing to drink at my place, nothing to eat. That gave us a foretaste of misery and I spent the worst moments of my life there. Recriminations, kisses without conviction, tears without end, remorse, disgust.

I exhorted her to return to have supper at her mother's, but she had a horror of the light of the sun, and then she didn't dare, incapable as she was of explaining her return before the appointed hour, since she had told them at home of that invitation to supper. She had had nothing since dinner at two o'clock; the sad prospect of going to bed fasting kept the wild beast of hunger awake. Brought up in a rich house, accustomed to luxury, ignorant of poverty, she grew exasperated. For me, hunger was an intimate since childhood, but I suffered horribly to see the adored one in a similar situation. I ferreted in my cupboard without discovering anything there; I examined the drawers of my bureau, and there, among the relegated souvenirs, faded flowers, love letters, discoloured ribbons, I found two sweets, kept in commemoration of some burial or other. I offered her the barley sugars wrapped in black paper and silver paper. What a lugubrious lovers' meal, those sweets with their decoration in mourning!

Crushed, destroyed, ruined by distress, I rose up, furious, and I fulminated against the decent women who had just closed their doors on us, expelled us.

"Why that hateful scorn? Have we committed a crime, an adultery? No. There is only an honest, legal divorce, in conformity with all the prescriptions of the law!"

"We have been too decent, you see," she said to console herself. "The world is only a herd of rogues. Public, brazen adultery is tolerated, divorce, no! Ah! Theirs is a pretty morality!"

We were in agreement. Yet the crime remained. It was hanging over our heads, cowering beneath the bludgeon-stroke!

I felt like a child who has removed a bird's nest. The mother was taken from the nest; the little bird lay on the ground and chirped, deprived of the warmth of the mother's wing!

And the father? He was left alone, in that ravaged nest, one Sunday evening like this, when the family would gather round the hearth, alone in the drawing-room where the piano remained unheard; alone in the dining-room where he took his solitary meals, alone in the bedroom. . .

"No," she answered me, "no. He is lounging on a good sofa at the chamberlain's, the brother-in-law of the cousin, and well-fed, bloated, clutching the fingers of his Matilda, the poor child so calumniated, he regales himself with unlikely stories on the bad conduct of his unworthy wife who did not adapt herself to a harem life! And the two of them, surrounded by the sympathies and the condolences of that hypocritical world, throw the first stone at us!"

And after profound reflection, I suggested that the Baron had led us well and truly by the nose, that he had rid himself of a wife who encumbered him to take another and, finally, that it was illegally that he had secured the dowry.

Then she grew furious:

"Don't say anything bad about him. All that's my fault!"

"Why not say anything bad about him? Is his person sacred?"

One would think so, for on every occasion that I attacked him she always became his advocate.

Was it the freemasonry of the classes which brought her back to the Baron? Or else were there some secrets in their intimate life, some mysteries which made her dread having that man for an enemy? This has remained inexplicable to me as well as her unswerving fidelity to the memory of the Baron, however perfidious he showed himself later on.

The sun set at last and we separated. I slept the sleep of the hungry, dreaming that I had a millstone hanging from my neck while I made desperate efforts to fly off to the sky.

2

Bad luck followed us. We made enquiries of the theatre director in order to obtain an evening début. He replied that he couldn't even enter, as a director, into relations with a wife who had escaped from the conjugal domicile.

Everything had been undertaken, everything had failed. So after her year had expired, her resources being exhausted, that woman would find herself on the streets. For me, a poor bohemian, to take her off them!

In order to verify that maddening news, she proposed to go and pay a visit to her friend, the great tragedienne, whom she would formerly meet frequently in society and who acted as a fawning bitch at the feet of the "Baroness with the blonde hair", calling her "her little elf".

The great tragedienne, an adulteress paled beneath calculated vice during her husband's lifetime, received the honest sinner in an outrageous manner and shut her door on her!

Everything was consummated.

There remained at present only revenge at all costs!

"Well," I said to her, "become a writer! Compose dramas and have them played on that very stage! Why descend when you can rise! Trample the third-rate actress underfoot. With a single leap rise above her head. Unveil in lashing prose that lying, hypocritical, vicious world which opens its salons to whores and closes them to the separated wife! That's a beautiful subject for a drama!"

But she was one of those soft, impressionable natures, without strength to strike back.

"No, no vengeance!"

Cowardly and vindictive at the same time, she left the care of her vengeance to God, which came to the same thing, except for the responsibility, which she shifted on to this kind of a man of straw.

I did not let go, and a fortunate chance came to us. A publisher came to offer me the arrangement of an illustrated book for children.

"Here," I proposed to Madame X, "arrange this text. There is a hundred francs to be earned, paid on the nail."

I brought her reference books, gave her the illusion of having executed the work herself and she earned the hundred francs. But what I had to do! For the publisher demanded that my name be on the cover of the picture book*, my name which had made my début as a playwright. It was literary prostitution. And my adversaries who had anticipated my incapacity as a writer would win the day this time.

---

* *För Våra Barn* · 34 bildar af Ludv. Richter med gamla och nya versar af August Strindberg · Stockholm · Seligmann and Co.

Then I forced her to write a column for a morning paper. She did it in a mediocre way. The article was inserted, but the paper did not pay for it.

I ran through the streets in order to discover a louis which I gave to the author—pious fraud—as if coming from the till of the paper.

Poor Maria! What a joy for her to be able to hand her scanty earnings to her distressed mother, who found herself, as a result of the collapse of her affairs, reduced to the hard necessity of letting furnished rooms. The old ladies began to envisage me as a saviour; from their drawers came copies of translations rejected by all the theatres, and I was now credited with unlikely faculties for being able to force my way into directors. Finally I was burdened with useless errands which disturbed me in my work and only served to plunge me into black misery.

My savings vanished as a result of the time I had wasted, of the daily consumption of my nervous resources, so that I was reduced to only having dinners and I resumed my old habit of putting myself to bed without having supped.

Encouraged by these few successes with money, Maria set about work and began a play in five acts. It seemed that I had poured, injected in her, all the unproductive germs of my poetic inspiration. Sown in that virgin soil, they rose, they grew, whereas I was becoming sterile, like the pollen-sac which spreads its fecundity, itself atrophying. And I felt torn to my entrails, on the point of dying, and the workings of my brain were disjointed, becoming enmeshed with that little feminine brain, regulated in a different way to a man's. I did not exactly know why I overestimated the literary qualities of that woman in urging her towards the art of letters, for I had read nothing by her hand except her correspondence addressed to me, sometimes personal, most often below the ordinary. She was on the way to becoming my living poem. She substituted herself for my vanished talent. Her person had grafted itself, joined itself onto mine, to the extent that she formed no more than a new organ for me. I no longer existed but through her, and I, the mother-root, led an underground life, nourishing the stem which rose to the sun in order to blossom into a splendid flower: and I rejoiced in that magnificence, forgetting that a day would come when the graft would separate from the exhausted stock in order to go and bloom again and shine elsewhere, supremely proud of the splendour which it borrowed.

The first act of her play was finished. I read it. Under the sway of my hallucination, I found it perfect and I expressed my admiration for it to the author in a loud voice, warmly congratulating her. She herself was astonished at her talent and I drew her a dazzling tableau of the prospects which awaited her future as a writer, when a sudden reversal was produced in our projects. Maria's mother reminded us of the existence of a lady friend, an artist-painter, the owner of a lordly estate, very rich, and, which was most important, closely connected with the leading actor of the Theatre Royal and his wife, both bitter rivals of the great tragedienne.

Under the moral guarantee of the landowner, who was a spinster, the artistic couple took it upon themselves to perfect Maria's studies until her début. And in order to enter into negotiations, Maria was invited to spend a fortnight at her friend's. She would meet there the great actor and his wife who—height of good-luck—had made precise and favourable enquiries of their director. The first news that had been reported to us was thus belied. It was, moreover, merely pure invention, having been created for the needs of the cause by Maria's mother, with the sole purpose of erecting an obstacle against the dramatic impulses of her daughter.

She was thus saved. As for me, I could sleep, breathe, work.

She remained absent for two weeks. To judge by her scanty letters, she was not bored. She had recited before her new friends who recognised her excellent aptitude for the stage.

As soon as she returned, she rented a room in the country for herself from a peasant woman who fed her. Thus she was delivered from her old wardresses and free to see me freely every Saturday and Sunday without witnesses. Life lavished a smile on us, despite the sadness which remained with us from the recent divorce, but in nature one feels the weight of social conventions less and under the sun, in the heart of summer, the darkness of the soul is more quickly dispelled.

In early autumn, her début was announced under the patronage of the two famous actors and the gossip stopped. The rôle which had been chosen for her did not please me at all. It was a costume rôle without importance in an old-fashioned play. But her teacher had counted on the sympathy of the public for her; she had a good scene in which the lady turned down a marquis who wanted to marry her to make of her only one more ornament in his drawing-room, a scene in which the heroine ended up by declaring that she preferred the noble heart of the poor young man to the fortune and the crown of the marquis.

Thenceforward forsaken as a teacher, I took advantage of all my time to devote myself to my scholarly studies and write a memorandum destined for some academy or other; that was indispensable in order to gain my titles as a titular librarian and a man of letters. With a frantic ardour, I thrust myself into my ethnographical research on the Far East. It was like opium for my brain exhausted by the litigation, the calamities, the lacerations that I had just undergone, and goaded by the ambition of becoming someone at the side of the beloved woman, whose future already appeared in seductive colours, I accomplished miracles of assiduity. I shut myself in the vaults of the royal castle from morning until evening, suffering, without complaining, from the humid and glacial air, braving want and lack of money.

Maria was going to make her début when her daughter died of an attack of encephalic tuberculosis. A further month of tears, of reproaches, of remorse.

"It's punishment," declared the grandmother, glad at being able to thrust that poisoned dagger into the heart of her daughter, for she had conceived a hatred of her because of the stigma that she imprinted on the name of the family.

Crushed with distress, Maria spent days and nights at the bedside of the agonising little one, under the roof of her ex-husband and under the auspices of her ex-mother-in-law. The poor father was shattered by the loss of his only joy; succumbing to the pain, he would sometimes want to see his bygone friend again in order to relive erstwhile memories with a witness of the past. One evening, some days after the burial of the little girl, my maid informed me that the Baron had come during the day and that he was waiting for me at home.

As I did not want any reconciliation, our liaison having been broken in exceptional circumstances, I refused with delicate and chosen explanations.

A quarter of an hour after the receipt of my letter, Maria, in mourning, with her face bathed in tears, came herself to ask me to give way to the supplications of the distressed Baron.

I found this mission in bad taste; I fulminated, arguing the opinion of the world and the ambiguity of such a situation. She accused me of having prejudices, finally begged me, appealing to the generosity of my heart and did so much that I adhered to that indelicate pact.

I had sworn to myself never to re-enter the old house where the drama had taken place. Now, the widower had removed. He was now living in the neighbourhood of my domicile and very close to Maria. In this way, the bias that I nourished against the former dwelling was not ruffled and I accompanied the divorcée to her former husband's.

The mourning, the grief, the serious and gloomy aspect of the house of death combined to remove all irregularity of character and all awkwardness from that meeting. The habit of seeing those two people together removed all suspicion of jealousy from me and the discreet and cordial behaviour of the Baron enveloped me with a perfect security.

We supped, drank, played cards and everything happened as in the good old times. The following day we assembled at my place; another evening at Maria's, newly installed in a room rented from an old maid. We reverted to our former habits and Maria was happy to see us in agreement. It calmed her and as we were always circumspect towards each other, thanks to our attentive manners, it came about that no-one amongst us found himself wounded in his intimate feelings. The Baron regarded us as secret fiancés and his love for Maria appeared quite dead. Sometimes he even went as far as to inform us of his sorrows of love, for pretty Matilda was kept an eye on at her father's and out of reach of the poor lover. . . And Maria teased him or consoled him alternately. As for him, he no longer made a mystery of the true character of his desires, formerly hidden from the world.

On parting, the intimacy took on such alarming proportions as to arouse in me, if not jealousy, at least a little repugnance.

One day, Maria informed me that she had remained to dine with the Baron, because she had had urgent business, motivated by her daughter's estate which the Baron inherited.

I reacted against those tendencies in bad taste, which I called indecent. She laughed in my face, reminding me, in mockery, of my revolts against prejudices and I ended up by laughing at it myself. It was ridiculous, out of place, but it was good form to jeer at the world and it was superb to see virtue triumphant.

From then on, she frequented the Baron as she pleased and I even think that to amuse himself he made her rehearse her rôle.

Until then all had happened without difficulties and soon my jealousy disappeared under the influence of habit and also because I still had that old illusion that they were man and wife. Now, one evening, Maria, alone, made her appearance in my place. I helped her off with her coat and, contrary to her habit she spent a moment in straightening her skirts. As I am versed in the secrets of women I sensed something. While speaking to me, she sat down on the sofa right in front of the mirror, and, chatting with a forced air, she furtively looked at her reflected image and rearranged her hair on the sly.

A cruel suspicion crossed my mind, and unable to contain my emotion, I burst out:

"Where have you come from?"

"From Gustav's."

"What did you do?"

A brusque movement, quickly repressed, and she replied to me:

"I rehearsed my rôle."

"You're lying."

She protested: "Your jealousy is absurd", she said. She overwhelmed me with reasons and I wavered. Unfortunately she precipitated our departure, for we were invited to the Baron's, so that my research was postponed.

At present, recalling that incident, I would be ready to swear, after a long examination, that she was "bigamous", to employ the most indulgent word. But, at the time, her artifices dazzled me and I was ensnared.

What had happened? . . . Most likely this:

She dined tête-à-tête with the Baron; they took coffee and liqueurs; she felt overwhelmed by that lassitude which follows digestion. The Baron advised her to stretch out on the sofa, which was not, moreover, to her displeasure. . . The rest was accomplished progressively. The solitude, the absolute confidence, the memories helping the husband and wife who did not have to overcome modesty; the bachelor, tempted, grew warm and that was that. Why deprive oneself of an enjoyment which does no harm to anyone, as long as it is unknown by the one who should know it? She was free, because she had received nothing in cash from the lover, and to fail in her word, what is that for a woman? Perhaps she also missed the loss of a male more abreast of her needs; very likely that after the comparison, her curiosity satisfied, she languished after the stronger in the combat of love in which the timid and the delicate, however impetuous he is, must be the underdog. Finally, it is more than probable that she, the bed-fellow, who had dressed a thousand times and undressed in the presence of that man, who knew even the slightest secret of her body, did not feel embarrassed to add a savoury dessert to that dinner offered behind closed doors. Especially when she felt free from all engagements and her sensitive woman's heart was filled with compassion for the needy man. And, my word of honour, if I had been in the shoes of that outraged, if not betrayed, husband, I swear by all the gods of antiquity and of modernism, that, reduced to a quandary by another and finding his mistress in my hands, she would not have left my bedroom intact, by jingo!

But as the cherished lips did not cease to proffer the great words of honour, of honesty, of good manners, I did not wish to lend credence to such suspicions. Why?

Because a woman, loved by a man of honour, always has the upper hand. He fancies he is alone, he wants to be the only one, and what one wants one believes.

I now recall a word which was thrown up at me by a person living in a house opposite the apartment of the Baron. Apropos of nothing, he made an allusion "to the ploughings with half harvest". Although it escaped me then, the insult was there all the same . . . and that was ten years ago.

"Why," I asked myself, "has that remained in my memory amongst thousands of phrases heard and forgotten since that period?"

Certainly, today, the fidelity of that woman appears unlikely to me in the highest degree, unacceptable, impossible.

Besides, during the hours which I spent tête-à-tête with the Baron, he always sought to appear deeply interested in whores, and on a certain evening when we had supped together at the restaurant, he

134

went so far as to ask me for addresses of bad places. No doubt trying to trick me!

Let us add that he had ways of a disdainful courtesy towards Maria; that then the manner of his wife was that of a cocotte, at the same time as her voluptuousness seemed to continually decrease in our intimate relations.

5

At last her début came. It was a success for many and complicated reasons. Firstly, and for everyone, the curiosity of seeing a Baroness mount the boards; the sympathy of the bourgeoisie in strife with the nobility, glad at the blow dealt against accepted conventions by the dissolution of the marriage; then the bachelors, the sexless, the enemies of conjugal slavery showered her with flowers: without counting the friends, the relatives, the intimates of the great actor, who found themselves so to speak engaged in the enterprise, since he had coached Maria for the theatre, since he had been her teacher.

After the performance, the Baron had invited us both to supper as well as the old maid with whom Maria lodged.

We were ecstatic at the result and the satisfaction intoxicated everybody. Maria, with the rouge which still remained on her cheeks, with the black which stuck to her lashes, her hair done *en grande dame*, displeased me. She was no longer the virgin-mother whom I had loved, but an actress, with brazen expressions, with common manners, talkative, interrupting everybody, obsessed by an outrageous fatuity.

She thought she had reached the summit of Art and only replied to my advice, to my observations by shrugs of the shoulder or a condescending:

"You cannot understand that, my little one."

The Baron had the air of some unfortunate lover. He would have kissed her, had it not been for my presence, and, after having drunk infinite quantities of madeira, he poured out his heart, expressing his regrets that Art, divine Art, demanded such cruel sacrifices.

The newspapers, well primed, ascertained the success and an engagement appeared probable as the inevitable conclusion. Two photographers fought for the honour of reproducing some of the attitudes of the débutante, and an insignificant publication, which was being launched, put a portrait of the new star, together with her biography, up for sale.

What astonishes me, when I still contemplate all those images of the Adored, is that none resembles my original. Had she then changed her character, her expression, in so little time . . . a year? Or could it be that she reveals somebody else in reflecting the love, the tenderness, the pity expressed in my eyes, when I look her in the face? In those photographs, I discover in her a commonplace physiognomy, hard, brazen, with expressions of a fierce coquetry, features which are inviting and which are provoking. One of the poses particularly frightens me. In it, she holds herself bent, leaning with her elbows over the back of a fairly low chair, exhibiting to whomsoever wishes to see it her naked throat, half hidden beneath a fan placed on the opening of the bodice. Her looks seem to be plunged into the looks of another who is not I, for my love mixed with respect and tenderness never caresses her with those ways of insolent voluptuousness with which whores are aroused; and that photograph seems to me like those indecent images which one is offered in secret at dusk in the doorways of cafés.

I refused to take it when she brought it to me:

"You do not want a portrait of your Maria," she said to me, with that pitiful air which brought home to me at times her inferiority never openly admitted. "The fact is then you no longer love me!"

When a woman tells her lover: "You no longer love me!" the fact is that she herself has ceased to love him.

And from then on I felt the progressive lowering of her affection.

She was aware that her futile soul had drawn from mine the courage, the steadfastness necessary for the goal that she wanted to reach and she was preparing to rid herself of the troublesome creditor. Yet while listening to me and feigning to scorn them, she was still robbing me of ideas:

"You cannot understand that, my little one!"

And she, ignorant of all things, who could only speak French, she whose education had been neglected, she who was brought up in the middle of the countryside, who knew nothing of the theatre or of literature, indebted to me who had given her her first lessons in the Swedish accent, who had unveiled for her the mysteries of prosody, of metrics, she was calling me bone idle!

For her second début which was to take place shortly, I recommended a rôle, a great melodramatic rôle, the finest in the repertory. She refused it. Sometime afterwards she informed me that she had definitely *chosen* the same rôle. Well! . . . I made an analysis of it for her, I designed her costumes for her, I showed her where her effects were, I indicated her exits to her and I pointed out to her the dominant traits of that figure which she had to bring out.

Then a silent struggle ensued between the Baron and myself. He, the director of the theatre of the Royal Guards, the instructor of the soldier-actors, alloted himself superior qualities in the matter of dramatic art, and Maria, esteeming his so-called ideas more, appointed him as a teacher and rebutted my advice. Ah! the fine personal aesthetics which he professed under the guise of naturalness! For it was banality, the common, the vulgar which he preached above everything else, that man, on the pretext of naturalness!

I quite admit this principle when it is a question of modern comedy. Then the characters move amongst the thousand miseries of life but it is impossible, insupportable, if it is a question of an English melodrama, for example. The great passions cannot be expressed in the same way as the witticisms with which drawing-room conversations are filled.

But it appears the distinction is too subtle for a mediocre brain which generalises the particular. Because this case is such, the rule holds good for all others! . . .

On the eve of her début, Maria honoured me with the exhibition of her toilettes. Despite my protestations, my prayers, she had chosen a dust-grey cloth which killed her, which gave her a cadaverous look.

As her only reply she rebutted me with this very feminine argument:

"But Madame X, the great tragedienne, created the part perfectly with a similar dress."

"True, but Madame X is not blonde like you. What suits blondes may not suit brunettes."

She did not understand and grew angry!

I predicted a failure for her and her second début was a fiasco.

How many tears then, reproaches, even insolences!

To complement this disaster, a week later, the great tragedienne took up again that same rôle in order to celebrate some anniversary or other and she was honoured with a luminous transparency, with a basket of flowers on stage and a cartload of wreaths!

Naturally it was I whom Maria blamed for this fiasco, for I was the ill-omened prophet of it and, in her distress at that discomfiture, she rallied more intimately than ever to the Baron, through the sympathy of one inferior for another.

I, the erudite, the dramatic author, the dramatic critic, initiated in every literature, in contact through my work and my activities in libraries with the most elaborate brains of the entire world, I was cast off like a rag, called ignorant, considered like a page-boy or like a dog.

However, she was engaged, despite the calamity of the second début, for a salary of two thousand four hundred francs a year and she was freed of worry. But at the same time her career towards the great Art was finished. Classed amongst the stand-bys, condemned to secondary rôles as a woman of the world or as a mannequin, she spent all her days at dressmakers. Three, four, five toilettes in a single evening were to absorb her insufficient wages.

Ah! the bitter disappointments, the heartrending scenes when she was distributed more and more flimsy parts, containing a dozen rejoinders to be given. Her room was converted into a dressmaker's workshop, filled with patterns cut from newspapers, with materials, with scraps. And there was the mother, the true woman of the world, who disdained and deserted drawing-rooms and dressing-up to consecrate herself to the sublime Art, who had become an apprentice seamstress—in her workshop, leaning over the sewing-machine, until midnight, in order to appear for a few minutes camouflaged as a woman of the world in the eyes of the bourgeoisie.

Then there was the life of idleness during the rehearsals backstage where she would wait for hours for an entrance in order to say a couple of words, standing, without the shadow of an occupation. Then there appeared the taste for gossip, chit-chat, smutty stories and the grave aspirations towards the heights were vanishing; the wings of the mind were falling and the ground was skimmed, the gutter was touched.

The débâcle went its way and the day when the dresses were turned inside out several times, when the means of procuring new ones no longer existed, her small rôles were withdrawn from her in order to lower her to a figurante.

And while poverty was coming, her mother, a prophetic Cassandra, made her spend sad days, and the world, which had attended that sensational divorce, the premature death of the child, rose up against the unnatural mother and the unfaithful wife. Soon the director of the theatre was to give way to the antipathy of the public: the actor, her own teacher, disavowed her, acknowledging that he had been mistaken about her talent.

So much fuss, so many disasters for the caprice of a woman declared of no consequence!

To add further to those miseries, Maria's mother suddenly died of a heart ailment, which the world naturally imputed to the chagrin which came to her from her depraved daughter.

Once again my honour was at stake. I grew irritated with the all-too-unjust world, and through a supreme effort I was to try and drag her from the mire. Now that she felt at the mercy of whoever would offer her a helping hand, she accepted my proposal to found a weekly paper for her devoted to theatre, music, literature, the arts. She could make her début there as a columnist and critic and so prepare herself an entrée to future publishers.

She invested two hundred francs in the enterprise. I took charge of the copy and the proofs. Well aware of my incapacity in the matter of administration, I left the sale and the advertising half to her and half to the theatre manager, the proprietor of a newspaper kiosk.

The first number, when paginated, appeared highly successful. A leader signed by one of our young master painters; an original correspondence from Rome, another from Paris, a music critique by an eminent writer, a collaborator in one of the leading newspapers of Stockholm; a literary review that I had signed myself, a gossip and first-night column from the hand of Maria.

All was then for the best. The important thing was the launching of the first number* on time; we were ready, but we were lacking the necessary funds and credit at the right time.

---

* *Gazetten,* first and only edition 23 Sept. 1876

Woe was me! for I had left my destiny in the hands of a woman! The day the newspaper was to appear she was in bed, sleeping in as she was wont.

Quite convinced that the paper was out, I went for a walk through town, meeting only quizzical people on my way.

"Well! where is that famous paper sold?" the numerous interested people asked me.

"Everywhere, for Pete's sake!"

"Or nowhere?"

I went into a newspaper shop.

"We haven't received it yet," the man answered me.

I dashed to the printing works. It hadn't left the press!

All was lost! A violent quarrel ensued with my administrator, innocent because of her inborn insouciance and her absolute ignorance in the matter of publications and moreover . . . was she responsible? She had relied entirely on the stage manager for everything.

The two hundred francs were squandered. I had wasted my time, my honour, my excessive and unpaid work.

In the general collapse I was left with a single idea: we were irreparably lost!

I proposed that she die with me. What was going to become of us? She had fallen into absolute penury as a result of all this; I was incapable of relaunching her once again.

"Let us die," I said to her. "Let us be ashamed of dragging ourselves through the streets, walking corpses, who obstruct the traffic of the living."

She refused.

"How cowardly, cowardly you are, my superb Maria! Infamous one who wants to keep for me the spectacle of your decadence beneath the scornful laughter of the world!"

I returned to the taverns. I got drunk there and fell asleep.

When I awoke I went to call on her. The drink had made me more perspicacious. For the first time, the change which had come about in her really struck me. Her room was untidy, her clothing sloppy, neglected, and her little adored feet were shod in down-at-heel mules on to which her stockings fell in spirals.

Oh! Misery of miseries!

Her language had become enriched with ugly terms, borrowed from actors' slang, her gestures smacked of the street, her expressions were hateful and her lips bitter.

She remained bent double over her work, no longer ever looking me in the eyes, as if she was brooding over black ideas.

Suddenly, without lifting her head, she said to me in a hoarse voice:

"Axel, do you know what a woman, in the conditions in which we are living, can demand of a man?"

140

Thunderstruck, believing I had misunderstood, I answered her hesitantly:

"No . . . what?"

"What can a mistress demand of her lover?"

"Love."

"And what else?"

"Money!"

The coarse word was enough to stop her from insisting and, sure of having understood her meaning, I went away.

"Whore! Whore!" I said to myself, walking up and down, with unsteady legs, through the streets saddened by autumn. We were at the last stage! . . . The bill for enjoyment! The trade unashamedly admitted!

All right if she had been wretched, in need. But she had just collected the inheritance of her mother, a set of furniture, some assets, some of which were dubious, no doubt, but which still represented some thousands of francs and, besides, her salary was still regularly paid her at her theatre.

All that was indeed inexplicable . . . when the image of Miss B., her landlady and her intimate friend, brutally came to my mind!

She was a person of thirty-five with the suspicious ways of a go-between, hateful, living one knew not how, always hard-up, always in the streets, however, in magnificent and extravagant dresses, worming her way into families in order to borrow the slightest sum in the last resort, and complaining everywhere about her sombre destiny. A shady woman who detested me, perceiving my sagacity.

As it happened, I recalled an incident which I had let pass as insignificant and which had happened some months previously. The said lady had wrung from a Finnish friend of Maria the promise to lend her the sum of a thousand francs. The promise had remained what it was, a promise. It was then that Maria, at the instigation of Miss B., and to safeguard the honour of her seriously ill-used Finnish friend, had pledged herself to obtain the money. She had, indeed, found the sum. But poor Maria had had many a reproach from her Finnish friend, and when arguments arose, Miss B. declared herself quite innocent of all that and put the blame exclusively on Maria. It was then that I had expressed my aversion and the suspicions that I conceived regarding that mysterious personage, advising Maria to break without delay from a woman who gave herself up to manoeuvres which did not fall short of blackmail.

But no, what excuses she then had to allege in favour of her perfidious friend! . . . Later, the whole story had been altered by her; it arose from a misunderstanding; then in the end the whole incident had become reduced, according to her, to an invention of my "sad fantasy"!

141

Perhaps that adventuress had suggested to Maria that day the distressing idea of "presenting the bill"! More than likely, for she had great difficulty in getting out that phrase which was so unlike her. I wanted to think so, to hope so. Still, if she had demanded the reimbursement of the money paid out by her for the newspaper, money which she had squandered, that would have been feminine mathematics, or if she had demanded marriage, which she was now against? But there was no doubt about it. It was really a question of paying for the love, the spasms, the kisses without number, the ruffled skirts. It was the bill for all that which she demanded! . . . Well, then, and what if I had presented her with the account for my work by the hour or piecework, for the expenditure of my nerves, of my brain, of my blood, for the expense of using my name, my honour, the list of my sufferings, the back-payment invoice for my career, broken perhaps!

But no, it was up to her to settle our account book first and I made no objection to it.

I spent my evening at the café, in the streets, wandering, meditating on the problem of degeneration. Why do we feel a piercing pain at the sight of a creature in decline? The fact is that there is something against nature in it, for nature demands individual progress, development and every step backwards betrays a decomposition of strength. Thus in social life where every individual aspires to reach material or moral heights. Hence the tragic sentiment which wrings us before decay, tragic as autumn, illness, death. That woman who was not thirty—I had seen her young, beautiful, frank, loyal, comely, strong, well brought-up; alas! I had seen her in two years degenerate so quickly, fall so low.

I was tempted for a moment to take the blame upon myself, in order to attenuate hers, which would have been a relief to me. But I was not really capable of victimising myself, for it was I who had inspired her with a cult of the beautiful, the love of superior things, of generous actions and the more she adopted the displeasing manners of actors, I was ennobling myself by assimilating the fine manners of the world, by imitating the polished gestures and language, by imposing upon myself that reserve which bridles the emotions and which is the distinctive sign of well brought-up people. In love, I preserved an outward chastity, being careful of modesty, always on guard against offending beauty, propriety, which make us forget the animal basis of an action, to my mind closer to the soul than to the body.

I am brutal, if need be, but never vulgar. I kill but I do not wound. I use the proper word when necessary, but I never gather sly asides; I invent my sallies myself, born at random, provoked by the situation, but I do not appropriate the witticisms of operettas or comic newspapers.

142

I adore cleanliness, tidiness, the beauty in life and I miss a dinner if I haven't a starched shirt. I never present myself either half dressed or in slippers in front of my mistress: I may offer her a meagre slice of bread with a glass of beer, but on a white tablecloth.

It was not I, then, who had lowered her below the norm by my examples. She no longer loved me. It was because of that that she had ceased to want to please me. She belonged to the public; she made up, dressed for the public, so that she became the public woman who ends up by presenting her bill for so many nights! . . . During the days which followed, I shut myself up in my library. I had put on mourning for my love, for my superb, mad, celestial love. All was buried and the battlefield on which the combats of love had been waged remained silent. Two dead and so many wounded to satisfy the needs of a woman who was not worth a pair of worn-out shoes. If at least her appetites had had procreation for a goal, if she had been led into giving herself through the unconscious instinct of unmarried mothers who give themselves for giving's sake. But she detested children, she found it degrading to give birth. A perverse nature, she debased the maternal feeling to a simple pleasure. Thus she was urged towards the extinction of a race because she felt she was a degenerate being, in decomposition, and it was the better to hide her disintegrating function that she spoke in flowery language on the necessity of living her life for superior ends or for humanity.

I detested her and I wanted to forget her! I walked along the rows of books without being able to drag myself from the accursed nightmare which pursued me. I no longer desired her, since she sickened me, but a profound pity, an almost fatherly tenderness, imposed upon me the responsibility for her future. What if I left her? . . . Left to herself, she would come to no good, either becoming the mistress of the Baron, or becoming the mistress of everyone.

Incapable of lifting her up, without the means to leave the mire into which we had sunk deep, I resigned myself to remain rivetted by her side, to contemplate her wasting away, while falling into ruin myself, since the desire to live and to work had died within me. The instinct for preservation, hope were dead. I wanted nothing, I desired nothing and, having become shy, I would even go as far as to the door of my restaurant, stop and return home, renouncing dining in order to go to bed earlier on my sofa and bury myself beneath the blankets. Like a mortally wounded animal, I lay stiff, my head empty, without sleeping or thinking, waiting for an illness or for the end.

One day, however, at the restaurant, hidden at the end of an isolated room, the retreat of chance lovers and of threadbare clothes which fear the broad daylight, I was taken out of my reverie by the sound of a well-known voice. Somebody was saying hullo to me

It was an unsuccessful architect, the wreck of a past bohemia, dispersed to the four corners of the world.

"So you're still alive?" he said sitting down in front of me.

"Just about . . . And you?"

"So-so . . . Leaving for Paris tomorrow . . . inherited from an idiot, ten thousand francs."

"May they serve you well!"

"Unfortunately, I've got no-one to devour the estate with."

"Not so unfortunately, since I possess the teeth and some extraordinary inventions to help you in this windfall."

"Really? You could accompany me? . . ."

"Immediately."

"Then . . . it's agreed?"

"It's a bargain!"

"Tomorrow evening at six o'clock. For Paris . . ."

"And then afterwards . . ."

"Blow our brains out."

"The devil! How did you get that idea from me? . . ."

"From the expression on your face which cries out for suicide."

"Good haruspex!—Let's go, buckle your trunk and long live Paris!"

In the evening when I arrived at Maria's, I informed her of the happiness which had come to me. It was with a compassionate joy that she received the confidence, congratulating me, repeating that it would do me good, would refresh my ideas. In short she appeared glad and overwhelmed me with her motherly attentions which touched me to the very bottom of my heart. After an evening spent tête-à-tête, an evening of listlessness, of recollections, in which we made few plans, since we no longer had any confidence in the future, we separated . . . — for ever? . . . The question was not touched upon; by tacit agreement, we left to chance the care of reuniting us.

6

Indeed, the journey rejuvenated me. In reviving the memories of the old times of my first youth, I felt myself ferociously gay, for I wanted to forget those two years of misery, and not for an instant did I wish to speak of her. All that drama of the divorce had become for me like excrement on which one spits and from which one withdraws without looking at it any more. Sometimes, I smiled furtively, like an escapee, firmly resolved not to let himself be. pinched again and I felt all the emotions of the debtor who clears off, without a care for his debts, to an unknown land.

In Paris, the theatres, the museums, the libraries, distracted me for a fortnight. As I received no letters from Maria, I flattered myself with the hope that she had consoled herself and that all was for the best in the best of worlds.

But at the end of some time, tired by madly gadding about, by new and strong impressions, saturated, everything lost its interest, and I kept to my room, reading the newspapers, oppressed by vague sensations and inexplicable uneasy feelings.

Then the phantom of the pale young woman, the mirage of the virgin-mother, rose up, no longer to leave me any repose. The image of the brazen actress had become effaced from my memory; it was the Baroness alone who emerged from the recollection, embellished, rejuvenated, having changed her wretched body into a glorious body, according to the dreams of the ascetics about the promised land.

I was living on those dolorous and charming dreams, when a letter from Maria reached me. In heartrending terms she announced to me that she was pregnant and that marriage alone could restore her honour.

Without a second's hesitation I packed my trunk again. I took the most direct train for Stockholm. I was going to get married.

Never did a doubt on the paternity become aroused in me. I had, for a year and a half presumed on mercy; I accepted the outcome of our mistakes as a grace, as the end of our sufferings, as a reality comprising heavy responsibilities, perhaps fatalities; but in the end it was a point of departure for the Unknown, something new. Besides marriage was from my youth the object of my most attractive preoccupations and constituted for me the only form of cohabitation of the two sexes, so that life together did not frighten me. Now that Maria was going to be a mother, my love took on a new ardour; it rose purified, ennobled from the filth of our illicit liaison.

On my return, Maria gave me the worst possible welcome and gave me a good dressing-down for the lies I had told her. Forced into a delicate explanation, I informed her that a urethal shrinkage was an ailment which diminished the dangers of fecundation without invalidating it. Many a time, moreover, in the course of the past season, we had undergone the terrors of false alarms; what was happening was hardly astonishing to us then.

She had a hatred of marriage, and, under the influence of her odious companion, she had learned that married woman is a slave, who works for nothing for her husband, and, as I had a great fear of slaves, I suggested a modern marriage to her, in conformity with our tastes.

Firstly, the three-roomed apartment, one for the mistress, one for the master, one neuter. Then, neither housekeepers nor servants in the house. The dinner was to come from a restaurant, the lunch and supper were to be prepared in the kitchen through the good offices of a servant who lived out. In this way the expenses would thus be easy to calculate and the causes of upsets avoided.

Then—and to forestall the unpleasantness of ever being suspected of having squandered the fortune of my wife—I proposed the dowry system. The dowry, which it is dishonourable in the lands of the north for a husband to accept, constitutes in civilised countries a sort of contribution from the wife which gives the illusion that she does not absolutely subsist thanks to her husband. And so, to eliminate any wrong impression altogether, the Germans and the Danes have established this custom: the bride brings the furniture, so that the husband preserves the feeling of being installed in his wife's home and that the latter will always imagine herself in her own home and that she maintains her husband.

Maria, having recently inherited from her mother a set of furniture comprising objects of no market value, but which were souvenirs for her and bearing the hallmark of antiquity, brought to my notice that since she had enough to furnish six rooms, it was useless buying new furniture for the three rooms. Since she was offering to stock them, I willingly accepted.

The important point remained: the awaited child.

Fortunately, the necessity of hiding the confinement found us in agreement on this point, that the newborn baby would have to be boarded out in town until the favourable moment when we could adopt it.

The marriage was fixed for the thirty-first of December, and, during the next two months, I would employ myself in discovering an honourable means of existence for myself.

To this end, and pressed by the prospect of soon seeing Maria obliged to renounce her theatre, I took up the pen again, so vigorously that at the end of the first month it was possible for me to deliver to the publisher a volume of tales immediately accepted.

With the help of good luck, I was promoted assistant librarian at the library, with the fixed salary of twelve hundred francs and upon the removal of the collections from the old building to the new building, I received six hundred francs as a bonus. It was perfect happiness, which, added to other happy events, allowed me to believe that wicked destiny had grown tired of persecuting me.

The most esteemed of Finnish reviews signed a contract with me for articles of literary criticism at the rate of fifty francs a piece, and the *Official Journal* of Sweden, published by the Academy, conferred the coveted appointment of art critic at thirty-five francs a column on me, without counting the proofs of the classical authors in course of publication, the revision of which was entrusted to me.

And all that was my lot during those two months, the most fatal of my life.

Soon my tales* were launched and won a frank success. The title of young master of the genre was bestowed on me and the book would be a landmark, it was said, for it was the first which had introduced the modern, realistic note into Swedish literature.

How happy I was then to be able to unite my poor adored Maria to an outstanding man who, to his titles of royal secretary and assistant librarian, added a name which was beginning to spread, holding promises of a brilliant future, which would allow her some day to reopen her artistic career, momentarily closed as a result of setbacks, perhaps undeserved.

Fortune was smiling at us with a tear in its eyes.

. . .

The banns were published. I packed my trunks. I said goodbye to my attic room, the witness of my miseries and my joys, and I was going to shut myself in that prison that no one fears, we less than all others, since we had foreseen in advance all the perils, removed all the stumbling-blocks.

And yet . . .

---

* *Från Fjärdingen och Svartbäcken* (1877)

THIRD PART

(1)

The inexpressible joy of being married! Sheltered from the inquisitive and foolish eyes of the world, always living tête-à-tête with the beloved! Oh! the maternal home refound, the security, the port after the storm, the nest where the little ones are awaited!

Surrounded by all those objects which belonged to her, souvenirs from the paternal house, I felt myself grafted on to her trunk and the portraits in oil of her ancestors gave me the impression that her family had adopted me, since her forefathers would be the forefathers of my children as well. I had everything from her hand; she decked me with the jewels of her father; she had me served in the porcelain from her mother; she made me a present of small keepsakes to which were attached memories of olden times, sometimes recalling celebrated warriors sung by the great poets of the land, which strongly impressed the mind of the commoner that I was. She was the benefactress, the bestower of all those generous gifts, and I was so dazzled with them as to forget that I had rehabilitated her, that I had brought her from the gutter, that I had made her the wife of somebody, of a man with a future, she the actress without a reputation, the condemned wife, whom I had perhaps saved from the supreme downfall.

Ah! the good household we made! The dream of free marriage realised. No double bed, no common room, no bathroom in common, so that all the turpitudes of the holy legitimate union were abolished. Such a good institution was marriage thus understood, revised and corrected by us. Through the separation of the bed we kept the fine occasions of endlessly wishing each other good-night and the ever perpetuated joy of greeting each other in the morning, enquiring after each other's sleep and health. And we also preserved in this way the pleasure of the discreet and delicate visits into the bedroom, always preceded by those courteous preambles, as a replacement to the more or less authorised rape of the double bed.

And how much work effectuated in the home beside the wife leaning over the layette of the forthcoming child, instead of the time formerly lost in meetings and in idleness.

After a month of absolute intimacy, the confinement arrived prematurely. We had a puny daughter, who could barely breathe. She was immediately boarded out to a midwife of recognised honesty, living in the neighbourhood. Two days afterwards we were told that the little one had gone off as she had come, painlessly, through lack of strength, resistance, not without having been previously baptised by the midwife.

The mother welcomed the news with some remorse mixed with a frank satisfaction. She was delivered from the incalculable worries which the prejudices which forbade her keeping a too-early child near her would cause her.

Now, by agreement, the new watchword was: no more children! Life together, as comrades, man and wife, without amorous privations, however, but each one for himself, on the road to reach his different goal. As she no longer had confidence in my innocuousness, we had recourse to the simplest and most innocent frauds.

This being established, and once all imminent danger was removed, we began to breathe, to reflect. My family having banished me, I had not dragged any importunate relatives along with me and, my wife possessing only an aunt in town, we escaped from those family encumbrances which are so painful and so embarrassing for a new home.

At the end of six weeks, I discovered that two intruders had slipped into my wife's intimacy.

Firstly there was a dog of the King Charles breed, a weepy-eyed monster, who welcomed me with frightful barkings whenever I returned home, just as if I were not one of the household. I detest dogs, those protectors of cowards who have not the courage to bite the assailant themselves; then that animal was particularly antipathetic to me in that he was an inheritance from the previous home, a perpetual reminder of the repudiated husband.

The first time that I imposed silence on him, my wife reproached me timidly, excusing the beast who remained as a legacy from her dead daughter: she would never have thought me so cruel and so on . . .

One day, I noticed that the monster had forgotten himself on the large carpet in the drawing-room. I administered a masterly chastisement to him, which brought me the qualification of slaughterer, for I struck animals deprived of reason.

"But what do you want me to do about it, my child: since brutes don't understand our language?"

She wept and confessed she was afraid of a wicked man like me . . .

The monster still continued to dirty the precious carpet.

From then on I took its education upon myself, persuading my wife that dogs become very docile and that with a little perseverance one achieves wonders of training.

She lost her temper and, for the first time, brought to my notice that the carpet belonged to her.

"Take it away then; I did not undertake to live in the lavatories of the house."

The carpet remained and the animal was more strictly controlled from then on; my chastisements had helped a little.

Further accidents occurred however.

In order to restrain the expenditure and to avoid the trouble of lighting the fire specially in the kitchen, I was content with cold dishes in the evening. But whilst passing through our kitchen by chance one fine day, what did I see? The maid was in the middle of cooking veal cutlets over the fully-lit stove.

"Who are those cutlets for?"

"For the dog, sir."

My wife arrived.

"Darling . . ."

"Ah! . . . Excuse me, I am the one who pays!"

"Very well . . . I understand. But I have a cold meal, myself, and I am worse fed than your dog . . . And I also pay."

That's rich! She paid!

From then on the King Charles was considered an idol, a martyr, and Maria shut herself up with a friend, a very new friend, in order to adore her animal which they decorated with a blue ribbon tied round its neck. And my good friends moaned together about human wickedness embodied in my odious personnage.

Then a mortal hatred seethed within me against that mischief-maker who got under my feet everywhere. My wife had made a bed for him, with feather cushions and a pile of shawls, which always encumbered the passage when I wanted to go and say good-morning or good-night to her. And on Saturdays, when, after a week of toil, I counted on spending the evening alone with my wife, chatting about the past and the future, my companion would remain for three hours in the kitchen with her friend, driving the maid mad, lighting the fire, upsetting the whole house, why? Because it was the monster's wash day.

"Isn't she really heartless to treat me like this?"

"She, heartless, the good soul who goes as far as to sacrifice her conjugal happiness for the care of a poor abandoned animal!" the friend expostulated.

There came a dinner at which infamy went beyond all bounds.

For some time now the food brought from the restaurant appeared extremely bad to me, but the darling one, with her irresistible good-nature, easily persuaded me that it was I who had become difficult. And I believed her since she was forever repeating to me that she had a sincere and frank nature.

At last, that fatal dinner was going to be served. There were only bones and tendons on the dish that was brought me.

"Look here, my child," I said to the maid, "what are you serving me there?"

"Yes, sir, I can see very well. It wasn't so bad when it was brought. But it was madame who ordered me to take out the best pieces for the dog . . ."

Beware of the woman caught in the act! Her anger will fall four-fold on your head!

She remained as if thunderstruck, unmasked as a liar and even a swindler, for she had always claimed to feed her beast from her own pocket. Dumb, livid, she only inspired me with pity. I was ashamed for her; but, never wanting to see her vilified, to see her beneath me, I decided, as a generous conqueror, to console her for this mis-adventure. Giving her a friendly tap on the cheek, I told her not to get angry for so little.

Generosity was not her weakness. She exploded. Ah! It was quite apparent that I was only a commoner without education, I, who was showing her up caught in the act in front of a servant, an imbecile who had misunderstood her orders. Finally, there was a guilty party, and it was I . . . An attack of nerves ensued, she became violent, rose brusquely from the table, threw herself on the sofa, screaming like a lunatic, sobbing and shouting that she was going to die.

Incredulous, I remained cold before this comedy.

"All this how-d'you-do for a dog!"

She howled in an alarming manner; a horrible cough shook her body, even more delicate since her latest confinement. In short, I ended up by becoming her dupe and I sent for the doctor.

He hurried round, sounded her, felt her pulse and went off testily. On the threshold of the door I stopped him:

"Well!"

"Hum! It's nothing," he said putting his overcoat on again.

"Nothing . . . But . . ."

"Nothing at all . . . Look here, you know quite well what women are . . . Good-bye."

Ah! yes, if I had known then what I know now, the secret that I have discovered to cure big and little outbreaks of hysteria. But I knew nothing then other than to kiss her eyes, asking for forgive-ness. Which I did. Why? She hugged me against her breast, calling me her good child, who had to be careful with her, for she was very fragile, very weak, and would die some day if her little boy was not more reasonable or renewed such violent scenes as this one.

To make her really happy, I took the monster and scratched its back, which earned me half an hour of looks full of a celestial joy.

From then on, the dog made its messes everywhere and often, without restraint, through a kind of feeling of vengeance. I sup-pressed my anger!

I was waiting for the fortunate chance which would deliver me from the torture of living in a pigsty like this . . .

The moment came. I returned for dinner one baleful day and found my wife in tears, deeply saddened. The dinner was not served. The maid was running after the dog, which had escaped.

I dissimulated my joy with great difficulty and sincerely pitied my wife, who was desolate. But she did not understand the simple fact that I could partake of her grief, despite my inward satisfaction at seeing my enemy removed. She saw through me and exclaimed:

"That makes you happy, doesn't it? You enjoy the misfortune of your neighbour, you know that you're wicked, fundamentally wicked, that you no longer love me."

"But no, my darling, I still love you, believe me, only I detest your dog."

"If you love me you should also love my dog."

"If I hadn't loved you, I would have beaten you!"

Ah! the terrible effect of that expression! Beat a woman! Just think, beat a woman! . . . She flew into a temper and even went so far as to invent that it was I who had let her dog loose, who had poisoned it perhaps!

After rushing about in a cab to all the police stations and even to the slaughterers, the mischief-maker was found again. There was a great rejoicing in the home for my wife and her friend, who regarded me at least as a possible poisoner from then on.

Finally, from that day on, the monster was imprisoned in my wife's bedroom and the love-nest decorated by myself with the taste of an artist was transformed into a kennel.

The apartment, already too small, thus became uninhabitable and the general effect of it was ruined. As I pointed this out, my wife retorted that her room was hers.

I then undertook a merciless crusade.

I made Madame dance to my tune, until she shuddered from the heat of her blood and she was the first to make advances:

"You never say hullo to me in the morning any more."

"Well, but I can't get to you."

She sulked. I sulked. I suffered for a fortnight from the bitternesses of a veritable celibacy and I obliged her to come right into my room to beg the favours she desired, which incurred her hatred for me until further notice.

Finally she surrendered and decided to have her dog killed. But instead of doing it there and then, she sent for her friend, performed the comedy of the supreme farewell, the last days of a condemned man on the eve of an execution, and went so far as to beg me on her knees to kiss the filthy beast as a token of reconciliation, for one never knows whether King Charleses have a soul and whether we shall see them in the other world.

Result: I restored life and liberty to the condemned, which incurred unbelievable testimonials of gratitude for me.

There were moments when I believed myself locked in a lunatic asylum but, alas! when one loves one does not look so closely.

And to think that that scene of the last moments of one condemned would be renewed every six months, reiterated during six years.

Young man, who have read this true story of a man, a woman, and a King Charles dog, you who have suffered reading these avowals, grant me your deepest pity, for that lasted three times three hundred and sixty-five days of twenty-four hours each; admire me, for I have remained alive! Finally, if it is admitted that I be mad—which my wife claims—say whose is the fault, if not mine, who have not had the courage to poison that dirty cur once and for all!

2

But let's pass on to the friend, an old maid of about fifty, mysterious, poor, with aspirations towards ideals I had given up.

She was my wife's consoler. It was on that breast that she went to weep, when I repudiated the dog. It was she who listened to the curses proffered by my wife against marriage, slavery, the servitude of women.

She was discreet enough and did not interfere too much in the routine of the household—at least as far as I know, and that's little —for the considerable work which I had in hand absorbed me absolutely and I heard nothing. However, I thought I knew that she was borrowing small sums from my wife, against which I had nothing to say, until the day when she came to take a load of silver plate to pledge it with a pawnbroker for her own benefit.

Only then did I make a respectful observation to Maria, giving her to understand that, even under the dowry system, I found that that was taking camaraderie rather too far, for, I, her husband, her associate, who was in difficulties, who had debts, I was not the object of a similar favour.

"Since it is permissible for anyone," I said to her, "to address such a demand to you, lend me some assets then. I shall also pledge them."

She objected that they were worthless as they were falling for the moment, and thus unsaleable. Besides she did not like to enter into business relations with her husband like this.

"Yes, but with a stranger, without guarantee, who lives off a retirement pension of seventy-five francs a year, that's all right! It is at least singular to refuse a service to the husband who is in the middle of making a future for himself which will consolidate the situation of his wife the day when she will no longer have anything and whose interests are juxtaposed to hers!"

At last she gave in. The loan valued at three thousand five hundred francs, represented by mediocre shares, was concluded.

From then on, she believed herself my benefactress and later she was to announce to whoever would listen to her that it was she who had assured my career by the sacrifice of her dowry! As if I had not shown signs of talent, both as dramatist and short story writer before knowing her. But it gave me pleasure to be beneath her, to be indebted to her for everything, for my life, for my happiness, for my future!

In our matrimonial agreements I had insisted upon the separation of our assets, particularly because of her affairs which were embroiled. The Baron, who had got into debt with her, instead of paying her cash, had become her guarantor for a loan. So that despite my precautions I found myself summoned to the bank the day after my wedding to reguarantee the sum. In vain did I protest; the bank did not recognise the solvency of my wife who had become a minor again through her second marriage; and to my inexpressible indignation I was constrained to sign the guarantee, substituting my name for the Baron's.

If I had known what I was doing then! But I was only a believer, an imbecile: I thought I was doing exactly what a man of the world would have done in my place.

3

One evening when I was receiving a friend in my room, the Baron came to see us. It was his first visit since our marriage. The presence of my predecessor in my home appeared in very bad taste to me, but since he did not recoil from his successor after all, I put on a fairly good face. Leading my friend back into the ante-room, I did not think it the thing to introduce him to the Baron. My wife reprimanded me for that, accusing me of coarseness. I replied by declaring that she, as well as the Baron, moreover, were absolutely lacking in tact.

A veritable quarrel ensued in which I was, in short, qualified as uncouth. As one thing led to another, we got round to talking about certain paintings removed from the Baron's house and which were decorating my walls. I claimed that they had to be returned to him.

"One cannot," my wife replied, "return gifts without wounding a friend. He certainly keeps the presents which you gave him, as a testimonial of friendship and confidence."

That pretty word confidence stunned me. At that moment my eyes fell on a piece of furniture which revived distasteful memories within me.

"Where does that desk come from?"

"I got it from my mother!"

She was telling the truth, but she was forgetting to add that it had passed through the apartment of her first husband.

What lack of delicacy, what height of bad taste, what improvidence in regard to my honour! Was it done on purpose to vilify me in the eyes of the world? Had I fallen into an ambush prepared by a shrew?

Defenceless against her infernal logic, I surrendered unconditionally, persuaded that her refined education ought to serve me as a guide in all the uncertain circumstances in which I was lacking in instruction. She had a reply to everything. "The Baron had never bought a household article . . ." All was hers! And since the Baron had adapted himself perfectly to living among the furniture of **my** wife, I could very well, I too, without any scruple, keep all the household articles belonging to my own wife!

The last phrase: "Since the Baron had accommodated himself to living among the furniture of **my** wife" caused me keen satisfaction. As the paintings hanging in my drawing-room had been placed in the limelight as proof of great confidence, testifying to the ideal character of our relations, they remained there and, to add to my naïveté, I considered it a pleasure to inform the curious who questioned me of the name of the donator of those landscapes.

If I had been able to know then that I, the commoner, I was the man of tact, the man of good taste, the bearer of those instincts which are revealed even in the low classes and which are too often lacking in society circles, despite the varnish with which they daub their rusticity! . . . If I had been able to know to what kind of a woman I had entrusted my destiny! . . . But I was totally unaware of it then!

4

As soon as she had got over her confinement, Maria, who was condemned to seclusion for some time, felt like bestirring herself. She went from theatre to theatre, under pretext of having to study, and frequented public entertainments, while I remained working at home. Under cover of her name as a married woman, all the circles, hitherto closed to the divorcée, were reopened. She sought to tie me to her apron-strings, for it made a bad impression never to see the husband. I scoffed at that, claiming my personal freedom, agreed upon in our verbal contract; I conceded her complete independence, every right to go wherever she wanted.

"One never sees the husband," it was repeatedly said.

"It's all right, one will hear of him!" I replied.

In short the husband had become a kind of trade-mark and the wife got used to looking down on him.

During my solitary hours in the house, I composed the ethno-graphical memorandum* which was to procure me promotion at the Library. I had entered into correspondence with the learned author-ities of Paris, Berlin, St. Petersburg, Peking, Irkutsk and, from my desk, I held the threads of a network of connections, spread over the old world. Maria reproached me for this work. She preferred that I write comedies and was angry with me. I advised her to wait a little for the end and not to condemn my work by declaring that I was wasting my precious time. But she did not want those scientific chinoiseries, which brought in nothing, at any price and, a new Xantippe, she set about plaguing my Socratic patience, claiming that I was indulging in the wasting of her dowry—always her dowry!— for trifles.

My existence glided by, mixed with bitterness and sweetness, with the daily worry about Maria's dramatic career. In March rumours began to spread. In the royal troupe cancellations of work were spoken of, which would take place at the end of May, the time for the renewal of engagements. Three months of extraordinary tears, in addition to the ordinary ones, went by; every day the house was full of all the actors of the Theatre Royal who had failed. My soul, which had become aristocratic through the development of knowledge and the increase of talent, shrank from that society of dregs, without quality, without instruction, odious through its vanity, in which outrageous banalities, borrowed from the slang of third-rate actors were retailed as new.

Disgusted with undergoing the torture of those idiotic conferences, I apologised to my wife for no longer being able to attend them. I

---

* *Relations de la Suède avec la Chine et les Pays Tartares*

advised her in the end to keep aloof from those lepers and from mediocrities, for they lowered us and deprived us of the courage we so badly needed.

I gained by being derisively qualified as "aristocratic".

"The fact is that I am an aristocrat indeed, my darling," I said to her, "in the sense that I aim for the heights, of talent of course, and not at all for the mole-hills of the so-called titled aristocracy; which does not prevent me from feeling all the sufferings of the disinherited."

When, today, I wonder how I was able to live for years, chained to a woman who pinched me, pulled my hair, robbed me with the complicity of her friends and of her dog, I attribute that to the little which suffices to content me, to the ascetic philosophy which I profess and which teaches me not to look too closely into men, and especially to my love. I loved her to the point of importuning her, for she sometimes made me feel that my obsessions annoyed her. But at the moments when she fondled me, when I was able to place my burning head on her knees, beneath the caresses of her fingers which played in my lion's mane, then all was forgotten, all was forgiven: I was happy and imprudently confessed that I could not do without her and that my existence was held by a thread the bobbin of which she held. And she gently got into the habit of believing herself a being of superior essence, and as a result of that optical error which provoked my voluntary abasement before her, I became like the baby of the house, so that she no longer accosted me except with cajoleries.

From then on I was at her mercy: she did not delay in abusing it even at the earliest opportunity.

When summer came, Maria installed herself in the country with her maid. In order not to remain alone during the six days of the week when I was kept in town by my duties at the library, she took her friend in as a boarder; in spite of me, for I was most afraid that she was not in a position to pay and our resources were most limited. But Maria called me "wicked"; claimed that I always spoke ill of everyone . . . , in short, I gave in, in order to avoid worse trouble and forced celibacy. I gave in . . . alas! as always.

Alone and celibate during the week, I greeted Saturday as a sabbath day. With a joyful heart, I took the train, I did half a league on foot beneath the burning sun, carrying bottles and provisions for the Sunday. On the way, I was delighted at the thought that I was going to see Maria at any minute coming to meet me and dashing forward, with open arms, with untied hair, with a rosy complexion, revived by the good, salubrious air and, mentally, I was already savouring the dinner done to a turn, ready on time, for I had not taken anything yet except morning coffee. Finally the cottage appeared in the firs on the edge of the lake. At the same time, I noticed Maria and her friend, dressed in light frocks, who were sneaking off in the direction of the bathing pavilion. With all the strength of my lungs I hailed them. They must have heard me, they were within reach of my voice. But they hurried up, as if they were fleeing from me and were engulfed in the cabin . . .

What did that mean?

Hearing me coming and going in the house, the servant made a timid appearance, looking sheepish, surely prepared to undergo disagreeable questions . . .

"Where are the ladies?"

"Bathing, sir."

"And the dinner?"

"Impossible to serve it before four o'clock, sir, the ladies have only just got up and Miss has taken all my time until now to dress her."

"You heard me calling them?"

"Perfectly, sir."

. . . So they had taken flight, chased by their troubled consciences and I spent two hours waiting for them, famished, broken by fatigue.

What a welcome after that week of work and regrets! And that piercing thought that she had run away, fled like a schoolgirl caught in the act!

At last she arrived! She found me asleep on the sofa, in a very bad mood, of course. She kissed me to forestall the storm as though nothing was the matter. But nerves cannot be commanded. You can't preach to a hungry man and a wrung heart is not dilated beneath perfidious kisses.

"Are you angry?"

"My nerves are angry, be careful with them."

"I am not your cook!"

"Far be it from me to want such a thing, but at least don't prevent the one we have from fulfilling her duties."

"You're forgetting, my dear, that Miss Amelia is within her rights when she requires the services of the maid. She is *our* paying guest."

"You didn't hear me calling you?"

"No."

She was lying! . . . It was heartrending.

Ah! the dinner—my sabbath dinner! . . . —a long torture. And the afternoon was spent in tears and Maria cursed marriage, the holy, happy marriage, the only happiness, weeping on the shoulder of her friend, covering her filthy "cur" with mad kisses.

Cruel, perfidious, lying—ah! the pretty sensitive heart!

And that was kept up with infinite variants, during the whole of the summer; I spent my Sundays between two imbeciles and a dog: I was persuaded that the misfortunes of the home arose from my unhinged nerves and that a visit to the doctor would be salutary for me.

162

I had promised myself long boating trips on the lake for the Sunday morning, but my darling was not visible before dinner. She was dressing, and my trip was solitary until dinner time; afterwards it was too late.

Ah! yes, the sensitive heart! which inflicted pin-pricks on me, which wept one morning because the gardener killed a rabbit for the meal and confessed to me in the evening on the pillow that she had prayed God that the poor animal might not suffer too much beneath the axe!

A pathologist has just classified the exaggerated love for animals associated with a simultaneous hardness of the heart for one's fellow beings amongst the symptoms of rational mania.

What does one think of this woman who prayed for a rabbit while martyring a man, with a smile on her lips?

The last Sunday that we spent in the country Maria took me aside, and flattering me for my generosity, appealing to my excellent, so clement character, she begged me to let Miss Amelia off paying her board, in view of her straitened circumstances.

I accepted without discussion, without saying that I was expecting the proposition, that I had foreseen the manoeuvre, that it was inevitable. But she, always armed to the teeth with repartees, even against answers which were not made to her, added to conclude:

"Besides I could, if it were necessary, pay for her!"

Agreed! But the worry and the troubles which she had reserved for me—could she pay for them as well? . . . —In short, one mustn't look so closely between husband and wife.

5

With the new year, a general crash shook the credit of the old country, and the bank from which Maria had lent me some shares went bankrupt. The termination of my loan ensued. I was obliged to cover the guarantee which I had furnished with my effective responsibility. It was a disaster. Fortunately, after interminable worries, the creditors granted a settlement, so that I managed to obtain a year's grace.

It was the terrible year, the most terrible of all.

Once calm was re-established, I sought to get back on my feet as soon as possible.

Simultaneously with my duties as librarian, I started a great novel* about contemporary behaviour; I filled the newspapers and the reviews with articles, while finishing the composition of my memoir. Maria, whose engagement at her theatre was expiring, obtained, through favour, its renewal for the year with a reduced salary of fourteen hundred francs . . . and there I was above her whom the crash had ruined.

In an execrable mood, she showered me with all her rancour, and, to re-establish equality between us, heeding only her independence, she attempted to obtain loans which only ended, as was to be expected, in recriminations against me. Through lack of intelligence, though motivated by excellent intentions, she was ruining me by seeking to save herself and to facilitate my task. And while being grateful to her for her goodwill, I could not abstain from reproaching her for her conduct.

Her cross-grained character inclined to underhandedness, and new incidents occurred which brutally revealed alarming states of her mind to me.

On the occasion of a masked ball which was given at the theatre, I formally made her promise not to disguise herself as a man. She promised me on oath, for I seemed to insist on it for reasons that I couldn't explain. Didn't I learn the following day that she had presented herself at the ticket office in a black suit and that she had supped with some gentlemen!

Besides the fact that the lie was most displeasing to me, the thought of that supper played on my nerves particularly.

"And so?" she retorted to my observations . . . "Aren't I free?"

"No," I replied, "you are married. And, since you bear my name, there is a solidarity between us. If you lose some of your reputation, my reputation also suffers by it, and even more than yours!"

---

* *The Red Room*, 1879

"Then, I am not free? . . ."

"No, there is no-one who is free in a society where everyone bears the fate of his neighbour rivetted to his own. In short . . . if you had seen me supping with some ladies, what would you say? . . ."

She declared herself free to act all the same, free to destroy my reputation as she liked, free in everything and for everything! Ah! the savage, who understands by liberty the sovereignty of the despot, who tramples the honour, the happiness of everyone underfoot.

After that scene, turning into a quarrel and ending in tears, in a fit of hysteria, another one followed all the more upsetting because I was not initiated into the mysteries of genetic life, the anomalies of which appeared sinister to me as all those which one cannot grasp at first sight.

One evening, then, when the maid was busy making Maria's bed in the room next to mine, I heard small cries of suffocation, smothered, nervous, laughter, as if provoked by ticklings. It produced a strange pain in me, and giving way to an inexplicable anxiety, all ready to dissolve into fury, I brusquely pushed the door, which was pushed to, and I surprised Maria with her hands plunged into the bodice of the open-bloused maid, with her avid lips near to the breasts dazzling with a pearly whiteness.

"What are you doing there, you wretches! You are really mad," I exclaimed with a thundering voice.

"Well! what? . . . I am playing with the maid," Maria answered me brazenly. "Is is your business?"

"Yes, it is my business. Come here."

And, face to face, I explained to her the incorrectness of her conduct.

But she attacked what she grossly called my "dirty fantasy". She accused me of being a depraved person, who only sees shameful actions everywhere. It is dangerous to catch a woman in the act. She poured night-pots of insults on my forehead.

In the course of that discussion, I reminded her of the love that she had formerly confessed, that senseless love for the cousin, pretty Matilda. In the most innocent of tones possible, she replied that she herself had been most astonished at that love, not believing, she said, "that it was possible for a woman to fall in love like that with another woman with such madness".

Calmed by that naïve admission, I recalled, indeed, that right in the middle of a gathering, Maria, at my brother-in-law's, had proclaimed her amorous sentiments for the cousin, without blushing, without even being aware that she was making a mistake.

But I grew angry, however. In restrained terms, I advised her to abstain from those manoeuvres, perhaps innocent in the beginning, but quickly breaking out and capable of having deplorable consequences.

165

She talked nonsense, called me an imbecile—she always dubbed me as the most ignorant of the ignorant—and finally declared to me that I was lying.

What was the use of explaining to her that the law condemned crimes of this nature to hard labour? What was the use of convincing her that those touchings, exciting the pleasure of the recipient, were, in medical books, classed among the vices?

It was I who was debauched, since I was instructed in all those vices! And nothing was able to drag her from her innocent games.

She was one of those unconscious villains which it would be better to lock up in institutions of special education for women, rather than keeping them in one's home.

6

Towards the end of spring she introduced a new friend into the house. This was one of her pretty theatre friends, a woman of thirty. Maria's companion in misfortune, she too was threatened with not being re-engaged and so she appeared to me worthy of pity. It hurt me to see this beauty, formerly so toasted, thrown on the streets for some unknown reason—unless it was because of the appearance on the stage of the Theatre Royal of a daughter of the great tragedienne and because a triumph always demands hecatombs of vanquished.

Nevertheless I found her antipathetic. She appeared to be a very conscious woman on the look-out for a prey. She seemed to want to flatter me, to fascinate me in order to bewilder the perspicacity of my gaze, the sagacity of which did not escape her.

And so from time to time there were scenes of jealousy between the old and the young friend and they vied in slandering each other, without my heeding them . . .

. . . Summer was ending when a new and indubitable pregnancy of Maria was revealed to us. According to our calculations the confinement would fall in February. It was a veritable thunderbolt. It was a question then of full sail ahead and reaching port before the fatal term expired.

I launched my novel in November. The success was resounding. Money rolled in and we were saved.

Arrived, singled out, known, acclaimed a master, I breathed after a year, after years of distress, and we envisaged the arrival of the child with an extraordinary joy. We had already baptised it prematurely and it received presents for Christmas. My wife displayed her pregnancy and our friends grew accustomed to asking after the "kid", just as though it were already there.

Having enough glory for my part, I resolved to rehabilitate Maria and save her compromised career. To this end I prepared a four-act play destined for the Theatre Royal. It contained the fine rôle of an amiable woman, in order to win back public favour for Maria.

On the day of the confinement I learned that the drama had been accepted and that the part was guaranteed for her.

Everything was for the best in the best of worlds and the broken tie between me and my relatives was reknit by the birth of the child.

The good time, the good season of my life, had arrived. There was bread in the house and even some flagons of wine. The mother, honoured, loved, starting to live again, and her faded beauty was blossoming afresh. All her wrongdoing towards the first dead baby was transformed into redoubled care for this one.

Summer came again and I was in a position to ask for a few

months' leave in order to rough it with my family in the greenery of an island on the edge of the Stockholm Archipelago.

At the same time I was reaping the harvest of my scientific works. My paper obtained the great honour of a reading at the *Institut de France* by the *Académie des Inscriptions et Belles-Lettres*. I was accepted as a member of several foreign learned societies and the medal of the Imperial Russian Geographical Society was conferred on me.

Having at the age of thirty reached a noteworthy position in letters and science, with a brilliant future before me, I felt happy to be able to lay my trophies at Maria's feet . . . but she grudged my having broken the existing equilibrium. Then I lowered myself more and more in order to spare her the humiliation of belonging to a superior man. Like the giant I allowed her to tug at my beard but she quickly took advantage of it. She liked to degrade me in front of the servants, in front of the friends received in the house—and women friends particularly. She was the one to show herself off, to expand, inflated by me and the more I lowered myself the more she trampled me down. I gave her illusions. She was the bestower of all my glory, which she ignored and pretended to scorn, and I enjoyed feeling beneath her. I liked to remain the husband of a charming woman to the extent that she ended up by really thinking herself in possession of my genius. And so it was in everyday matters. Being a very strong swimmer, I taught her to swim. I acted as though I were afraid in order to encourage her. She enjoyed ridiculing me, telling of her bravado in public and it brought me infinite pleasure.

Yet time passed by. In my adoration of the woman-mother, I did not heed the link which tied me to a woman of thirty. The dangerous period was beginning, however, and alarming signs were already apparent, perhaps without consequence for the moment but not exempt from germs of discord.

After the confinement the incompatibility of our bodies was joined to the incompatibility of our brains. Embraces became odious. She turned into a brazen coquette when very excited. She liked to make me jealous or indulged in worrying fancies, perhaps under the pressure of her frenetic and disorderly desires.

One fine morning we set out to sea in a sailing-boat, together with a young fisherman. I held the rudder and the mainsail while the boy took charge of the mizzen. He was with my wife. The wind dropped and a long silence settled on the boat. I noticed at once that the young fisherman was slyly sending, from under his cap, sidelong glances in the direction where my wife had probably placed her feet . . . Her feet? . . . and perhaps she was also showing him the bottom of her leg, for I was not in a position to see anything from where I was. I observed my wife. Her eyes were passionately scrutinising the boy's body. I made a brusque movement, as if I were dragging myself from some dream, in order to remind her of my presence. And Maria, taking hold of herself, lowered her eyes towards the tops of the boy's big boots and, clumsily, she freed herself from the awkwardness with this stupid remark:

"Do a pair of boots like that cost a lot? . . ."

How can I qualify such a silly reflection, I ask myself . . .

I proposed that we change places, with some pretext or other, in order to break the thread of her sensual ideas.

I tried to forget this moving and agonising scene, and I convinced myself that I'd seen incorrectly, though the memory of similar scenes came to my mind, when she would touch me with her burning eyes, following the lines of my body beneath my clothes.

My suspicions were to be reawakened, however, a week later, following an incident which almost destroyed all my hopes of having at last created a mother in this perverse being.

One of my friends came to spend twenty-four hours with us. He behaved in a friendly fashion towards Maria. She repaid his courtesy with demonstrations of a coquetry which was disagreeable to me. At nightfall, we parted, wishing each other good-night and Maria pretended to go to bed.

Half an hour later, I heard voices on the balcony. I hurried out and I caught my wife and my friend sitting down to a bottle of cognac. I put on a fairly good face, but the following day I showered her with reproaches for her insolence in so ridiculing me before the world.

She laughed, declared me to be a man of prejudices, attacked my "fanciful and dirty, etc." imagination . . . In short, she displayed arguments from her choicest repertoire.

I lost my temper, she performed her small scene of hysteria, to the extent that I asked her forgiveness for *my wrongs*. I say *my wrongs*, for I reproached her for her behaviour, indeed condemnable!

Her final word finished me off!

"Do you think then, my darling, that I would want to go through the troubles of a separation for a second time?"

With the thought of all the pangs recently undergone, I fell asleep in the peace of deceived husbands.

What, then, is a coquette? . . . A woman who makes advances. And coquettry is only an advance. Nothing more.

And jealousy? . . . That's the fear of losing the most precious thing one possesses . . . The jealous man? . . . That's a ridiculous man, for the ridiculous reason that he cannot make up his mind to lose his most precious possession . . .

169

(7)

I went from one success to another: the debts were paid and money poured in, but despite the large amount of my income that I put into the household, our affairs were always embroiled. Maria, who held the book of accounts and the till, was always asking for more. From there, terrible scenes.

Her dramatic career was decidedly broken. Naturally, I had to suffer all the consequences. The fault was mine . . . If she hadn't married me . . . Ah! Ah! The rôle that I had written for her was forgotten—and, indeed, she had absolutely ruined it, acting it without any kind of nuance.

It was about this time that, thanks to a play of the celebrated Norwegian male bluestocking*, that good joke called "women's emancipation" came up for discussion. Then, all the softened minds had the monomania of seeing *subjugated* women everywhere. As I refused to become the dupe of that absurd story, I was qualified as a *misogynist* for the rest of my life.

Following a quarrel in which I went as far as to tell Maria some home truths, she abandoned herself to a fit of violent hysterics. The greatest discovery of the nineteenth century in neuralgic therapeutics had just been made. And, as with all great things, how simple it was!

At the height of the howling of my patient, I grabbed a carafe of water and in a thundering voice I pronounced the magic formula.

"Get up or I'll drench you!"

At that very moment the howling stopped . . . and a look full of admiration, affectionate gratitude and mortal hate darted from the eyes of the Adored.

At first I was afraid but the reawoken male does not let go easily . . . For a second time I shook the carafe, shouting:

"Stop your row or I'll soak you! . . ."

She got up but it was only to call me a rogue, a wretch, a scoundrel, etc., signs that the cure had been wholly successful.

Husbands—deceived or not—believe me your sincere and most devoted friend. I hand you down the precious means of curing violent hysterics forever . . . Bear it in mind, it can come in handy.

From that day on my demise was inscribed in the notebook of a woman. She began to detest me—the Adored! I would be put to death, a redoubtable witness of feminine artifices. My material and moral destruction was decreed by the whole sex and my avenging fury undertook the ungracious and difficult task of torturing me to death.

---

* *Ibsen*

170

At first she installed her friend as a lodger in the house, in a furnished room of our apartment—and this after dreadful struggling between us. Maria even wanted to have her at our table—which I decidedly and vigorously opposed. However, despite my observations and precautions, I brushed against the skirts of the pretty friend everywhere in my house—to the extent that I could well imagine myself a bigamist. And the evenings which I would have liked to devote to my wife, I had to remain at home, for Maria shut herself in her friend's room, where they had a good time at my expense, smoking my cigars, drinking my punch. As for the friend, I began to detest her bitterly and as I did not hide—not enough—my way of thinking, I attracted Maria's invective whenever I happened to be lacking in courtesy towards "this poor child".

Now that she had estranged my wife from her husband and her own child—veritably abandoned to the hands of a vicious shrew of forty-five—the pretty friend debauched my cook: they got drunk together on my beer.

I found my servant sleeping at the edge of her stove, ruining the food, and their incredible consumption of my beer rose to almost five hundred bottles in a month. The pretty friend was no more than a man-eater who had chosen me as her prey.

One day Maria showed me a coat she wanted to buy. I liked neither the cut nor the colour and advised her to choose something else. The friend, who was present, kept it for herself and I forgot the incident. A fortnight later I received a bill in the name of my wife mentioning a coat. This signified that Maria, after having well and truly acquired all her procedure, had allowed herself to be led into blackmailing her husband through a ruse well-known in the *demi-monde* of actresses.

As usual, I was the one who had to undergo the wrath of the guilty, when I invited Maria to break off all relations with that adventuress . . .

Things went from bad to worse.

Some time later, my wife, imploring mercy, posing as the submissive wife, asked me very humbly to allow her to accompany, as a reference, the "poor child" who was going to an old friend of her late father in order to solicit a loan. The request appeared odd to me and—scenting a most dangerous trap, in view of the bad reputation of the friend, who was said to have had relations with old men—seized with horror, I begged Maria, in the name of her innocent child, to wake up from a torpor which would cause her to roll into some abyss . . . The only reply I obtained was a re-edition of the old patter: "It's your ignoble fantasy . . . etc.".

Everything went from worse to worse.

On the occasion of a luncheon offered by the beauty, who wanted to provoke a proposal of marriage by a famous actor, a new surprise came to drag me from my lethargy.

The champagne had been flowing freely and the ladies had got drunk as was her habit. Maria was slumped in an armchair, holding her pretty friend on her knees and kissing her time and again on the lips. Then, interested by the strange spectacle and as if to prove an accusation, the renowned actor drew a friend of his towards him and, designating the two women, exclaimed:

"Eh! You see? ..."

It was, without any doubt, an allusion to certain rumours and implications were hidden beneath the bantering tone.

What could I do?

When we arrived home, I begged Maria to cure herself of her voluntary blindness and, for the honour of our child, to avoid similar behaviour, scabrous for her reputation. Then, openly, she confessed that it gave her pleasure to see beautiful girls and to kiss their breasts, that the friend wasn't the only one of her companions whom she treated like this and that at the theatre, in their dressing-rooms, she had the same favours for other actresses; that she intended to continue for it was an ingenuous game which donned licentious appearances only in "my ignoble fantasy".

Impossible to make her understand what she was doing! There was only one way left for me. To bring on a new pregnancy in order to revive the maternal instincts in her . . . She became violently angry because of it, but her embarrassing situation kept her in her home for some months yet.

When her confinement was over, she inaugurated another style. She strove to pay court to men from that time onwards—yet too brazenly to make me seriously jealous—either because the fear of the consequences of her perverse appetites was making her disguise herself as a coquette, or because her feminine instincts had reappeared.

She now declared a war to the death on me—without an engagement, idle, capricious, an execrable despot.

Didn't she want, one day, to prove to me that it was cheaper to have three servants than two? At the end of my resistance against a lunatic, I took her by the arm and put her out.

She swore to wreak vengeance on me. She hired a third supernumerary maid and nothing more was done in the house. Everything went to rack and ruin, to the noise of the squabbling of our three servants, who got drunk on beer the whole day long and gave their lovers nuptial repasts at my expense.

To add to this picture of conjugal happiness, one of my children fell ill, which earned me the favour of seeing five servants in the home, not to mention two doctors. This put me five hundred francs in debt in a month. I redoubled my efforts to face it all but my nerves, I felt, were beginning to weaken.

She overwhelmed me into the bargain with eternal reproaches on the dilapidation of her imaginary dowry, obliged me to make an allowance to her aunt in Copenhagen, who came and accused me of having spent "her fortune", maddened me with unbelievable arguments, declaring that Matilda's mother had formally formulated on her death-bed that Maria was to share her part of the inheritance with her, the aunt! I could understand none of it. But one fact remained: it was that lazy, good-for-nothing and covetous aunt who fell into my care, when "the fortune" from that will had never existed except as a mirage. Nevertheless I accepted and I also went as far as to act as guarantor for a long-standing friend, the mysterious adventuress, who bore the number one. I committed myself to everything, since the Adored had now thought up the idea of selling me her favours and, to obtain an embrace I confessed my guilt for everything, for having wasted her dowry, squandered her aunt's fortune, broken her dramatic career by marrying her, even having undermined her health.

From that moment on there was the triumph of legal prostitution in my home, introduced into the marriage.

And it was following all these concessions I made her that she elaborated the legend on my misdoings which later was to have currency in the scandal press, hawked by all her friends whom I had successively thrown out . . .

A mad rage seized her. She wanted to ruin me. At the end of the year, I had made over to her twelve thousand francs for the expenses of the home and I was now obliged, nonetheless, to take advances from my publishers.

If I had complained of our exorbitant budget:

"One doesn't have children then," she retorted, "one doesn't put one's wife into penury! And to think that I had a fine position and that I left it to marry that! . . ."

But I had an answer to that:

"As a Baroness, my child, your husband brought you only three thousand francs and debts. I bring you more than three times that!"

She added nothing; she made me fast! To the extent that, when night came, I agreed to all she wanted. Yes, three thousand constitutes three times two thousand, yes, I am a wretch, yes, I am a miser, a "fair friend" who had risen to success at the expense of an adored woman, especially adored when in undress for the night!

To get rid of her bile, she composed the first chapter of a novel which dealt with the theme of the woman slave, exploited by a guilty man, whereas her silhouette of a soft blonde, of a madonna, of a little mother, passed into all my writings, which sang her praises, erecting into an immortal legend that marvel of a woman, entered by the grace of god into the dolorous existence of a poet . . . And her accursed personage, during this time, paraded, surrounded by an undeserved gloriole, beneath the pens of the critics who did not tire of exalting that good genius of a pessimistic novelist!

And the more I suffered from the perversities of my Maenad, the more I sought to aureolise her head of Saint Mary! The more reality brutally crushed me, the more the hallucinations of the Adored inflamed me! . . . Oh! love!

8

Sometimes I was led to believe that that woman had begun to hate me and that she wanted to get rid of me to take a third husband.

Sometimes I even went as far as to suspect her of having taken a lover, for unknown reflections were discovered in the expressions of her physiognomy and the coldness of her attitudes with me reinforced those suspicions.

Suddenly, ferocious jealousy rose up, upsetting the marriage; and hell, wide open, loomed before us for the future.

She suddenly declared herself ill. She was smitten, she said, with a vague, imprecise, elusive illness, which she ended up by locating somewhere, alternately in the back or in the spine, at some other moment in the kidneys, she couldn't say exactly where.

I sent for the children's usual doctor, an old university friend. He diagnosed that she had rheumatic knots on the muscles of her back and prescribed massage. I found nothing to object to in this measure since her case was clearly determined, and Maria began the daily sessions at once. As I was not in the know about the delicate methods of her treatment, I remained immersed in my literary works and the cure went on without my paying any attention to it. The illness of my wife did not necessarily seem to me to be, moreover, of the gravest, since she came and went, as she was wont, visiting the theatres and her friends, whose homes she was always the last to leave.

One evening, amongst friends, a guest complained of the lack of feminine doctors in modern society. He claimed it was odious for a woman to have to undress before a stranger, and turning to Maria:

"Isn't it? . . . It's a very disagreeable sensation?"

"Hm! . . . in front of my doctor! . . ."

Only then did I grasp the nature of those sessions of massage, and merely at the sight of Maria's expression of voluptuous ferocity, observed for some time already, I felt my heart anguished by a horrible suspicion.

So she undressed in front of that fellow of loose morals, openly recognised as an arch-libertine.

And I didn't know it! . . .

Alone together, I begged her to give me particulars.

In a frivolous tone, she told me what went on.

She kept her underskirts on, but her chemise was pulled down and her entire back was naked.

"And you're not ashamed?"

"Why should I be ashamed?"

"Because you pretend you are ashamed in front of me."

Two days afterwards, my doctor came to the house to see to one of my children. From my room, I surprised a more than strange conversation between the doctor and my wife. And laughter and muffled words murmured hand over mouth . . .

Immediately my door opened and the two interlocutors penetrated into my room, with banter on their lips.

Overwhelmed with black ideas, I clumsily engaged the conversation which touched lightly on sick women.

"You're an expert, old boy, in women's illnesses . . . eh?" I said to the doctor.

Maria looked at me. Her look was that of a fury. I discovered so much hatred in it that a shudder passed down my spine. The doctor gone, she broke loose and dashed at me.

"Whore!" I spat in her face, irresistibly.

The word had escaped me against my will, the expression of an unflecting intuition. And so, by ricochet, the insult touched my heart and, when I noticed, there, in front of us, the children, I implored forgiveness on my knees, on my knees and in tears.

She played the fury. Two hours of supplications couldn't sway her.

In order to make amends for the immense wrong which I acknowledged and under the influence of her growing hatred, I conceived the project of procuring a journey of pleasure and recreation in Finland for her, a theatrical tour of a few weeks.

I began negotiations then with theatre directors and, the affair concluded, I looked for the necessary money.

She left, won patriotic victories and family laurels.

Having remained alone with the children in the country, I fell ill, and believing myself at my last gasp I called her back by telegram, which did not impinge on her journey, since her performances had all been given.

She returned and, finding me on my feet and restored, she accused me of having dragged her from the innocent pleasures which she was enjoying with her family by a lying telegram! . . .

However a new deviation came about in her indecipherable character, after that return, which gave me fresh apprehensions.

Contrary to her habit, she gave herself absolutely to my embraces.

"How come that all fear of pregnancy has disappeared?" I asked myself without wishing to question her about it . . .

The day after and the following days, she spoke to me only of her enjoyment of Finland, and in a surge of intoxication at the memory, she told me that she had made the acquaintance of an engineer on the boat. An enlightened, modern talker, that man had convinced her that sin did not exist in the world, that everything depended only on the circumstances and Destiny.

"Very well, my darling, but our actions still continue to have consequences for all that. I admit that sin does not exist since there is no God in a personal form, but we are still held responsible before the men whom we have wronged: and, despite the absence of sin, crime remains, as long as the law is still in force. Despite the suppression of the theological notion of sin, revenge, or better, vengeance, none the less persists, always directed against whoever has inflicted injury on us.

She suddenly became serious, yet feigned not to have understood. At last she retorted:

"It's only the wicked who avenge themselves!"

"Agreed: but there are so many wicked people in the universe that one is never sure of meeting with a hero who receives wounds without returning them."

"All the same Destiny dominates our actions."

"Agreed, but it is also Destiny which guides the dagger of the avenger."

. . . At the end of the month, a miscarriage occurred.

Adultery seemed sufficiently proven to me! And from that moment the suspicions accumulated and harshened, while her attacks took on alarming proportions.

Then she thought up a way of convincing me that I was "mad"! To hear her, my suspicions only came from an overworked brain.

Once more I accepted her forgiveness for my wrongs and, as a token of reconciliation, I composed the drama of a woman with a great rôle impossible to ruin especially for her. On the seventeenth of August I delivered the manuscript to her with a deed of gift. The drama belonged to her in all rights. She was free to have it performed, anywhere, on the condition that the rôle would be entrusted to her. It was a gift of two months' frantic work. She received it without gratitude as a sacrifice performed on the altar of Her Majesty the Downfallen Starlet!

During this time, the home was going straight to ruination and I couldn't do anything about it since all advice, all intervention on my part was repelled like outrages. And I remained inert, impotent before the ravages operated by the servants, the squandering of the provisions, the absolute lack of supervision of the children.

To the economic miseries were added the quarrels.

On her return from her trip to Finland, the expenses of which were deducted from my personal account, she brought back two hundred francs, the product of her performances. As it was she who held the till, I carried the sum in my head for the household budget. But well before the time fixed she came to ask me for money again. Surprised by that unexpected demand, I risked a discreet question on the employment of her money. She had lent it to her friend and, citing the law, she claimed to have the free disposal of what she earned through her work.

177

"And what about me then!" I said to her . . . "But to subtract money from the household is not to dispose of it."

"It's not the same thing for a woman!"

"That only counts for a subjugated woman, doesn't it! For the woman-slave who tolerates a man bringing her everything to do with subsistence? Those are the consequences of that good joke the emancipation of woman."

All that Emile Augier had predicted in *Les Fourchambault* relative to the dowry system had been accomplished. The husband had become the serf. And to think that there are men who have allowed themselves to be deceived to the extent of digging their own graves! You poor fools!

While the ribbon of the misery of my marriage was being unravelled, I took advantage of my literary successes to uproot the prejudices and to topple the outdated superstitions which weighed on our old-fashioned society; in a volume of satires*, I threw a handful of stones onto the most noteworthy charlatans of the capital, including the sexless women.

I was incriminated as a pamphleteer; Maria lost no time. In order to extricate herself personally from the matter, she made an alliance with the enemy. Day and night she played the respectable woman, complaining of me everywhere: what a misfortune to be rivetted to a scandalous man! And now she was forgetting that behind the libeller there was a great novelist-dramatist.

A sacred martyr, she showed worry for the future of her unfortunate children, who would undergo the consequences of the dishonest actions of a father who had squandered her dowry, broken her artistic career and ill-treated her into the bargain. At the same time, a newspaper launched an item in which it informed the public that I had become mad, while a brochure made up to order, paid for in cash, spread the whole sad legend from Maria and her women friends, registering all the insanities imagined by that muddy brain of a woman.

She had won the game.

And now that she saw me succumbing beneath the blows of the enemy, she rose up, attributing to herself the rôle of holy mother of a prodigal child, and, charming with everybody except with her husband, she rallied all my false or sincere friends around her. Isolated, at the mercy of a vampire, I renounced all kind of defence. To raise my hand against the mother of my angels and against the Adored! . . .

No, never!

I gave in. Then she surrounded me with her tendernesses, only out of the house, for in the home there were only outrages and scorn for me.

---

* *The New Kingdom* (1882)

Broken by the excess of work and the maltreatment, I fell ill. Head-aches, nervous irritability and stomach pains! . . . The doctor diagnosed catarrh of the stomach.

It was a fairly unexpected outcome of the intellectual over-exertion!

A curious detail, that ailment only manifested itself after my formal decision to go abroad, the only means for me of escaping from the net of those innumerable friends who brought perpetual condolences to my wife. In short, I only suffered from that mysterious malady the day after a visit to the laboratory of one of my old friends, from whom I had taken a phial of cyanide of potassium destined to cause my death: and I had placed that phial under lock and key, in one of the pieces of furniture of my wife!

Paralysed, thunderstruck, I remained outstretched on the sofa, looking at my children who were playing, thinking of the beautiful days of former times and preparing myself to die, without leaving a word in writing to reveal the causes of my decease and my sad suspicions.

I resigned myself to disappear, assassinated by a woman whom I pardoned.

The lemon was squeezed. From the corner of her eye Maria was observing me, wondering if I would not soon be leaving for the other world, so that she might be able to enjoy in peace the revenue which the sale of the complete works of the celebrated poet would raise for her, and the State pension which she would certainly manage to grab for the children . . .

. . . Puffed up with pride as a result of the success that she won at the theatre with my drama, a solid success which had earned her the qualification of great tragedienne, she obtained the permission to play a new rôle of her own choice. She failed completely, and as she recognised that it was I who had created, rehabilitated her, her debtor's hatred only increased. She made the rounds of all the manage-ments in search of an engagement, without succeeding in finding one, and ended up by forcing me to re-open the negotiations with Finland. Again I was ready to leave my country, my friends, my publishers, to settle in the midst of her friends, my enemies. But the Finns wanted nothing of her: her career was ended.

Now and during this time she was leading the existence of an idle woman, freed from all her duties of wife and of mother, and when my health forbade my attending the meetings of artists, she went there alone. Sometimes even she only returned in the morning, drunk, and making such a row as to wake up the whole house and I heard with nausea the noise of her vomitings in the children's room where she slept.

What could one do in such a case? Denounce one's wife? No. Divorce? No, since the family had become an organism like that of a plant for me, a whole of which I was an integrating part. Alone I could not exist, nor alone with the children, without their mother; the transfusion of my blood was operated through great arteries, flowing out from my heart to ramify into the uterus of the mother and to spread into the little bodies of my children. It was a system of blood-vessels which interwove into each other. If one cut off a single one of them, life would escape from me with the blood which the sand would drink. That was why the adultery of the wife was a horrible crime. That was why one might be tempted to obey the watchword: "Kill her!" given by the famous writer, when the father is mortally wounded by his uncertainty of his descendance, falsified by a mother without scruples.

Inversely, Maria, won over to the exorbitant ideas for the extension of feminine liberties and rights, rallied to the new theories, namely that the wife who deceives her husband is not guilty, since she is not his property.

I could not lower myself into spying and I did not want any proof for that would be tantamount to a death blow for me. Then I enjoyed fooling myself ceaselessly, living in an imaginary world which I poetised at my will.

And all the same I felt wounded: I knew that the descendance of my race was polluted and that the children which, before posterity, would bear my name, which would be fed from the revenue of my work, were not mine. I loved them nevertheless, for they had entered into my existence in order to be the life of the future, and now that that hope of surviving myself was withdrawn from me I hovered in space, a phantom breathing air through adventive roots.

Maria seemed to grow impatient at the adjournment of my funeral and, although she spoiled me like a mother in the presence of witnesses, she pinched me in secret as the little juggler is pinched by his father in the wings. In order to hasten my decease she ill-treated me. She invented a new torture, attacking my accidental weakness, treating me as senile; at the peak of her mania of grandeur, she threatened to strike me, declaring herself stronger than me. She went as far as to dash at me. But I got up then, and, taking hold of her by the wrists, I threw her onto the sofa.

"Admit then that I am still the stronger despite my weakness!"

She made no concession and, with a sheepish air, furious at being mistaken, she left me, defying me.

In the struggle, she preserved all her advantages of a woman and of an actress in relation to me. Think of it, reader, the man condemned to a hard labour at all hours was without defence against an idle woman, who had all her day to spin intrigues: so that at the end of a certain time he found himself shut into a network woven on all sides around him.

Besides, when she accused me of impotence throughout the world, with the goal of having herself pardoned for her crime, didn't modesty, honour, pity order me to keep silent about her bodily defect, contracted at the moment of her first confinement, aggravated by the three following, and known in anatomical terms by the name of a rupture of the perineum. A man, who never entrusts his matrimonial secrets to anyone whatsoever—would he get it into his head to hawk about the flaws of his wife!

Impotent! It was always I whose fervour, unabatedly, solicited her favours and how many repugnant concessions to quench it! . . . She had no cause to complain, certainly; but, with the nature of a bitch, she had to have a taste of everything even at the cost of her happiness or of that of her children!

"In love," said Napoleon, a great connoisseur of women, "there are no victories except when one takes flight!" But flight is not possible for guarded prisoners, and for those condemned to death it is quite impossible . . .

While I was reposing, my brain recovered and, freed from my work, I prepared myself to escape from that fortress guarded by a shrew and my friends, her dupes. Having recourse to a ruse of war, I had our doctor receive a letter, admitting to him the apprehensions I had of soon becoming mad and proposing, as a palliative, a trip abroad. The reply was to ratify my proposal and I hastened to communicate this decree without appeal to Maria:

"The doctor's ordered it for me!"

It was a term that she herself employed when she prescribed the doctor to order what she liked.

She grew pale as she received the news.

"I do not want to leave my country."

"Your country? . . . That's Finland and besides I can hardly see what you could miss in Sweden, where you have neither a relative nor a friend, nor a theatre."

"I don't want to leave . . ."

"Because? . . ."

After a hesitation she finished:

". . . because you frighten me! I don't want to remain alone with you."

"A lamb that you lead on a string frightens you? Come, come . . . it's not the real reason."

"You're a wretch and I don't want to stay beside you without protection!"

She must have had a lover, or else the fact was that she feared lest I survive if her crime were discovered.

So I frightened her, I who played the fawning dog, I who dragged myself in the mire to adore her white foot, I, who had let my leonine mane fall beneath the scissors to reduce it to the tuft that a horse wears, I who had turned up my moustache and worn turned-down collars in order to be able to better enter into combat with her redoubtable lovers!

Her fear inspired me with still more fear and revived my suspicions:

"That woman has a lover whom she does not want to leave or else she dreads her judgement," I said to myself inwardly.

After endless disputes she wheedled the promise from me that we would at least return in the course of the year.

And I promised.

The will to live returned to me and I set about work in order to end a collection of poems* which were to appear in the winter, after my departure.

And in the heart of that summer, my strength having returned, I sang; I sang the Adored especially, whose blue veil floating on her straw hat on the day of the first meeting had become for me the ensign that I hoisted to the top of the mast setting out towards the stormy sea.

One evening, in a small gathering I read the poem in the presence of a friend. Maria listened to me, piously enraptured. The reading over, she burst into sobs, rose and came to kiss me on the forehead.

A consummate actress, she had thus fooled my friend. An imbecile, he ranged me from that day amongst the jealous madmen, when heaven, he would say, had granted me the most loving wife!

"She loves you, old boy," the young man assured me!

And four years later he made a display of this scene amongst the most convincing proofs to be given on the fidelity of my wife.

"I swear to you that she was sincere at that moment," he would repeat.

"Sincere in her remorse, yes! . . . before that love which sang of the whore, transmuting her into a madonna! . . . I can well imagine!"

You poor thing, get away with you!

---

* *Poems in Verse and Prose* (1883)

9

However, and at last, the house was rid of women friends.

The last, the beauty, had disappeared in the company of my best friend, an illustrious scholar who had returned from an expedition with four decorations and an assured future. Homeless again, the beauty who had been dwelling in my apartment for nothing grasped the opportunity, attached herself to the poor fellow, reduced to forced celibacy for a year, and having seduced him in a hired cab in the sombre night under pretext of taking him somewhere, she forced him to wed her by creating a disturbance in the house of a third party where they had both been invited. Out of trouble, the beauty did not delay in throwing off the mask. At a soirée, being drunk, she forgot herself and called Maria a depraved being. A friend who was attending the soirée felt obliged to report the remark to me.

In three phrases Maria proved the accusations absurd, and I from then on closed my door to the lady, thereby depriving myself of all relationship with my friend the scholar, definitely lost to me.

Although I was hardly curious to research into those words "depraved being", it was nonetheless a thorn planted in my bleeding flesh. However, new insults fallen from the same impure mouth concerning the shady conduct of Maria during her trip to Finland, added to my old suspicions, which, when related to the incidents of the miscarriage, of that conversation which we had held on the philosophy of Destiny and to the freedom that she left me in our relations, confirmed me in my decision to flee.

Maria, having perceived the excellent profit which could be realised out of an infirm poet, appointed herself sister of charity, sick nurse, and, when necessary, mental nurse.

She wove herself a saint's crown, acted with full powers behind my back and—I discovered this later—extended her attentions to the extent of raising loans, for my so-called account, from my friends. At the same time, precious pieces of furniture were disappearing from the apartment, which were left with adventuress number one, to be put up for sale by her.

All that attracted my attention and for the first time I asked myself this worrying question:

"Could it not be that Maria was making secret outlays, in view of the mysterious transactions that I am discovering and the enormous expense of the household? In that case, to what end? . . ."

I was now drawing the salary of a minister, more than an army general, and I was dragging penury about like a ball on my leg. Our way of life however was of the simplest! We had the food of the lower middle-class, badly prepared, often uneatable, the drinks of the worker, the beer and the schnapps; the cognac was of bad quality in

183

our home; our guests had even given the house a reputation for that; I only smoked a pipe; I never had an enjoyment, except on the evenings of great rejoicing, once a month, when I went out to bestir myself.

Only once, being beside myself, did I bother to examine the question. I consulted a well-informed lady about it. As I was asking her if the budget of my household was not too high, she laughed in my face on hearing the enormous sum of our expenditure, and assured me that it was pure folly.

So there was reason to believe in extraordinary and secret outlays. But on what? Relatives, aunts, women friends, lovers whom she was then maintaining? Who would reveal that to a husband, everyone, for I know not what reasons, appointing themselves the accomplices of the adulteress! . . .

At last, after interminable preparations, the day of the departure was fixed. But then, another difficulty which I had foreseen cropped up, bringing in its wake a series of lachrymose scenes! The King Charles was still alive. How many worries had he not brought me already? Especially because the care which he was given was taken from that which was due to the children.

However, the moment had come when Maria's idol and my evil genius was going to end his days, old, ulcerated, stinking, dirty, to my inexpressible joy! Basically, I was convinced, Maria wanted the death of that animal; but thinking of the innocent pleasure that his disappearance would give me and in view of the annoyance that she felt at the very idea of offering me an enjoyment, she prolonged that affair of the King Charles and invented ingenious tortures to make me, in any case, pay dearly for the days of hoped-for bliss.

She arranged, then, a farewell feast, organised heartrending scenes, and finally left for town, carrying off the monster, after having had a chicken killed, the bones of which were served to me at dinner, in view of the fact that I was of a sickly constitution. After having absented herself for two days, she announced her return in cold terms . . . as was befitting, when addressing "the assassin". Drunk with happiness, delivered of six years of bitterness, I went to meet her at the boat, sure now of seeing her there alone again. She welcomed me as a poisoner, with big tears, and repelled me when I wanted to kiss her. Taking hold of a large parcel of unusual form, she made her way towards the house as though behind a procession, in a step rhythmed by some invisible funeral march. The parcel hid the corpse! Heavens! The burial was in store for me, a final stroke of destiny! One man was necessary to build the coffin, two men to dig the grave and, holding myself aloof, I was obliged to attend the funeral of the assassinated. How edifying it was then! Maria retired within herself and prayed the good God for the victim and for the murderer. To the laughter of the populace, she planted a cross on the tomb, the cross of the

Saviour, who had delivered me—at last!—of a monster, innocent in itself but terrible as the incarnation of all the wickednesses of a woman whom cowardice prevented from tormenting a man openly.

After some days of high mourning, without kisses—for she did not want to kiss a poisoner—we left for Paris.

FOURTH PART

(1)

I had chosen Paris as the principal goal of my journey in order to meet friends of long standing there, initiated into my eccentricities, intimates, versed in my stray impulses, knowing full well the fancies of my mind, my paradoxes, my audacities and consequently in a position to judge the present mental state of their poet. Furthermore, the most celebrated Scandinavian writers had then settled in Paris and I wanted to place myself under their protection in order to be able to better outwit the criminal schemes of Maria, who aimed at nothing less than to have me locked up in an asylum.

During the journey, Maria's anger did not wane and having no witnesses to be careful of she treated me like a negligeable object. With an ever preoccupied expression, with distracted looks, she remained indifferent to everything. In vain did I take her through the towns where we were to spend the night; she was interested in nothing, saw nothing, scarcely heeded me. My attentions embarrassed her and she seemed to be languishing. For what? For that country where she had suffered, where she did not leave a single friend . . . but a lover perhaps!

Besides, she behaved like the least practical and most badly brought up of women; I discovered that she had none of those superior qualities of organiser, of administrator, qualities which she attributed to herself. She had us led to the leading hotels, and for the single night that we had come to sleep there, ordered the rearrangement of the furniture, insisted upon the *maître d'hôtel* for a cup of badly-served tea, made a formidable din in the corridors, which brought humiliating observations upon us. In order to remain in bed until lunchtime, she made us miss the few agreeable trains we might have taken; through her fault, our baggage went astray in faraway stations and when we left the hotel she generously left a mark for the service.

"You're a coward," she replied to my observations.

"And you are only a negligent woman without education!"

Ah! The frightful pleasure trip that that beautiful journey was!

Arrived in Paris, in the midst of my friends who refused to let themselves be charmed by her attractions, she noticed that she had the worst of it and felt herself caught in a trap. What irritated her most was a relationship which I had struck up with one of the most illustrious literati of Norway*, who surrounded me with affection. She abhorred him, naturally, since one day the word of that man could rise in my favour.

One evening, at a dinner of artists and men of letters, the latter proposed a toast to me as the leader of contemporary Swedish literature, and that in the presence of my poor Maria, the martyr of

* *Bjørnson*

188

a marriage concluded with the ill-famed pamphleteer, so her sexless women friends said. It saddened me to see her crushed beneath the acclamations of the guests which resounded in my honour, and when the orator wanted to make me promise to remain at least two years in France, I could no longer resist the dolorous looks of my wife. To console her a little, to offer something of a reparation, I replied that in my home no important resolutions were ever taken except by the two of us, which earned me a warm look from Maria and the sympathy of all the ladies present.

But my friend did not want to give up. Insisting on the prolongation of my stay, in an oratorical flourish, he begged the guests to join with him and they all raised their glasses in order to support the proposal.

I admit that I have not yet been able to explain to myself that friendly obstinacy, although I then grasped something of the silent combat which was being waged between my wife and him, while not knowing the reason for it. That man was probably better informed than myself and with his ready-witted perspicacity, he had penetrated my secrets no doubt, being married himself to a woman of very singular morals.

Mysteries hitherto hidden!

After a stay of three months in Paris, where she felt ill at ease, the value of her husband being admitted, indisputable, my wife began to hate the great town. She put me on my guard incessantly against "the false friends who would end up one day or another by bringing me misfortune" so she said.

With a new pregnancy, hell was to reopen for me.

However, this time, I did not think it possible to doubt my paternity. I was in a position to fix the date and certain incidents even reminded me of the moment of the conception, with the circumstances.

We left for French Switzerland; and there, as soon as we were settled in a middle-class pension, in order to avoid thereby all quarrels relative to the housekeeping, she made up for lost time, for once more she held me, isolated and without protection.

From the first moment she presented herself to everyone as the guardian of a harmless lunatic. She struck up an acquaintanceship with the doctor, warned the master and the mistress of the pension, and even cautioned the whole lot of the servant girls, lackeys and boarders. I was sequestrated, deprived of contact with the people who could have been on a level with my intelligence or in a position to understand me. At the dining-table, it was she, the good imbecile, who avenged herself for the silence which she had to observe perforce in Paris. She took the floor at every turn, talking nonsense for which I had reproached her a thousand times already. And when that world of illiterate bourgeois gave its assent to her sillinesses out of politeness,

I could only fall silent and there she was perfectly convinced of her superiority.

However, she had a puny, sickly expression as if a worry was gnawing her, and her hatred towards me was absolute.

All that I loved, she detested. She decried the Alps since I vaunted them, she abhorred walks, she shunned every tête-à-tête with me. She practised anticipating my wishes in order to thwart them; she said "yes" when I said "no" or vice versa; in short, she hated me to the point of disgust!

And I, alone in that foreign country, I was constrained to solicit her company; when our conversations were suspended for fear of a quarrel, I was content to see her at my side, to feel the sensation of not being isolated in that place.

The pregnancy declared, I no longer believed myself obliged to be careful in our love-making; as there were no more reasons for refusing me, she invented allegations in order to tease me and when she saw my satisfaction after our free embraces, she grudged me that full joy which had come to me from her.

It was also too much happiness for me, whose nervous malady resulted especially from continence! At the same time my gastralgic ailment was aggravated to the point that I could take nothing other than broth and at night I would wake up with frightful stomach cramps and insupportable burnings that I sought to calm by absorbing cold milk.

My refined brain, developed through a perfected instruction, became unhinged at the contact with an inferior brain and every attempt to attune it to my wife's brought me spasms. I then tried with strangers. Alas! they dealt carefully with me in conversation, as one deals carefully with a madman!

Then, during three consecutive months I kept silent. At the end of that time I noticed with horror that my voice had faded, through lack of exercise, and that I no longer had the use of the spoken word.

As compensation, I started a brisk correspondence with my friends in Sweden. Their reserved language, their dolorous sympathy, their paternal advice demonstrated to me the conviction that they had of the breakdown of my mental state.

She triumphed. I was on the point of being a dodderer and the first symptoms of persecution mania came to light.

... Mania? Why that word? I was persecuted! So, it was perfectly logical that I thought myself persecuted!

The long and short of it was that I returned to childhood. Extremely weak, I spent hours on a sofa, with my head placed on Maria's knees, girdling her waist with my arms, in the position of Michaelangelo's *Pietà.* I pressed my brow against her breast, she called me her child and I repeated: "Yes, your child". The male was

190

waning in the arms of the mother who ceased to be a woman. Sometimes she looked at me like a triumpher, sometimes she eyed me softly, moved by the sudden tenderness which comes to the executioner before his victim. She was like the female spider who devours her husband after having conceived by him.

During those agonies, Maria led a mysterious way of life. She stayed in bed until lunchtime, about one in the afternoon. Then she left for town, without a definite goal and only returned for supper, most often late. When I was asked where my wife was, I replied: "She's in town."

And everyone went off laughing up their sleeves.

Never did a suspicion cross my mind. I did not think of spying on her.

After supper, she spent her evening in the drawing-room, prattling with strangers.

At night, she drank cognac with the maid and I could hear them chattering in hushed voices without managing to impose upon myself the degradation of going to listen at their door . . .

Why? Because there are actions which one ought not to allow oneself.

Why? Because that has slipped into my education as a kind of male religion.

Three months melted away and I woke up most suprised to see the expenses of our household so high. Now that the outlays were controlled it was easy for me to calculate.

The pension cost us twelve francs a day. That was three hundred and sixty francs a month then and I had given Maria a thousand francs a month. There had thus disappeared six hundred francs a month in false expenses.

"That money has gone in extraordinary expenses," she replied, furious, when I asked her for the accounts.

"Come now, three hundred and sixty francs of ordinary outgoings and six hundred extraordinary ones! You take me for a simpleton then?"

"You have given me a thousand francs, it's true, but you have taken back most of it for yourself."

I began a sum.

"Agreed! Let's see . . . tobacco (very bad), including cigars at ten centimes: ten francs . . . postage: ten francs . . . And then . . . what . . ."

"Your fencing lessons! . . ."

"I had one: three francs."

"Horse racing! . . ."

"Two hours: five francs."

"Books! . . ."

191

"Books? Ten francs . . . that makes . . . thirty–eight, let's put down a hundred francs. That leaves five hundred francs for the false expenses . . . That's hard to swallow! . . ."

"Then, you suppose that I am robbing you? . . . You're nothing but a wretch, now!"

What could I reply?—Nothing! . . . I was a wretch and, the following day, all her women friends in Sweden were informed by her of the progress of my madness.

Thus the legend was gradually being formed. From year to year my personality was becoming defined in its contours and, instead of the innocent poet, it was a mythological figure which was sketched, blackened, shaded, verging on the criminal type.

An attempted escapade in Italy where I was to meet some fellow artists failed and we returned to the banks of Lake Geneva for Maria's confinement. The child brought into the world, my wife, taking on the aureole of a martyr, of a subjugated wife, of a slave without rights, begged me to have the newborn baptised. She was not unaware that in my clamorous writings I had just openly confessed the disgust that I have of the superstitions of Christianity, which consequently forbids my practising the rites of that Church.

Although she was not at all religious, although she had not put her foot inside a church for ten years, although she had not communicated since I know not when and only said prayers for dogs, chickens or rabbits, she dreamed only of that baptism in great pomp. No doubt, it was because she knew of my desire to be rid thenceforward of those ceremonies, which I judged hypocritical for my part and clashing with my doctrines!

With tears in her eyes, she implored me, appealing to my kindness, recalling my generosity, and I gave in on the condition that I at least would be exempted from attending the ceremony. Whereupon, she kissed my hands, thanking me with effusion for that token of love, for that baptism was a "veritable case of conscience" for her, something like a vital question.

The baptism took place. Now, after her return from the ceremony, in the presence of witnesses, she laughed at "that comedy", playing the freethinker, ridiculing that rite, boasting of not knowing anything about that persuasion into which her son had just been received.

She scoffed at it once the game was won and the "vital question" was reduced to a victory won over me, which from then on gave my adversaries a hold over my person.

I had vilified, compromised myself once more to satisfy the caprices of a woman maddened for power!

But now came the most serious thing of all. A girl arrived from Scandinavia, imbued with all the mad ideas of emancipation, and since she presented herself as a friend right from the start I was a lost man.

She brought with her the cowardly book of someone sexless, who, disowned and rejected by all factions, behaved as a traitor to men by concluding an alliance with all the bluestockings of the civilised world. After reading *Man and Woman* by Emile de Girardin, I had for my part grasped all the consequences of that movement in favour of women.

To want to unseat man, replace him by woman, going back to matriarchy, to dethrone the true master of creation, he who created civilisation, spread the benefits of culture, the progenitor of great thoughts, of the arts, of the crafts, of everything, to raise the dirty beasts of women who have never taken part in civilising work—or almost never—with a few futile exceptions—that was to my mind a provocation to my sex. And at the very idea of seeing those bronze-age minds, those anthropomorphs, semi-apes, that horde of evil-doing animals coming to the forefront, the male rose up within me. A curious fact to be noted, I was cured of my illness, dispelled by a hate-ridden wish to resist against an enemy inferior in intellect and all-too-superior in her complete lack of moral sense.

Since it appears that in a war to the death between two peoples the less honest, the more perverse, must win the day, since the chances of winning the battle are very dubious for a man in view of the inborn respect he professes for woman, not to count the advantages he offers her, a breadwinner who allows her free time to prepare herself better for the fight—I took the question seriously; I equipped myself for the new combat and I immediately prepared a volume which was to my mind like the glove thrown in the face of emancipated women, of those madwomen who desire freedom at the price of man's bondage.

Spring approached and we changed our *pension*. I soon found myself in a sort of purgatory, where twenty-five women who watched over me provided me with the necessary elements for the diatribe* which I composed against those usurpers of the husband's rights.

At the end of three months the volume was ready. It was a collection of stories on marriage preceded by a preface in which I enunciated a lot of disagreeable home truths, in the following style:

Woman is not at all a slave since she and her children are fed from the work of man. Woman is never subjugated since she chooses her rôle, since nature has bestowed her lot upon her, which is to remain under the protection of man during the accomplishment of her maternal functions. Woman is not the equal of man in intellect and man is not the equal of woman in the realm of procreation. Woman is thus superfluous in the great work of civilisation since man understands his business better than she and, according to the theory

---

* *Married* (1884)

of evolution, the greater the differences in sex, the stronger is the offspring. So "masculinism" or the equalisation of the sexes is a step backward, a retrogression, an absurdity, the last dream of the romantic and idealistic socialists.

Woman, the male's necessary appendage, man's spiritual creation, has no right to the rights of the husband, since she forms "the other half" of humanity only in the numerical sense, proportionally forming merely the sixth part of a sixth. Let women then leave man's labour market unviolated, while he remains with the obligation of providing for the upkeep of the wife and children—and may it be well noted that every job grabbed from a man will have as its inevitable consequence one more spinster or prostitute.

Imagine the fury of the *masculinists* and think of the redoubtable faction they formed, since they were able to try and get the book confiscated by provoking a lawsuit.

Unfortunately all their wits did not suffice to realise that enterprise, disguised under the charge of blasphemy against religion, for they had already hoisted the nonsense of the sexless to the rank of religion.

Under these circumstances Maria was decidedly opposed to my going alone on a trip to my native country, since my resources did not allow me to transport all my family with me. What she basically feared was that I escape from her close watch, and furthermore, maybe, that my appearance in court before the public would victoriously refute all the wicked rumours she had sown on my mental state.

But she fell ill with a vague complaint which forced her to remain bedridden. Nonetheless I decided to leave to appear in person and I left.

The letters I wrote to her during those distressing six weeks in which I was threatened with a sentence of two years hard labour, were full of a love which distance and forced celibacy had reawoken. My overworked brain transformed her into poetry, replaced around that face an aureole of brilliant gold, and abstinence with its regrets bedecked her in my thoughts with the white clothing of the guardian angel. Everything disappeared, the base, the ugly, the wicked and the Madonna of my first amorous visions appeared afresh to the extent that in an interview I went so far as to confess to an old journalist friend "that I had become more humble and purer under the influence of a good woman". I leave you to judge whether that phrase made the rounds of the newspapers of the united kingdoms.

She must have laughed on reading that, the infamous one!

The public at least got its money's worth.

Maria's replies to my love letters testified to the keen interest she took in the economic side of the matter but the more the ovations which were made to me at the theatre, in the street, before the court increased, she changed her colours, voiced the stupidity of the judges and showed her profound regret at not being one of the jury.

As for the expressions of love which I proffered to her, she kept a prudent reserve, admitted nothing, not committing herself to discuss the subject, limiting herself to revolving around the words "to understand one another, to comprehend one another", attributing our conjugal disasters to the fact that I had never understood her. And I'd swear that it is she who never grasped a single word of the language of her learned author.

Now, among the letters there was one which had awoken my old suspicions. And so I gave her to understand that, once escaped from the clutches of justice, it would be pleasanter for me to settle down abroad.

She flew into a temper, insulted me, threatened to take away her love for me, implored my great mercy, prostrated herself, evoked my mother's memory, admitting that at the thought of "never seeing *her* country again" (not Finland!), an icy shudder had enveloped her from head to foot—and that she would die of it. And I wondered:

"Why that shiver at that thought?"

Even now I still couldn't explain it.

At last the jury acquitted me and—supreme irony—at the end of the banquet which was offered me, it was to Maria that a toast was raised, as the "well-deserving instigator of my appearance in person".

No! . . . That was exquisite!

I returned to Geneva where my family had been living during my absence. To my great surprise, Maria, whose correspondence depicted her in bed, still ill, came to meet me at the station, alert and fresh, with only a slightly preoccupied expression.

I immediately came alive again and the evening and that happy night repaid me for all the harassment undergone.

The following day I realised that we were living in a pension full of students and strumpets. Listening to their chatter, I gathered that Maria had enjoyed herself by playing cards and drinking in this shady society, and I was distressed by the shocking intimacies which reigned in this low place. She posed as the little mother (her old game still!) with the university students and she had joined up with the worst of the ladies whom she introduced to me—a fat tart who sat down at the dining-table in a state of manifest drunkenness.

And it was this brothel that my children had been frequenting for six weeks. And the mother saw nothing, having not even the slightest scruple! And her illness—simulated—did not prevent her from mixing in with the suspicious meetings of those dubious individuals!

As for me, whenever I raised my voice about it, my position was clear. I was nothing but jealous, a conservative, an aristocrat! . . .

And the struggles of yesteryear began again worse than ever!

195

A new subject for quarrels was now to be offered to us: the education of the children. The maid, a peasant's daughter, who had not the slightest trace of knowledge was promoted to the office of educator, and, in concert with the mother, she committed the cruellest sillinesses. The two women, very lazy, loved to sleep in of a morning. As a result, the children were condemned to remaining awake in their beds in the morning, and, when they persisted in wanting to get up, they were whipped. Seeing this, I decided to intervene; without a word of warning, I went to sound the reveille in the rooms of the little ones, who greeted me with their joyful cries, like a liberator. My wife invoked individual freedom—which consisted in impinging on the freedom of others, according to her.—Nothing moved me.

The monomania of the weak and inferior brains, who want to equalise that which can never be equal, was to run riot at the same time in my family. My eldest daughter, precociously intelligent, accustomed to dip into my illustrated books since her first year, continued to enjoy her birthright. And because I could not grant the same favour to the youngest one, still incapable of handling a precious book, the mother claimed I was lacking in equity.

"Everything should be equal," she said.

"Everything? Ah! . . . the size of the clothes and the shoes also!"

The reply didn't come, but soon accusations of "ineptitude" replaced it.

"To everyone according to his capacities and merit! This for the adult and that for the minor!"

But she didn't want to understand and I was designated as an *iniquitous* father who "hated" the youngest.

To tell the truth, I was fonder of the eldest, because firstly she was the eldest, she was linked to the memories of the first fine days of my life, she had reached the age of reason and, quite likely also, because the birth of the youngest dated from a period when the fidelity of the mother had become suspect to me. Besides, the *equity* of the mother manifested itself in a complete indifference to her children. She was always out when she wasn't sleeping. She remained a stranger to them and the children became attached to me, whose affection was always increasing to the point of awakening the jealousy of their mother. In order to help matters, it was by her that I habitually had all the toys and the toffees which I could bring home distributed, in order thereby to win for her their devotion.

The babies were then truly a part of my way of life, and in the black minutes when isolation was to overwhelm me, the contact of those little living beings was to reattach me to existence, to woman at the same time. Because of them, all idea of separation was unthinkable, a baleful situation for me, for I was thereby going to descend to the last degree of bondage.

The outcome of the assault that I had made on the fortresses of the *Masculinists* made itself felt. I was attacked in the Swiss newspapers to the point of having my stay rendered intolerable. The sale of my works was forbidden and, persecuted from town to town, I fled into France.

Now, in Paris, the friends had become apostates. They made an alliance with my wife against me. Tracked down like a wild animal, I changed my battlefield and, almost in penury, I managed to reach a neutral port, a village of artists near Paris. I had run into a trap where I remained a recluse for ten months, perhaps the worst in my life.

The society that I met there was composed of young Scandinavian painters, former apprentices to divers trades, of origins as diverse as strange; and, what was worse, of women painters, without scruples, emancipated from everything, frantic admirers of hermaphroditic literatures, so that they believed themselves the equals of man. To distract attention from their sex, they attributed certain male exteriorities to themselves, smoked, got drunk, played billiards, etc., and indulged in the games of love between one another.

That was the last straw!

So as not to remain alone, I struck up a relationship with two of the monsters; one of them was a self-styled woman of letters, the other a dabbler in painting.

It was the woman of letters who first paid a visit to me as one does to a great writer, which awoke the jealousy of my wife, at once prepared to attach that ally to herself, who seemed enlightened enough to appreciate the value of my reasons launched against the half-woman.

At that moment a series of incidents came to resuscitate the black ideas and my monomania, henceforth famous, was shortly to manifest itself in all freedom.

There was at the hotel an album containing caricature-portrayals of all the noteworthy Scandinavians, drawn by national artists. Mine, which was found there, was decorated with a horn, surreptitiously formed with a mesh of my hair.

The author of that portrait was one of our best friends. I was thereby able to conclude that the infidelity of my wife was notorious, known to all the world, except to me alone. I asked the owner of the collection for an explanation of the matter.

Previously forewarned of my mental state by the attentions of Maria, he swore to me that that forehead ornament was seen by me alone, that it did not exist in the drawing, that I was getting upset without cause; and pending further information the matter remained as it was.

One evening Maria and I were having coffee in the little garden of the hostelry in the company of an old Scandinavian gentleman recently arrived from the home country. It was broad daylight and I was sitting so as to be able to follow all the expressions of Maria's physiognomy. The old gentleman was relating to us everything which had happened since our departure from Sweden. In passing he happened to pronounce the name of the doctor who had formerly massaged Maria. Interrupting the old man, my wife, who had not let the name of the doctor pass by unnoticed, asked him a question out of bravado.

"Ah! You know Dr. X . . ."

"Yes . . . He is a fairly sought-after doctor . . . I understand he enjoys a certain renown . . ."

"As a romeo, yes!" I said.

Maria's face paled; an impudent smile was fixed on her lips, upturned at the corners, revealing the naked teeth. And the conversation languished as the result of a general embarrassment.

Remaining alone with the old gentleman, I implored him for information on the rumours spread about that affair which intrigued me. He swore to me by all the devils that none of those rumours had reached his ears. Finally, by dint of insistence, after an hour of supplications, I withdrew this rather enigmatic phrase of "consolation" from him:

"Besides, dear chap, if we suppose that there is one, rest assured that there were several."

And that was all. But from that day the name of the doctor no longer passed Maria's lips, formerly so prompt in telling stories, in pronouncing that name in public, as if she had wanted to practice hearing it pronounced one day without blushing, obeying some obsession of thought which got the better of all her scruples.

My attention brutally attracted by the revelation, I gave myself some time to search my memory and find there the supporting evidence. And, at once, the memory of a literary work, which had appeared in the course of the lawsuit which was brought against me, came to throw a ray of light, uncertain, I admit, but sufficient however to find a leading channel going back to the source of those rumours.

It was a drama by a celebrated Norwegian bluestocking*, the promoter of the egalitarian folly, which had fallen into my hands: and I had read it without ever perceiving an analogy with my own position. Now, on the contrary, all was easily translated, the more I gave free rein to the most atrocious suppositions for the reputation of my wife.

---

* Ibsen

Here is the résumé.

A photographer (an appellation which my *romans à clef* had earned me) had wed a girl of dubious morality. Previously the mistress of a great landowner, the woman, by means of secret funds which were paid out to her by her former lover, supported the household and started to exercise the trade of the husband, an idler who spent his time in cafés, getting drunk with bohemians.

Such was the travesty of the facts, turned inside out with the help of the publisher, well informed on the detail that Maria did translations, but unaware of the other fact, namely that I corrected those translations, gratis, and simply paid out the fruit of her work to her in full.

The matter became aggravated the day when the unfortunate photographer came to discover that his daughter, a child whom he adored and who had come into the world prematurely, was not his and that his wife had odiously deceived him in leading him into marrying her.

To add to this baseness, the deceived husband allowed himself to accept a large sum from the ex-lover, as compensation.

Thereupon, I scented Maria's loan, enhanced by the Baron's guarantee, a guarantee that I had counter-signed on the day after the legal wedding.

As far as the story of the child and of her illegitimate birth was concerned, I did not quite grasp what analogy there could be, for my daughter had only come into the world after two years of marriage had gone by.

But, I thought about it! . . . And the one which didn't live! . . . There it was, the clue! . . . The poor little dead one! . . . She who had provoked my marriage, otherwise problematic! . . .

A risky conclusion, but a conclusion all the same. It was true! Maria's visits to the Baron after their separation, the relations of the Baron with the newly-weds, the paintings which were seen hanging on my walls, the loan . . . and! . . . and the rest!

Firmly resolved to act, I prepared a big scene for the afternoon. I wanted to offer Maria the drawing-up of a requisitory or rather an argument for both our defences, since we were equally attacked by the man of straw of the *Masculinists* who had been bribed into doing that honest task.

When Maria penetrated into my room, it was in the most cordial way possible that I welcomed her.

"What's the matter?" she asked.

"A serious matter which concerns us both equally."

Whereupon I revealed the play to her in all its developments, adding this: that the actor entrusted with the rôle of the photographer had thought he had to "make himself up like me".

She remained silent, pondering plans, a prey to a very visible emotion.

Then I began the defence.

"Supposing it is true, tell me and you're forgiven. If it were that the little dead one were a child of Gustav's, you were free at that period, only being tied to me by vague promises, and then you hadn't yet received anything from me. As far as the hero of the drama is concerned, he seems to me to behave as a kind-hearted man; that man is incapable of making an unfortunate future for his daughter or for his wife. As for the money which he accepted, by way of a subsidy for the child, I can only see in it a proper compensation for damage caused."

She had given me her complete attention and that profoundly bourgeois mind was to bite at the bait, without swallowing it however. To judge by the calm which relaxed her features, contracted by the thought of remorse, the argumentation I had chosen on the rights she might have had to dispose of her body, not having received any money from me, appeared to suffice her. As far as the deceived husband was concerned, she also acquitted him with the qualification of "a kind-hearted man". He had a "noble heart", she claimed.

Without succeeding in wheedling from her the admission that I was provoking, I continued and I arrived at my peroration, holding out to her the ladder by which to escape, asking her for advice regarding the measures to be taken to rehabilitate *us both*, proposing to produce the defence in the form of a novel, in order to wash us of all those infamies for the world and for our children . . .

I had been speaking for an hour. She had remained sitting at my table, handling a pen-holder between her fingers, excessively nervous, without saying a word, except for some isolated exclamations.

I went out for a quiet walk and to have a game of billiards. On my return I found Maria still in the same place, immobile as a statue. It was two hours since I had left.

On hearing me, she started up.

"It's a trap that you've laid for me there?" she said.

"Not in the slightest. Do you think then that I could ruin the mother of my children forever!"

"Ah! the fact is that I believe you capable of everything. You want to get rid of me as you've already tried once before by introducing me to Mr. Y . . . (here a name not yet mentioned . . .) yes Mr. Y . . . who was to try to seduce me so that you might catch me in the act of adultery? . . ."

"And . . . who told you that?"

"Helga!"

"Helga!"

200

It was the last "woman friend" of Maria at the time of our departure! The vengeance of Lesbia!

"And you believed her?"

"Certainly . . . But, you see, I have really *tricked* you both, Mr. Y . . . and you."

"That's to say you have deceived me with a third?"

"I didn't say that."

"But you have admitted it! Since you have deceived us both, you have deceived me! It's logical at least!"

She struggled like someone guilty by exacting proof from *me*. Proof! . . .

Now, I was floored by the revelation of such an imposture, surpassing everything wretched which I had dreamed of at the bottom of the human heart. I lowered my head, I fell on my knees, I implored mercy.

"You have been able to believe the gossip of that woman! You have believed that I wanted to get rid of you. I who have always been the faithful friend, the assiduous spouse, I who cannot live without you! You have complained of my jealousy . . . and all the women who were running after me, seeking to seduce me, I have denounced them to you, all of them, as evil minds. You have believed that! . . . You have believed that! . . ."

She was seized with pity! Carried away by a surge of momentary sincerity, she admitted never having believed all those tales.

"And yet you have deceived me . . . Say it, I forgive you! . . . Deliver me from the terrible, dark ideas which are haunting me! . . . Say it . . ."

She said nothing, limited herself to objurgations against Y . . ., that "wretch"! . . ."

A wretch, my most intimate, dearest friend!

I desired death! Odious existence was insupportable for me! . . .

Throughout dinner, Maria was more than pleasant to me. As soon as I went to bed, she paid me a visit, sat down on the edge of my bed, clutched my hands, kissed my eyes, and with a broken heart, she finally burst into sobs.

"You're crying, my darling, tell me your trouble; I'll console you! . . ."

She stammered some disconnected words, haltingly, about my generosity, my feelings, my extreme indulgence, the great pity that I extended on the miseries of the world.

What a senseless anomaly! I was accusing her of adultery; she was caressing me, overwhelming me with eulogies!

The fire was lit however and the conflagration burst forth.

She had deceived me!

I had to know with whom!

The week which followed counts among the bitterest of my bitter life.

It was a question for me of waging a frightful combat against all the principles, inborn, inherited, or else acquired through education, in committing an offence. I resolved to unseal the letters which arrived addressed to Maria, in order to know where I stood! And despite the absolute confidence that I testified to her, for I authorised her to read all my correspondence during my absences, I still recoiled from that infraction of a sacred law, the most delicate obligation of the tacit social contract, never to violate the secret of a letter!

Nevertheless I was sliding down the slope. A day came when I no longer respected the secret. The letter was there, between my trembling fingers, unsealed, trembling as if they had unfolded the paper on which the mortal downfall of my honour could be read.

It was a composition of the adventuress, of the friend number one.

In mocking and scornful terms, she expatiated on my madness, vowing that the good God would soon deliver Maria from her martyrdom by quenching the last flickers of my troubled mind. After having copied down the most shameful phrases, I resealed the envelope and put off the presentation of the letter until the evening post. The moment having come, I gave the missive to my wife and I sat down near her to observe her.

Arriving at the point where a mention was made of the desire which was felt for my death—right on top of the sheet on page two—she laughed, with a ferocious laugh.

So the Adored could not see any other way out of her remorse than my death. Her supreme hope, to extract herself from the consequences of her crimes, consisted in seeing me promptly die. And when that event was accomplished, she would then draw my life insurance, the pension of the famous poet and would marry again or would remain, according to her fancy, a merry widow! The Adored! . . .

So *moriturus sum,* and I was going to hasten the catastrophe by giving myself up to absinthe, which alone made me happy, as well as to billiards which soothed my burning brain.

Meanwhile, a new complication arose, more terrible than all the others. The lettered friend, who affected to have taken a liking to me, made the conquest of Maria, who fell warmly in love with her to the point of giving birth to gossip. At the same time the comrade of the friend became jealous, and that was not conducive to attenuating the ugly rumours.

One evening, in bed, Maria, bewildered by our embraces, asked me if I was not in love with Miss Z . . .

"Ah! no, certainly not! An ignoble drunkard! You can't mean it?"

"I'm mad about her!" she replied. "It's strange, isn't it? . . . I'm afraid of remaining alone with her!"

"Because? . . ."

"I don't know! She's charming . . . An exquisite body . . ."

"Then . . ."

. . . .

A week later, we had invited some friends from Paris, artists without scruples, without prejudices, with their wives.

The husbands came, but alone, the wives excusing themselves with pretexts too vague not to wound me cruelly.

It was an orgy. The scandalous conduct of the gentlemen riled me to the marrow.

They treated the two friends of Maria as whores. In the middle of the general drunkenness, I perceived my wife who was letting herself be kissed time and again by a lieutenant.

Brandishing a billiard cue over the heads of the imprudent pair, I demanded an explanation.

"He is a childhood friend, a relative! Don't make yourself ridiculous, my poor friend," retorted Maria. "Besides, it's the custom in Russia to kiss one another like this, point-blank, and we are Russian subjects."

"It's not true! Lie," exclaimed a friend . . . "Relatives, them, not on your life! Lie."

I was *almost* a murderer. I was going . . .

. . . .

The mere idea of leaving the children without a father or mother held back my raised arm.

Alone together, I avenged myself and I administered to my Maria the chastisement she deserved:

"Whore!"

"Why?"

"Because you let yourself be treated as such!"

"You're jealous?"

"Yes, certainly; I am jealous; jealous of my honour, of the dignity of my family, of the reputation of my wife, of the future of my children! And your bad conduct has just banned us from the society of decent women. To let oneself be kissed like that in public by a stranger! Don't you know that you're nothing but a madwoman, since you can see nothing, can hear nothing, can understand nothing, and renounce all feelings of duty? But I will have you shut away if you don't mend your ways, and to begin with, I forbid your seeing your friends from now on."

"It was you who encouraged me to seduce the latest comer."

203

"In order to lay a trap for you and surprise you, yes!"

"Besides, have you proof of the nature of the relations which you suspect are established between my friends and myself?"

"Proof, no. But I have your admissions, which you have cynically told me. And then your friend Z . . ., hasn't she declared in front of me that she would be condemned to deportation for her morals if she were living in her own country?"

"I thought that you didn't recognise the 'vice'?"

"Let those wenches enjoy themselves as they like, it doesn't concern me, since it doesn't affect my family! But from the moment that that "peculiarity", if you prefer it, causes us trouble it becomes a pre-judicial action for us. As a philosopher, there do not exist any vices for me, it's true, except in the sense of bodily or psychic defects. And when the Chamber of Deputies of Paris recently dealt with that question of the unnatural vices, all the noteworthy doctors rallied to this opinion, that the law has no business to interfere with those things, except in the case when citizens are affected in their interests."

But one might as well have preached to the fish! What was the use of thinking one could make that woman who only obeyed the urge of her bestial instinct understand a philosophical distinction!

In order to make a clean breast of those rumours in circulation, I sent off a letter to a devoted friend in Paris, beseeching him to tell me everything.

His reply frankly signified to me that, according to the accepted opinion of the Scandinavians, my wife might have an inclination towards illicit love and that the two Danish damsels were in any case recognised as established tribads in Paris, where they frequented cafés in the company of other lesbians.

In debt in our pension, without resources, we had no possibility of escaping. Fortunately for us, the Danes, who had seduced a most beautiful local girl, brought the hatred of the peasants upon themselves, and were obliged to decamp. But the acquaintanceship, already formed for eight months, could not be brusquely broken like this, and as those two well-brought-up girls of good family had become companions in misfortune for me, I wanted to prepare an honourable retreat for them. To that end a farewell dinner was served in the studio of a young artist.

At dessert, drunkenness did not fail to appear, and Maria, carried away by her feelings, got up to sing a romance composed by her to the so well-known air of *Mignon*. In it she said her farewells to the Adored.

She had sung with zest, with such a true feeling, with her almond-shaped eyes, moistened with tears, sparkling in the reflection of the candles, she had opened her heart so widely, that, upon my word, I myself was moved and charmed by it! There was such a touching naïvety and sincerity in her song that every licentious idea disappeared on hearing that woman sing amorously of woman! A strange fact, she had not the manner nor the physiognomy of the man-woman, no, she was the loving and tender, mysterious, enigmatic, unfathomable woman.

And one ought to have seen the object of that love! A redheaded type, male face, hooked, hanging nose, fat chin, yellow eyes, cheeks puffed out from an excess of drink, with a flat breast, crooked hands, the most detestable, the most execrable thing it is possible to imagine, a type with which a farm hand would not have contented himself.

Her romance sung, Maria went to sit down beside the monster, who got up in her turn, took her head between her hands and with wide open mouth, sucked her lips by way of a kiss. "It's carnal love at least," I said to myself, and, clinking glasses with the redhead, I got her dead drunk.

She fell on her knees, looked at me with her big frightened eyes, with the hiccuping laughter of a cretin, with her body bundled up against the wall.

Never did I see such a monstrosity in human form and my ideas on the emancipation of women were thenceforth fixed.

After a scandal in the street, where the painter's strumpet was discovered sitting on a milestone and howling terribly between two vomitings, the party was closed, and the following day the two friends had left.

. . . .

Maria went through a horrible crisis which only inspired me with pity, so much did she languish for her friend, so much did she suffer, offering the veritable spectacle of an unfortunate lover. She wandered alone in the wood, singing songs of love, sought out the favourite places of her friend, offered all the symptoms of a deeply wounded heart, so much so that I was seized with fear for her reason. She was unhappy and I did not succeed in distracting her. She avoided my caresses, pushed me away when I wanted to kiss her and I held that friend in mortal hatred, for she dispossessed me of the love of my wife.

Maria, more unconscious than ever, did not dissimulate the subject of her grief. Every echo resounded with her plaints and with her amorous pangs. It was unbelievable.

In the course of all these miseries, an assiduous correspondence was kept up between the friends, and one fine day, enraged at the enforced celibacy they made me undergo, I laid hands on a letter from the friend. It was a complete love-letter! My chick, my pet, the intelligent, the delicate Maria, with such noble feelings, etc.; her brutal husband was only a stupid brute! There was a question of attempts at abduction, at escapades . . .

I then rose up against the rival and, that very evening, a struggle, good Lord! a hand to hand struggle, was engaged in the moonlight between Maria and myself. She bit my hands. I dragged her, in order to drown her like a cat, to the edge of the river when all of a sudden the images of the children were evoked and gave me back my reason.

I prepared myself for suicide, but I wanted, before dying, to write the story of my life.

. . . .

The first part of the book was completed, when the news was spread in the village that the Danes had rented an apartment for the summer.

At once, I had the trunks packed and we left for German Switzerland.

4

Ah! The sweet land of Aargau! . . . Arcadia where the postmaster grazes the flocks, where the army colonel drives the only hire-cab into town, where the girls all want to have a rose wedding, where the lads fire at targets and beat the drum. Land of Cockaigne, land of golden beer, of salted sausages, fatherland of the game of skittles, of the Hapsburgs and of William Tell, of the *fêtes champêtres,* of naïve songs bursting forth from simple hearts, of pastors' wives and of presbytery idylls.

Calm was reborn in our agitated minds. I recovered, and Maria, weary of war, enveloped herself in a candid indolence. The game of backgammon was introduced and imposed in the house as a palliative and we substituted the tossing rolling of the dice for dangerous conversation. The good harmless beer replaced absinthe and exciting wines.

The influence of the milieu made itself immediately felt. I spent hours on end in astonishment that life could be so gay after so many tempests, that the elasticity of the mind could offer such a resistance to so many shocks, that the oblivion of the past could be brought about to such an extent that I believed myself the happiest husband of the most faithful of wives.

Maria, through lack of society, through lack of women friends, resumed playing her rôle of mother without boredom, and, at the end of a month, the children were dressed in clothing cut and sewn by their mamma, who no longer tired of devoting all her time to them.

She began to have weak spells: her ardour for pleasure diminished, mature age was making its appearance! What affliction the day she chanced to break her first incisor! Poor Maria! She wept, clutched me in her arms, begging me not to stop loving her! She was in her thirty-seventh year! Her hair was becoming thinner, her breasts were sagging, like waves after the storm, the stairs were becoming tiring for her little foot and her lungs were no longer functioning with the same pressure.

And I loved her more, thinking that she was going to be mine alone, ours, although I glimpsed my renewal, my second spring, despite my increasing virility and my health which was flourishing. At last she was mine. She would be obliged to grow old surrounded by my attentions, sheltered from seductions, sacrificing her existence to her children! . . .

The symptoms of the convalescence were becoming accentuated with touching signs. Foreseeing the danger of being married to a young man of thirty-eight, she honoured me with her jealousy, started to titivate herself and no longer neglected taking trouble with herself in order to receive me at night.

She had nothing to fear from me however, who am of a monogamous, essentially monogamous constitution; and far from abusing the situation, I did my utmost to spare her the atrocious pangs of jealousy, reassuring her by multiplied testimonials of my rejuvenated love.

5

Autumn having arrived, I decided to leave for a trip of three consecutive weeks during which I would have to change places every day.

Still a prey to the monomania of believing me in shattered health, Maria sought to dissuade me from undertaking such a tiring tour.

"You will die from it, my child," she repeated to me.

"We'll soon see."

That journey was a point of honour for me, an experiment by which I intended to reconquer the love for the male by reawakening it . . .

. . . I returned after unbelievable hardships, refreshed, tanned, robust, vigorous.

She welcomed me, with her eyes full of admiration and defiance, then of disagreeable disappointment.

And I, for my part, after three weeks of continence, treated her as a mistress, a refound woman. I took her gallantly by the waist and I returned victoriously in possession of my rights despite a journey of forty hours in a through train. She didn't know what face to put on, amazed, afraid of revealing her true feelings to me, haunted by keen fears at the thought of seeing the man-tamer resuscitate in the husband.

When I came to myself again, I noticed a transformation in Maria's expression. Examining her, I discovered that she had had false teeth put in, which made her younger than before. Finally, certain details of her dress bespoke a careful coquetry. This stimulated my attention. I sought and I discovered a foreign girl of fourteen at the most, with whom Maria had struck up a relationship of warm friendliness. They kissed, went for walks, bathed together . . .

An immediate flight was imperative.

And there we were installed on the shores of Lake Lucerne in a German pension.

Here a fresh and most dangerous relapse.

In the house a young lieutenant was living. Maria paid court to him, played backgammon with him, walked melancholically in the garden while I worked.

At a dinner, at the *table d'hôte*, I thought I could perceive tender looks being exchanged between them, without the accompaniment of conversation. It was ingenuously, as though they were making love with their eyes. I attempted a frank experiment and, brusquely thrusting my head between the two of them, I looked my wife in the face. In order to throw me off the scent, she let her looks slide along the lieutenant's temple up to the wall-paper on the partition, on which a brewery advertisement was fixed. Then, troubled, without rhyme or reason, she attempted this remark:

"Is that a new brewery?"

"Yes . . . but don't count on tricking me," I retorted.

She bowed her neck as if under the pressure of a bit, and remained stupefied, dumb.

Two evenings later, she pretended a lassitude, gave me the evening kiss and returned to her room. I went to bed, I read and I fell asleep.

Suddenly, I woke up with a start. Downstairs in the drawing-room I heard the piano resounding, then a voice, the voice of Maria.

I got up and enjoined the maid to go at once and fetch my wife.

"Tell Madame not to delay, or else I'll go myself, with my cane, to show her how to behave and to whip her publicly."

Maria came up that very instant, ashamed, playing the innocent, asking me the reasons for that strange message, which forbade her the society of strangers, when there were other ladies present.

"It's not that which irritates me, it's the treachery in managing to make me leave the drawing-room, when you want to remain there alone!"

"If you insist, alright, I am going to bed."

What candour, what sudden submission! . . . What had happened? . . .

A winter of snow, sad and solitary, followed on from autumn. We were left alone, the last boarders in the modest pension, and as a result of the cold we had our dinner in the large common room of the restaurant.

One fine morning, during the meal, a man of strong build, a rather handsome man, a servant, according to all the outward signs, sat down at a table and asked for a glass of wine.

Maria, following her loose behaviour, eyed the guest attentively, measuring up his body and losing herself in reverie. The customer went off, visibly embarrassed by an attention which appeared honorific to him.

"Handsome man!" said Maria, turning to the head waiter.

"He's my former porter!" replied the latter.

"Really! He has a magnificent presence and is not too common for his position! Indeed, he is a fine man!"

And there she was launching forth into details, exalting masculine beauty in such terms that the landlord remained thunderstruck.

The following day, the superb ex-porter was already at the table in his same place when we made our entrance into the room. Dressed up, in his Sunday best, with his hair and beard immaculate, he seemed already forewarned of his conquest, and that lout, after having greeted us, not without having received in return a gracious greeting from my wife, squared his shoulders and posed as if he were Napoleon!

He returned the following day, determined to open fire. With the taste of a porter, he started a gallant, back-door conversation, addressing himself directly to my wife, without stopping for the habitual small manoeuvre which consists in previously pulling the wool over the husband's eyes.

It was unbelievable!

What I know is that Maria engaged herself in the conversation, gracious, comely, enchanted by the great favour, tranquilly, in the presence of her husband and children.

Once more I sought to open her eyes, begging her to safeguard her reputation, which earned me her usual reply on my "dirty imagination".

A second Apollo came to the rescue. He was the proprietor of the village tobacconists, a big man, from whom Maria made small purchases of mercery at times. Craftier than the servant, he tried to win me over and at the same time showed himself more enterprising. At the first meeting, after having looked Maria well in the face, in a brazen manner, he exclaimed at the top of his voice, turning towards the landlord:

"Ah! God! What a beautiful family!"

Maria's heart was inflamed and the fellow reappeared every day.

One evening, he was drunk, and consequently more emboldened. He approached Maria while we were playing backgammon and leaning towards her, asked her for explanations on the rules of the game. I made a remark to him in as polite a manner as possible and the fellow returned to his former place. Maria, of a more sensitive heart than mine, believed herself obliged to make amends to the *insulted* merchant and, turning towards him, she addressed some question to him at random:

"You can play billiards, sir?"

"No, madame, or so badly . . ."

Thereupon he got up, came forward and offered me a cigar. I refused.

He then returned towards Maria and with the same gesture:

"And you, madame? . . ."

Fortunately for her, for the tobacconist, for the future of my family, she also refused, but with what coy thanks!

However did that man get it into his head to offer a cigar to a woman of breeding, in the room of a restaurant, in the presence of the husband!

Was I a jealous madman? Or was my wife behaving in a scandalous manner, to the point of provoking the appetites of men . . . and of the first comers? . . .

Having returned to our rooms, I made a scene, for she was like a sleepwalker and I wanted to wake her up. She was going straight to her perdition without knowing it. And, as in the last pages of a book, I drew her the tableau of her sins old and new, analysing her slightest actions.

Without saying a word, pale, with hollow eyes, she listened to me to the very end. Then she got up and went down to go to bed. But this time—the first time in my life—I degraded myself; I lowered myself to the point of spying on her. I went down the stairs behind her, I took up my stand in front of the door of her room, with my eye at the keyhole.

The maid was sitting in the full glow beneath the lamp, right in front, within my sight. Maria was very agitated, she was moving about, was talking excitedly of the injustice of my suspicions, pleading her cause like one accused who defends herself. She repeated my expressions as if she wanted to get rid of them by spitting them out.

"And to think that I'm innocent, innocent of all that . . . Ah! it's not, however, the opportunities to do wrong that I've lacked . . ."

Thereupon she brought two glasses, some beer and had a drink with the servant girl. Then she sat down near her and undressed her with her eyes. She drew closer to her, placed her head on the very developed breasts of that new "friend" and took her by the waist and asked her to kiss her . . .

. . . Poor Maria! Unhappy one who sought her consolations far from me, far from me who alone could bring her deliverance from her remorse. Suddenly she drew herself up, listening, and pointing towards the door:

"There is someone there!" she said.

I went away.

When I returned to my observation post, I perceived Maria half undressed, showing her shoulders to the servant, whom this did not seem to impress. Then she began her defence again.

"He is now mad without any doubt! I wouldn't even be surprised if he attempted to poison me . . . I feel intolerable pains in my stomach . . . But no . . . , I daren't believe it . . . I ought to flee to Finland perhaps. . . Oughtn't I? . . . But he would die of it, for he loves his children!"

What was all that then except chewed remorse? . . . Harassed by all those clandestine thoughts, she was seized with horror and sought a refuge in the bosom of a woman! A perverse child, a treacherous rogue, unfortunate above all!

I remained awake the entire night, overwhelmed with suffering. At two o'clock in the morning, Maria started to moan while dreaming, to moan atrociously. Seized with pity, I knocked on the wall to deliver her from all her spectres and it was not moreover the first time.

In the morning, she thanked me for my intervention. While

caressing her, I pitied her, I asked her if she did not want to confess herself to her friend at last . . .

"About what? . . . I have nothing to say."

If she had admitted everything at that instant, I would have forgiven her, so much did her remorse inspire me with pity, so much did I love her, in spite of everything and perhaps because of her misery. She was only an ill-fated woman! How dare I raise my hand against an unhappy woman!

But, instead of delivering me from my frightful doubts, she offered me a frantic resistance. She herself had come to the point of believing me mad, the instinct for preservation forcing her to forge a fable which donned the real contours of a fact, and which ended up by serving her as a palladium against remorse.

6

Round about the new year we made our way towards Germany. We halted on the shores of Lake Constance.

In Germany, land of soldiers, where the régime of the patriarchate was still in force, Maria did not feel at home. No-one understood her sillinesses on the alleged rights of woman. Here they had just forbidden girls from attending university lectures; here the dowry of the officer's wife had to be deposited with the war ministry as inalienable family fortune; here all State employments were reserved for man, the provider.

Maria struggled as if I had made her fall into an ambush. At the first attempt that she ventured at hoodwinking me in a circle of women, she was given a sharp dressing-down. At last, there I was then, supported by the faction of the women and my poor Maria bit the dust. As for me, I recovered myself in the intimate relationship with the officers, adopting virile manners under the influence of the conversion and the male reasserted itself within me after ten years of moral emasculation.

At the same time I reassumed the freedom of my mane, abolishing the tuft that she had demanded; my voice, half quenched by the continual habit of cajoling a nervous woman, regained the sonority of its timbre, my hollow cheeks filled out with flesh and all my physical constitution developed at the approach of my forty years.

Linked in intimacy with the ladies of the house, I grew accustomed to taking the floor, in such a way that Maria, hardly sympathetic to those women, found herself relegated.

She then began to fear me. One morning, the first in the last six years of our marriage, she presented herself fully dressed in my bedroom, catching me in bed. I understood nothing of that sudden transformation; a stormy quarrel took place; she betrayed herself by letting me guess the undercurrent of jealousy she had begun to feel for the servant who came every morning to light the fire in my stove. At the same time she affirmed her disgust for my new ways:

"I detest virility and I am beginning to hate you when you assume importance."

Yes, yes, always, it was the page, the lap dog, the cripple, her "child" whom she had cherished, however little; the virago could not love the man in her husband although she adored it, however, in others.

Yet I was seen by the women in a better and better light. I sought out their society, letting myself be penetrated by that radiating warmth of true women, of those who inspire respectful love, the unreflecting submission that man grants to feminine women alone.

Now, at that very moment, the possibility of an early return to the homeland came up again for discussion. My former apprehensions were resuscitated: seized by the fear of reestablishing contact with the friends of yesteryear, it was of importance to me to know if I counted lovers of my wife amongst them. In order to put an end to my uncertainties, I resolved to begin a minute enquiry. Previously, I had questioned some friends in Sweden, with regard to those covert rumours which were bruited about the infidelity of my wife, without managing, naturally, to elicit a frank reply from them.

They had only pity for *the mother*! Who cared about the ridicule which was going to ruin the father?

I then hit upon the idea of employing the resources of the new psychological science, combined with the reading of thoughts, in my research, and at our evening meetings I put the ladies in the know, using the manipulations of Bishop and his colleagues as a parlour game. Maria was distrustful. She accused me of being a spiritualist, railing at me, calling me a superstitious free-thinker, riddling me with badly-chosen invective, seeking by every means to divert me from those practices which she felt were to be ill-omened for her!

In order to fool her, I pretended to obey her and, putting hypnotism aside, I attacked her unexpectedly, when we were alone together.

One evening, when we were both in the dining-room, sitting face to face, I gradually led the conversation onto gymnastics and, after having interested her sufficiently enough for her to become a little impassioned with regard to the discussion, either through the force of my will, or through the association of the ideas, which had to follow the impulse I gave them, she came to speak of massage. From there, her thought jumped directly to the pain provoked by massage and, recalling the treatments at her doctor's, she exclaimed:

"Oh! yes it hurts, massage: I can still feel the pain when I think of it . . ."

That was enough. She bowed her head to hide the mortal pallor; her lips were moving as if to articulate something else; her eyes flickered: a terrible silence came about which I sought to prolong. It was the train of thought that I had set in motion, launched at full steam by my skilful hand in the desired direction. In vain she tried frantically to apply the brakes. The gulf was there: the engine could not stop. With a supreme effort, she got up, dragged herself from the obsession of my looks, and dashed out without saying a word.

The blow had struck home!

Some minutes afterwards, she came back, with her face relaxed. Pretending that she was going to make me feel the beneficial effects of massage on my head, she took her stance behind my seat and rubbed my skull. Unfortunately for her, there was a mirror in front of us, I glanced at it furtively, enough to recognise in it a pale, frightened spectre whose haggard eyes were scrutinising my features . . . and our inquisitive looks crossed.

215

Then, contrary to her habit, she sat down on my knees, put her arms around me, fondly, and declared that she was dropping with sleep.

"What have you done wrong then, to caress me today?" I said.

She hid her brow in my breast, kissed me and went off, wishing me: "Good-night".

It certainly wasn't proof to produce before a judge, but it was enough for me who knew the ways of her being so well!

All the more so since the masseur had just been thrown out of my brother-in-law's house for his conduct with his wife.

7

I did not want to return to my country at any cost, to find myself involved in adventures prejudicial to my honour; for my position would oblige me to have daily dealings with men suspected of having been the lovers of my wife. To escape the ridicule which attacks the deceived husband, I fled to Vienna.

Alone in the hotel, the image of the ex-adored pursued me. Incapable of working, I gave myself up to correspondence and sent her off two letters every day; as many love letters. The foreign town produced the effect of a tomb on me. I went for walks there like a phantom among the crowd. Suddenly my imagination set to work to people that solitude. I created a poetic story to introduce Maria into those dead surroundings. At once all the inert matter of the buildings and the men lived again! I imagined that Maria would become a renowned singer. To realise that dream and to make the grand décor of the capital a background for her face, I paid a visit to the director of the Conservatorium of music, and I, the blasé, who detested the theatre, I spent all my evenings at the Opera or at concerts. A keen interest was awakened in me when I reported all that I contemplated, all that I heard to Maria. On my return from the performance at the Opera, I sat down at my desk in order to give her detailed accounts on the way in which Miss So-and-so sang her aria that evening, always drawing comparisons to Maria's advantage.

When, in the meantime, I saw the room of a museum of painting, I saw her again everywhere. At the Belvedere, I remained for an hour in front of the Venus of Guido Reni, who resembled my Adored so much, and, finally overcome with nostalgia for her body, I packed my trunks and returned as quickly as possible to her side. Ah! I was bewitched by that woman; there was no means of escaping her!

What a happy homecoming!

It appeared that my love letters had inflamed Maria. I dashed to meet her in the little garden. I kissed her ardently and taking her forehead between my two hands, I said to her:

"You work magic then, little sorceress?"

"What! . . . That journey was an escapade? . . ."

"An attempt at flight, yes! But you are stronger than I . . . I surrender!"

In my room I found a spray of red roses on my table.

"You love me a little bit then, monster?"

She had the timid air of a girl; she blushed . . . It was the end for me, for my points of honour, for my efforts to extricate myself from her chains which I missed too much when I freed myself from them.

. . . .

An entire month of full, magic spring, with the twittering of the starlings, spent in unheard-of love, in interminable embraces, in duets sung at the piano, in games of backgammon and the finest days of the last five years paled into insignificance! What a spring in our autumn! Did we ever dream that winter was so close to us!

8

From then on I struggled in her nets.

Reassured, now that I had got drunk on her intoxicating philtre, Maria relapsed into her former indifference. Negligent in her dress, she no longer bothered to show herself to advantage, despite the admonitions that I made to her, for I foresaw that coldness would result involuntarily from all this. Her passion for her fellow-sex also reappeared, more perilous and more deplorable than ever, for this time she had designs on minors.

One evening, the local commandant and his daughter of fourteen, our hostess and her daughter who was fifteen, as well as a third girl of the same age, accepted the invitation that I gave them to attend a modest evening of music and dancing at my home.

Towards midnight—I still shudder with horror at it—I perceived Maria, slightly drunk, among the girls assembled around her, gloating licentiously over them and kissing them on the mouth, in the way which lesbians are accustomed between themselves.

In a shadowy corner of the room, there was the commandant following her with his eyes, weighing up her movements, ready to explode. In a flash of thought, I foresaw prison, hard labour, the irreparable scandal, and I dashed into the middle of the group formed by the girls and my wife. I dispersed them by inviting them to dance . . .

At night, alone, I upbraided Maria. A stormy conversation followed and was prolonged until the morning. As she had drunk too much, she revealed her plans, in spite of herself, and confessed horrible things, hitherto unsuspected, to me.

Carried away by anger, I repeated all my accusations, all my suspicions, adding this, which I myself find too much on reflection:

"And that mysterious malady," I exclaimed, "which brought me such violent headaches . . ."

"Wretch! You're accusing me then of having given you s . . !"

I admit that I was not thinking of that. I only intended to speak of those symptoms of poisoning by cyanide of potassium that I had observed in myself.

But at that moment a recollection passed through my mind; I remembered an incident in our relationship which had at the time appeared so unlikely to me that it was unable to leave a lasting imprint in my memory . . .

Now my suspicions became aggravated and were combined all of a sudden with a certain phrase of an anonymous letter received some time after my trial and in which Maria was called "the whore from Soedertelje".

Whatever could that mean? I had done some research without result. Let's see a little what fresh clues there are? . . .

When, at Soedertelje, the Baron, the ex-husband, made the acquaintance of Maria, the latter was almost engaged to a lieutenant who was considered not to be of the healthiest in body. That poor Gustav must have acted a rôle of dupe there! . . . And that would become evident enough from the warm gratitude which Maria, even after the divorce, had kept for him, when she admitted to me that *he had saved her from dangers* . . . which she never mentioned, moreover.

But "the whore from Soedertelje! . . ." I thought about it . . . And the reclusion to which the young couple found themselves condemned, that aloof life, without connections, without invitations into the world, that banishment from the society to which they belonged! . . .

Could it not be that Maria's mother, a former governess, of a common family, who had seduced the Finnish baron, Maria's father, when she was ruined and had found refuge in Sweden to free herself from the debts which pursued her, could it not be that that widow, whose penury was. so well hidden, had lowered herself into selling her daughter at Soedertelje?

That old woman, still a coquette at sixty, only inspired me, moreover, with aversion mixed with pity; avaricious, avid for enjoyment, with the ways of an adventuress, she regarded men as objects of exploitation, being a veritable man-eater: she surreptitiously charged me with the upkeep of her sister, as she had previously swindled the Baron, her son-in-law, by offering a fictitious dowry which came from a plot against her creditors.

Poor Maria! It was in that shady past then that her remorse, her unrest, her black ideas had taken root. And by comparing recent facts with those old facts, I believed myself in a position to judge those bloody quarrels which took place between the mother and the daughter, in which they verged on assault and battery; and I understood those enigmatic confessions of Maria, in which she admitted the irresistible rage when she wanted to put her foot on her mother's throat!

Did she want to oblige her mother to keep quiet? Probably. For she had threatened her with breaking up our marriage by admitting "everything" to me.

And those antipathies of Maria for that mother whom the Baron qualified as a "slut!", an epithet which was never made clear to me except by the half-admissions of the Baron who said that she had brought her daughter up to practice all the artifices of the coquettes to grab a husband.

Everything united then to confirm my decision to flee. It had to be, it had to be! I left for Copenhagen in order to gather together all the information possible on that woman to whom I had delivered my name for posterity.

Seeing my compatriots again after several years of absence, I noticed their opinion about me was already made up; they had been hoodwinked by the assiduous attentions of Maria and her women friends. She had become the holy martyr. I was the madman, the imaginary cuckold!

To discuss . . . It was as if I were banging my head against a wall! I was listened to, I was smiled at, with a benevolent air, I was contemplated like a curious animal. And without having been able to elicit the slightest enlightenment, abandoned by everyone, by the envious for the most part, who desired my downfall, the only means of making room for them, I returned to my prison where Maria was waiting for me with an anxiety too visible not to teach me by itself and by its very aspect, more than I had been able to learn in the course of that sad journey.

For two months I champed at my bit and, for the fourth time, in the middle of summer, I fled, this time to Switzerland. But it wasn't an iron chain that I could break which tied me, it was a rubber cable which stretched. The more strongly it was pulled, the more violently it brought me back to my point of departure. When I came back once again, she severely scorned me, because she was convinced that a new flight would cause my death, her only hope.

It was then that I fell ill, that I imagined that I could see death very closely, and that I decided to draw up a memorandum of all the past. I clearly discovered then that I was the dupe of a vampire and I made a resolution to live, to wash myself from that filth with which woman had defiled me, and to return to life in order to avenge myself, when I had gathered up the proof of her treacheries from everywhere.

A hatred was kindled in me, a hatred more fatal than indifference since it constituted the reverse of the love which was slipping away to such a point that I would be tempted to formulate the axiom thus: I hated her because I loved her. At a Sunday dinner in an arbour of the garden, the electrical fluid, piled up for ten years, exploded as a result of I know not what. No matter! For the first time I struck her. A storm of blows rained on her face and as she decided to resist I broke her wrists and made her fall to her knees. She uttered a horrible cry. But the instantaneous pleasure that I felt quickly changed to horror when I heard the children maddened with fear starting to cry their heads off. It was the most painful moment in my life of miseries. It was a sacrilege, an assassination, a crime against nature, to beat a woman, a mother! And to see her children . . . there! It seems to me that the sun ought not to have lit up the scene . . .

Life disgusted me!

Yet all the same, a calm as after a storm, a satisfaction as after an accomplished duty came about, descended into my mind! I regretted my action, I didn't repent it! Like cause, like effect.

In the evening, Maria went for a walk in the moonlight. I went to meet her: I kissed her. She did not push me away, melted into tears and, after a chat, accompanied me into my room where we made love until midnight.

What a strange couple! I beat her at midday. In the evening we went to bed together!

What a curious woman who kissed her executioner with full lips!

Why hadn't I known it sooner? I would have been beating her for ten years and I would be the happiest of all husbands.

That's a tip.

Ponder it, colleagues in cuckoldry! . . .

She was organising her vengeance, however! Some days later, she came into my room, started the preliminaries and after innumerable detours, admitted having been *raped* once in Finland, only once, during her journey.

There was my analysis confirmed!

She begged me not to believe that this had been renewed and not to suspect that she had had several lovers.

Which signified: several times several lovers.

"So, you have deceived me and, to hoodwink the world, you have spread the fable of my madness! The better to hide your crime, you have wanted to harass me until I die of it. You are a scoundrel. I am sure of it now. Let us be separated by divorce!

She fell at my knees, weeping hot tears, imploring my forgiveness:

"Alright. I forgive you, but let us be divorced!"

The following day she appeared calm; the day after that she re-asserted herself; the third day which followed that catastrophe, she behaved as one innocent.

"Now that I have shown myself generous enough to admit everything, I have nothing to reproach myself with."

She was more than innocent, she was a martyr, who treated me with an offensive condescension.

Unconscious of the outcome of her crime, she did not grasp the dilemma. Either I was to remain a laughing-stock to the world as a cuckold, or I was to leave, the misfortune was to remain, and I was a lost man.

Ten years of tortures in exchange for a few blows and a day of tears—that wasn't fair!

For the last time I made off, lacking the necessary courage to say good-bye to my children.

It was at midday, on a delightful Sunday, that I embarked on the boat for Constance, firmly resolved to find friends in France, to write the novel of that woman there at once, the true type of the age of the asexual.

At the last moment, Maria turned up at the boat, with tears in her eyes, agitated, feverish, unfortunately so pretty as to turn my head. I remained cold, impassive, dumb; I accepted her perfidious kisses, without returning them.

"Say at least that we're friends," she said to me.

"Enemies for the little life that I have left!"

We had to part.

And, when the boat pulled away, I could see her running along the quay, still seeking to hold me back by the magic power of those looks which for so many years had been able to deceive me! She came and went like an abandoned dog, the frightful bitch! And I awaited the moment when she would throw herself in the water, when I would join her for us to drown together in a supreme embrace, but she turned her back, disappeared into an alley, leaving me the impression of her bewitching face, of her silhouette with its tiny feet which were placed for ten years on my throat, without my ever uttering a single cry, unless it was in one of my works where I had misled the public by dissimulating the true crimes of that monster, always celebrated hitherto by her poet.

In order to steel myself against grief, I went down at once into the saloon of the boat. I took a place at the dining-table, but at the first course sobs choked me and I was obliged to leave, to go up on deck.

There I could see the little green hill where the white cottage stood with its green shutters. It was there that my little ones were living in a devastated nest, without protection, without anything to live on . . . Then those stabbing pains chilled me and pierced my heart.

I felt like a silkworm chrysalis, unravelled by the great steam engine. At every stroke of the piston, I grew thinner and the cold increased while the thread lengthened.

It was death which was approaching!

I was like a foetus prematurely detached from the umbilical cord! What an integral and living organism is the family! I had already foreseen this at the time of the first divorce, when I myself recoiled and when remorse almost killed me! But She, the adulteress, the murderess, she had not recoiled! . . .

At Constance, I took the train for Basle! Oh! That Sunday afternoon!

If there were a God, I would beg him never to inflict such hours of suffering on my bitterest enemy!

Now it was the locomotive which unwound my intestines, the lobes of my brain, my nerves, my blood vessels, all my viscera in such a way that I was like a carcass on arriving at Basle.

At Basle a sudden urge overcame me to see again all the places in Switzerland where we had stayed, in order to satiate myself with the memories which she or the children had left me.

I spent a week at Geneva, one at Ouchy, hunted from hotel to hotel by my memories, without respite or mercy, pushed like one damned, a wandering Jew, spending my nights weeping, evoking everywhere the dear images of my children, visiting the places that they had visited, throwing bread to *their* seagulls on Lake Geneva, wandering like a shadow.

Every day I waited for a letter from Maria which didn't come. She was too cunning to put written proof in the hands of her enemy. And I addressed love letters to her, several times a day, all full of forgiveness . . . without sending them off however.

Upon my word, Judges, I admit that if I ever sank into madness, it was during those hours of distress and desolation that it must have happened!

At the end of my resistance, I began to imagine things and I imagined that the admission of Maria was only a trap to get rid of me and start life again with another, that mysterious, unknown lover or the Danish tribad, the mistress, as a last resort! And I could see my children under the thumb of a *step-father* or in the clutches of a *step-mother*, who would grow fat on the revenue from my complete works and would sketch a story of my life, observed through the eyes of a hermaphrodite who had taken my wife from me. All my instinct for self-preservation was then resuscitated; I had recourse to a ruse. As it was impossible for me to work unless I was in the midst of my family, I decided to join them, to stay with them for the time necessary to write a whole novel, while gathering the most precise notes regarding Maria's crime. In this way I would use her without her suspecting anything. She would be the instrument of my vengeance which I would throw away far from me after use.

To this end, I sent her a telegram, clear, without sentimentalities, in which I announced to her the rejection of our application for a divorce, and, with the pretext of signatures to be given, I fixed a rendezvous for her at Romanshorn, on this side of Lake Constance.

. . . .

The telegram sent, I lived again: I took the train the next morning and I arrived on time. All that week of suffering was forgotten; my heart functioned as usual, my eyes shone, my chest expanded when I saw again, on the horizon, the hills of the other shore where my dear children were. The boat approached, but I couldn't see Maria. At last there she was, on the deck, with her face devastated, aged ten years. What a blow it dealt to my heart to see the young woman suddenly grown old! Her gait was dragging, her eyes were reddened with tears, her cheeks hollowed, her chin was drooping!

At that moment, pity alone suppressed all feelings of hatred or aversion. I prepared myself to welcome her with open arms, when, suddenly, I recoiled and drew myself up, assuming the relaxed attitude of a swell who turns up at some rendezvous or other! The fact was that in a flash, while eyeing Maria carefully and more closely, I discovered a striking resemblance in her to her friend, the Dane. Everything was there; the mien, the pose, the gesture, the arrangement of the hair, the expression of physiognomy! Had the tribad played this last trick on me? Did Maria not come from the arms of her mistress?

The recollection of two incidents that occurred at the beginning of the summer confirmed this supposition. I had caught her one day asking an inn-keeper in the neighbourhood if there were not a place free in his pension.

For whom? Why?

Then she had asked me if she could go and play the piano a little, in the evening, in the neighbouring pension.

Without constituting evident proof, these details put me on my guard and, while conducting Maria to the hotel, I rehearsed the rôle I intended to play.

Crushed, declaring herself ill, she kept her composure nonetheless. She asked me clear and judicious questions on the procedures employed in matters of divorce and, soon discarding her pitiful mien, she decided to look down on me as much as was possible, when she was convinced that my conduct revealed no trace of grief.

During this interrogation she smacked so much of her friend that I was about to give her news of the wench. There was above all a tragedienne's pose which caught my eye (a pose much relished by the friend), accompanied by a gesture of the hand leaning on the table ... Ah!

I got her to drink some strong wine. She took gulps which soon forced her to weaken.

Then I seized an opportunity to ask her for news of the children. She burst into tears, admitting that she had just spent an odious week listening to the little ones asking for their papa from morning to nightfall and that she did not think she was in a position to be able to live without me.

My wedding ring was no longer on my ring finger. She noticed this and suffered a violent shudder.

"Your wedding ring?" she asked me.

"I sold it in Geneva. I treated myself to a girl with the money so as to reestablish the balance for a moment."

She grew pale.

"Now we're quits. So ... let's begin again? ..."

"That's it ... That's how you understand fairness! You have committed an action which has baleful consequences for the family, since doubts on the legitimacy of my children have arisen within me and you are thereby guilty of having destroyed the descendance of a race. You have polluted four people for life, your three children with a dubious birth, and handed over your husband as a laughing-stock, as a deceived husband! ... What are the consequences of my action?"

She wept. I proposed to let the divorce take its course, while she would remain in the house as my mistress.

I would adopt the children by testament.

"Isn't that the free union that you had dreamed of, you who have ceaselessly cursed marriage?"

She reflected for a moment. The proposition repelled her.

"What? Didn't you tell me one day that you wanted to find a position as governess in the household of a widower? Here is the widower you want."

"That calls for reflection ... I need time ... We'll see. Meanwhile are you coming back to us?-"

"If you invite me."

"You only have to come."

And for the sixth time I returned to the fold, firmly resolved to utilise this respite which was to be left to me in order to finish off my story and arm myself with precise information on that mysterious affair.

(12)

The story is now terminated, my Adored. I have avenged myself; we are quits . . .

September 1887—March 1888

STRINDBERG'S PREFACES

PREFACE

This is an atrocious book. I admit that without objection, for I bitterly regret having written it.

What caused the book to be born?

The just necessity of washing my corpse before it is shut forever in the bier.

I remember that four years ago one of my literary friends, a declared enemy of the indiscretions . . . of others, let slip this phrase before me, one day when the conversation touched upon my marriage:

"That's a subject for a novel, ready-made for my pen, believe me."

From that minute dates my resolution to fashion my novel myself, since I was indeed almost certain of being approved of by my friend.

Dear friend, don't think badly of my claiming here my rights of ownership as the first occupier!

I can still remember how—this time sixteen years ago—the late mother of my future wife, then a baroness and separated, said to me as she saw me watching her daughter smirking in a group of young men:

"Isn't that the subject for a fine novel for you, sir?"

"With what title, madame?"

"A woman of fire," she answered.

Lucky mother, deceased in time, here are your wishes fulfilled. The novel is written. Now I myself can die.

1887   *The Author*

A NEW PREFACE

The other day I met the hero of this novel. I reproached him vigorously for having incited me to publish the story of his first marriage. Now that he is married a second time, the father of a pretty little girl, he looks ten years younger than he did ten years ago.

"My dear friend," he replied to my misgivings, "the sympathy that the heroine of this book won on its publication absolves me in my own eyes. Judge thereby how incredibly strong was my love since it could survive so much ferocity, since it even transmitted itself to the readers. This hasn't stopped a French Academician from stigmatising the tenacity of my affections as a weakness, the perseverance of my fidelity towards my family, including my children, as a sign of inferiority in view of the brutality, the instability and the dishonesty of the wife. Would that man judge the insignificance of a Caserio superior to the eminence of a Carnot simply because the former stuck his knife into the living flesh of the latter?

"Besides, in this book that you have wanted to write, love forms only a woof in a shred torn from a cloth, the richness of which is only known to my compatriots, to those who have followed my literary career as it developed parallel with the misfortunes of my adventures in love—without ever being troubled by them. I could have deserted the field of battle. I remained steadfast at my post. I struggled against the enemy at home and in bed. Isn't that courage, I ask you?

"The 'poor defenceless woman' had the four Nordic Nations at her disposal where she had only friends, to combat a sick man, alone, fallen into indigence, whom they wanted to lock in a lunatic asylum because his superior intelligence revolted against gyniolatry, the penultimate superstition of the free-thinkers.

"The benign, who dissimulate their mediocre vengeance under the pompous qualification 'divine Justice' have condemned my *Manifesto* in the name of their *Nemesis Divina,* claiming on false grounds that I had deceived the husband of the first marriage.

"Then let them read the scene in which you have shown the husband getting rid of his wife by throwing her into my arms—at me, who had clean hands, whereas I had confessed to him my innocent love for his abandoned wife! Let them recall—this detail has its importance—the pages in which I took upon my young shoulders the whole weight of the blame in order to save the position of the officer and the future of his child, and let them say if it is in the logic of any vengeance whatsoever to punish an act of devotion.

"I must have been young and foolish to act as lightly as I did, I agree. But that will never happen again, I assure you . . . Moreover . . . let's leave it, and then . . . no . . . good-bye!"

He went off rapidly. There remained behind him an impression, as it were, of absolute good faith.

I no longer regret having narrated the novel of that kind of idealist, vanished from the world and from literature, and I at last renounce a previous decision which was to write *A Madwoman's Manifesto*, because it now appears to me too contrary to common sense to allow the criminal to testify against her victim.

Paris-Passy, October 1894   *The Author*

Translator's note

Axel (Strindberg) divorced Maria (Siri). The Baron married Matilda.

232